Second Language Socialization and Learner Agency

BILINGUAL EDUCATION & BILINGUALISM

Series Editors: Nancy H. Hornberger, *University of Pennsylvania, USA* and Colin Baker, *Bangor University, Wales, UK*

Bilingual Education and Bilingualism is an international, multidisciplinary series publishing research on the philosophy, politics, policy, provision and practice of language planning, global English, indigenous and minority language education, multilingualism, multiculturalism, biliteracy, bilingualism and bilingual education. The series aims to mirror current debates and discussions.

Full details of all the books in this series and of all our other publications can be found on http://www.multilingual-matters.com, or by writing to Multilingual Matters, St Nicholas House, 31-34 High Street, Bristol BS1 2AW, UK.

Second Language Socialization and Learner Agency

Adoptive Family Talk

Lyn Wright Fogle

MULTILINGUAL MATTERS
Bristol • Buffalo • Toronto

For Cameron

Library of Congress Cataloging in Publication Data
A catalog record for this book is available from the Library of Congress.
Fogle, Lyn Wright.
Second Language Socialization and Learner Agency: Adoptive Family Talk/Lyn Wright Fogle.
Bilingual Education & Bilingualism: 87
Includes bibliographical references and index.
1. Second language acquisition--Case studies. 2. Socialization--Case studies.
3. Adoption--Case studies. 4. English language--Study and teaching--Russian speakers--Case studies. 5. Bilingualism--Case studies. 6. Code switching (Linguistics)--Case studies. I. Title.
P118.2.F64 2012
401'.93--dc232012022004

British Library Cataloguing in Publication Data
A catalogue entry for this book is available from the British Library.

ISBN-13: 978-1-84769-785-1 (hbk)
ISBN-13: 978-1-84769-784-4 (pbk)

Multilingual Matters
UK: St Nicholas House, 31-34 High Street, Bristol BS1 2AW, UK.
USA: UTP, 2250 Military Road, Tonawanda, NY 14150, USA.
Canada: UTP, 5201 Dufferin Street, North York, Ontario M3H 5T8, Canada.

The policy of Multilingual Matters/Channel View Publications is to use papers that are natural, renewable and recyclable products, made from wood grown in sustainable forests. In the manufacturing process of our books, and to further support our policy, preference is given to printers that have FSC and PEFC Chain of Custody certification. The FSC and/or PEFC logos will appear on those books where full certification has been granted to the printer concerned.

Typeset by The Charlesworth Group.
Printed and bound in Great Britain by The MPG Books Group.

Contents

Acknowledgements

This project has traveled with me across geographical and professional contexts, and I have many people to thank. First and foremost, Kendall King has remained a constant mentor and guide. Kendall has the enviable ability to ask just the right question at the right moment. Her questions provided the framework for this study and book and continue to inspire and challenge me.

I would also like to thank the co-editors of the Bilingual Education and Bilingualism series for Multilingual Matters, Nancy Hornberger and Colin Baker, for including this work in the body of scholarship that has influenced and shaped my own thinking on these topics. I am very grateful to the anonymous reviewer whose comments helped me tighten my focus on the contribution this study makes to an understanding of agency in language socialization. A great amount of gratitude goes to Tommi Grover who was instrumental in getting me through the publication process.

Several readers provided useful insights on earlier drafts of the chapters. First, I am grateful to Elizabeth Lanza who, in the midst of an extremely busy schedule, found time to read several chapters and provide valuable commentary in key places in the manuscript. Rachael Stryker, who I have yet to meet in person, provided extremely helpful suggestions on adoption and kinship. Her enthusiasm for the work on language and adoption helped me keep going during the initial revisions. Thank you to Michael Keiffer for the nuanced comments on metalanguage and literacy. Hansun Zhang Waring and Ginger Pizer also provided invaluable support and useful suggestions on earlier drafts. Conversations with Sol Pelaez were instrumental in helping me draft the final conclusion.

Alison Mackey and Anna De Fina provided stimulating commentary on language acquisition and identity respectively. Their encouragement was instrumental in my decision to write this book. Thanks also to Julie Abraham for inspiring and mentoring me as a young student.

Natalia Dolgova Jacobsen was a great help during the data collection. Masha Chechueva, Matt Withers and Zachariah Zayner spent many hours preparing the transcripts. Research assistants at Mississippi State University, Taylor Garner, Anna Bedsole and Emily Mills, helped with proofreading and editing the final versions of the manuscript. Thank you to Cameron for helping me find the balance through it all and to Noah for all the giggles.

    And finally, the families who participated in this project took the unprecedented step of opening up their private conversations and allowing me to observe what being an adoptive family was like. I cannot thank them enough for their willingness to participate in this project, and I hope that their perspectives and experiences will contribute to a better understanding of language learning and older adoptees.

Transcription Conventions

(adapted from Tannen *et al.*, 2007)

((words))	Double parentheses enclose transcriber's comments.
/words/	Slashes enclose uncertain transcription.
/???/	Indicates unintelligible words.
Carriage return	Each new line represents an intonation unit.
-	A hyphen indicates a truncated word or adjustment within an intonation unit (e.g. repeated word, false start).
?	A question mark indicates a relatively strong rising intonation (interrogative).
!	An exclamation mark indicates rising intonation (exclamatory).
.	A period indicates a falling, final intonation.
,	A comma indicates a continuing intonation.
..	Dots indicate silence (more dots indicate a longer silence).
:	A colon indicates an elongated sound.
CAPS	Capitals indicate emphatic stress.
<laugh>	Angle brackets enclose descriptions of vocal noises (e.g. laughs, coughs, crying).
Words [words] [words]	Square brackets enclose simultaneous talk.

1 Introduction

At the turn of the century, transnational adoption emerged as a growing and important phenomenon in contemporary society that has changed the way people view family and kinship and, by extension, culture (Howell, 2007; Volkman, 2005). The rates of US adoptions from abroad nearly tripled in the years 1990 to 2004 (Vandivere *et al.*, 2009), and the phenomenon of transnational adoption has touched numerous lives around the world. In addition, transnational adoption has been a topic of intense media attention and public discourse in Western cultures. Celebrities such as Madonna and Angelina Jolie and Brad Pitt have been both admired and maligned in the popular press for the motives and methods of their multiple adoptions from various nations (Russell, 2009; Simpson, 2009). Further, cases such as Artyom (Justin) Hansen, who was returned to Russia alone on a plane by his US adoptive mother, incited anger and fear on the part of parents, government officials and the general public both in the US and in Russia (Levy, 2010). In short, transnational adoption has become a touchstone issue for understanding the West's position in a globalizing world.

In this maelstrom of high-profile media attention, it has been hard to hear the voices of everyday adoptive families and harder still to understand what life in an adoptive family is like. How do adoptive families create lasting bonds and how, for example, do older adoptees manage the transitions to a new country, language and home? This book focuses on one important aspect of transnational adoption – the second language acquisition of English by older children adopted from abroad by US adoptive families. In examining everyday conversations audio-recorded by three Russian adoptive families, I discuss the role language plays in forming a family across linguistic and cultural differences, how learning and using a second language (for children and adults) relates to establishing bonding relationships in the family, and how children themselves develop agency in language socialization processes. I provide detailed linguistic analyses of discourse level processes (such as storytelling [narrative talk], talking about language [languaging episodes] and switching between languages [code-switching]) in these families' everyday conversations to show the active role that children play in shaping language learning and identity formation. This research contributes to how we view second language learning and socialization as well as how we understand learning processes in the transnational adoptive family.

Language Socialization

The language socialization paradigm originally sought to integrate psycholinguistic perspectives on first language acquisition by children with anthropological insights on socialization (Ochs & Schieffelin, 1984; Schieffelin & Ochs, 1986). Language learning from this point of view is considered an essentially social phenomenon that is mediated by culture and language. Language socialization, or the socialization of children or other novices to language and through language (Ochs & Schieffelin, 1984), has most often focused on top-down processes, or the role of experts (parents) in shaping novices' (children's) behaviors and practices. Recent approaches to the study of socialization in childhood, however, have begun to emphasize the active role children play in their own learning processes and the co-constructed and collaborative nature of socialization (Corsaro, 2004; Kulick & Schieffelin, 2004; Luykx, 2003; Luykx, 2005). Concomitantly, recent studies in second language socialization, or the process in which non-native speakers of a language (or individuals who have lost competence in a language they once spoke) seek both competence in the second language and to become members of a community in which it is spoken, have emphasized the contradictory and conflicted nature of such processes as learners may reject or resist target language norms (Duff, 2011). Drawing these two strands together, this book takes as a starting point the notion that young second language learners can actively shape the interactional contexts in which they participate, and in so doing, create opportunities for learning for themselves and socialize adults into meeting their linguistic, interactional and identity needs.

Focusing on the ways in which children and other learners affect the world around them is important for understanding second language learning processes, as well as the processes of socialization that occur in contexts such as the transnational adoptive family. In the chapters that follow, I illustrate two main points: (a) that second language socialization, or the apprenticeship of young transnational adoptees into the linguistic and cultural norms of the US family, is a bidirectional and often child-directed process (i.e. parents often accommodate linguistically to children's direct influence), and (b) correspondingly, life in adoptive families requires quotidian negotiations that entail the creation of new family practices and norms. Through the analysis of interaction in these three families, I demonstrate both the collaborative and co-constructed nature of language socialization processes and elaborate on the transformations that Duff (2011) notes are characteristic of second or additional language processes (see also Garrett & Baquedano-Lopéz, 2002; Kulick & Schieffelin, 2004).

Most studies of the second language socialization of young English language learners have been conducted in classroom settings. The past two decades of research on young English language learners' experiences in schools has ushered in a new focus on the complex social worlds and identities associated with second language learning. Norton and Toohey (2001), for example, argued that being a good language learner was the result not only of the acquisition of linguistic competence (i.e. the language code), but also of having access to conversations and discourses that make it possible for learners to become members of their new communities. Sociocultural and ethnographic approaches to second language learning have emphasized a focus on learner participation in communities of practice, such as classrooms and peer groups, as a way to understand these complex and sometimes confounding processes (Duff, 2008b; Hawkins, 2005; Toohey, 2000; Willett, 1995). In studying the language socialization processes that occur in adoptive families, this book sheds light on socialization and learning processes in middle-class US families that connect with school and classroom practices and, specifically, how children in the family environment achieve a sense of agency that facilitates language learning in interactions with adults.

The way that students act and behave, the extent to which their own participation patterns match those of their teachers and the amount of control and power they feel they have both in the classroom and in interactions with others can play a role in how students are perceived by their teachers, how much access they have to learning opportunities and how much they learn (Harklau, 2000; Hawkins, 2005; Philips, 2001). In many cases, these ways of participating in the classroom are related to home socialization. Further, language socialization research in monolingual middle-class homes has shown how children are socialized in these families into practices that coincide with the expectations and goals of formal schooling (e.g. theory building and narrative practices) (Ochs & Capps, 2001; Ochs et al., 1992). New perspectives from bi- and multilingual families have pointed to the ways in which children themselves socialize other family members (parents and siblings) into discourse practices and language choice in family interactions (Fogle & King, in press; Luykx, 2003, 2005), the point of focus for this book. Here I start with discourse practices known to be important sites of language socialization and, in some cases, precursors to literate activities in the classroom (i.e. narrative activities, metalinguistic talk and code-switching) and show how, as the adoptees in this study become competent participants in these activities, they also find ways to change and transform these practices in interaction with their parents.

Focusing on the unique and vulnerable population of transnational adoptees opens the door for a better understanding of how mainstream language ideologies (of parents) intersect with language learning processes of second language-learning children and how socialization into middle-class, mainstream norms prepares these learners for contexts outside of the family (see Fogle, in press). It also provides a micro-level view of what cultural change can encompass as the language-learning children in this study achieve and exert their agency in the new home. The fact that middle-class, Western parents are known to use a 'self lowering' or accommodating style when interacting with children (see Ochs & Schieffelin, 1984) guides my analysis of how the children are able to influence their parents and establish agency in family interactions as parents and other family members accommodate to certain linguistic strategies (e.g. resisting, questioning and negotiating) that transform the family discourse.

Agency and Identity in Second Language Socialization

A primary finding in studies of school-based second language socialization has been that the achievement of agency by learners is necessary to facilitate learning processes. Learners who are able to act, in the sense that they are able to recruit assistance and scaffolding and gain opportunities to use language, do better in classroom environments than learners who remain silent and do not actively seek out language learning opportunities (Hawkins, 2005; Rymes & Pash, 2001). Language learning and being a 'good learner' in school settings entails negotiations among learners' individual agency, structures put in place by the teacher and school and ideologies that mediate learning and interactional processes (McKay & Wong, 1996; Toohey, 2000).

But what do we mean by learner agency in second language studies? The construct is most often invoked in studies of second language learning to explain learner behaviors that facilitate learning, such as participation and actively seeking out assistance (e.g. Hawkins, 2005; Pavlenko & Lantolf, 2000). However, Morita (2004) and others (Harklau, 2000; McKay & Wong, 1996) have effectively shown how learner actions that do *not* lead to participation and positive learning outcomes (such as resistance through silence and subversion) are also agentive. Agency as a construct, therefore, can both afford and constrain language-learning opportunities depending on the sociocultural context and the intentions or goals of the learner. This contradiction results in the construct of agency as yielding potentially *no* explanatory power in understanding language learning processes without a more nuanced discussion of the conditions under which learner agency emerges, the types of agency that are possible in the particular context and, crucially, the effect of the action.

Sociolinguists have expanded on notions of agency in the social sciences by considering the linguistic construction of agency, both embedded in grammars and instantiated in interaction. Ahearn (2001) defines agency as the 'socioculturally mediated capacity to act', and Al Zidjaly (2009: 178) elaborates on this definition by suggesting that these processes are also linguistic, explaining that 'agency is best conceived as a collective process for negotiating roles, tasks, and alignments that takes place through linguistic ... or nonlinguistic mediational means'. Like Al Zidjaly, my analyses of children's agency will be primarily linguistic with a focus on the interactional strategies children use not only for action in the family, but also to transform the interactional context in which they participate. I will further argue that it is the outcomes of agentive actions in which we are most interested in second language learning.

Three adoptive families participated in the research presented in this book, and each family context gave rise to a different type of agency that gained importance in negotiating the interactional context and language-learning opportunities for the children. In the first family, The Sondermans (Chapter 4), I examine the children's resistance to the father's prompts and questions. In the second family, the Jackson-Wessels (Chapter 5), I look at elicitation of parental talk and control through children's questioning practices as a type of agency. And finally, in the third family, I discuss the children's negotiation of language choice and the use of Russian as an agentive practice. These different types of learner agency – resistance, control and negotiation – do lead to important language learning and identity construction opportunities in the adoptive families despite the fact that they do not always coincide with the parents' desired practices and norms. In this way, the second language socialization processes in these transnational adoptive families, where bonding and becoming a family are central to family interactions, are negotiated and collaborative.

Families both reflect and construct ideologies and processes found on the macro or societal level (see King et al., 2008), and the microinteractional roles that are established in families have been posited to connect with larger, macro-level identities (Ochs & Taylor, 1995; Ervin-Tripp et al., 1984). In this book I focus on how the micro-level roles that children take on in the family (as resistor, questioner or negotiator) influence parents to change their linguistic and interactional strategies. I argue that these interactional-level identities do relate to the children's larger, desired identities as they establish certain child-directed discourse practices as the norm over other, parent-directed ones. These processes lead to new opportunities for learning for the children and open up spaces for them to talk about and be the type of individuals they want to be. Specifically, it gives the children in these different families opportunities to connect their prior lives in Russia or Ukraine with their current families and, in the third family (Chapter 6), to make space to continue speaking Russian in the home environment.

The Case of Transnational Adoption

Since the 1990s, more than 444,000 children have been adopted by US families from abroad (Vandivere et al., 2009: 7). Popular authors such as *Boston Globe* journalist Adam Pertman (2001) have written about the pervasive nature of such changes to the US family, claiming that adoption contributed to the trend of multiculturalism in the US by bringing together families across racial, ethnic and cultural lines. Sociologists and anthropologists have also taken up this argument, theorizing that adoption is at once reproductive of societal norms (through the formation of nuclear families and kinship relations in contractual agreements) while, at the same time, it disrupts notions of the culturally and racially homogenous family through lesbian and gay adoptions and transracial and transnational adoptions (Esposito & Biafora, 2007; Stryker, 2010; Volkman et al., 2005). The adoptive family, then, contributes to multiculturalism and diversity in the US at the micro level of the individual family at the same time as it reflects societal notions of family and kinship.

But how do we do we understand these larger societal-level processes as they coalesce in individual families? And even more, how do we (e.g. researchers, clinicians, teachers and parents) support and guide families who find themselves reinventing and rethinking what it means to be a family and to belong, especially when they are doing so across linguistic, ethnic, racial and cultural differences? Language plays a key role in establishing social identities and relationships, such as those entailed in membership in a family (De Fina et al., 2006; Tannen et al., 2007). And from a sociocultural point of view, language also mediates cognitive processes of learning (Lantolf, 2000; Lapkin et al., 2010; Vygotsky, 1986). Therefore, language is a key resource for becoming and displaying who we are, as well as learning new concepts, ideas and even linguistic structures. In this book, these two processes (i.e. identity construction and learning) are intimately tied and occur during the everyday interactional routines of transnational adoptive families.

In the families who participated in this study, as I have discussed thus far, transformations emerged in daily negotiations over language choice, values and norms within the family sphere. Take for example the following excerpt from a dinner conversation that occurred in the Sonderman[1] family (detailed in Chapter 4). John Sonderman, the US father, was an English-speaking psychotherapist who had studied Russian for two semesters in an intensive university course in preparation for adopting his two boys, Dima and Sasha. Dima (age 10 at the time of recording) and Sasha (age eight) had arrived from Ukraine about a year earlier (in 2004). Both boys had been fluent in Russian and Ukrainian prior to the adoption, and John had used only Russian for about the first six months after the children's arrival. In Excerpt 1, however, they both resist and seem unable to respond to their father when he prompts them to speak Russian.

Excerpt 1.1 Hakuna Matata[2]
(Original utterance transcribed using Cyrillic script for Russian. Transliteration to Roman script follows on the next line. English translation is on the third line. All Russian words are in italics.)

1	John:	Testing testing testing, *один два три* testing.
		Testing testing testing, *odin dva tri* testing.
		Testing testing testing, *one two three* testing.
2	Sasha:	Uh-huh.
3	Dima:	Hah.
4	John:	*/Счас/ по-русский – мы по – мы говорим.*
		/Schas/ po-russkiy – mi po – mi govorim.
		/Now/ we will – we are speaking Russian.
5	Dima:	Uh-uh.
6	Sasha:	*Да!*
		Da!
		Yes!
7	John:	*Да.*
		Da.
		Yes.
8	Sasha:	*Сичас ми по-русский и ми /говорихим/.*
		Sichas mi po-russkiy i mi /govorihim/
		Now we are /speaking/ Russian.
9	John:	*говорим*
		govorim
		speaking
10	Sasha:	*говорим.*
		govorim.
		speaking
11		[bla, bla, bla]
12	John:	[A:h]!

13	Dima:	Hahhh.
14	Sasha:	Huhh.
15	Dima:	I don't want to.
16	John:	*Ты помниш?*
		Ti pomnish?
		Do you remember?
17		*[Помниш]?*
		[Pomnish]?
		[Remember]?
18	Sasha:	*[ti pomne]* ((approximate repetition))
19	Dima:	*[pomne]* ((approximate repetition))
20	John:	*[Ты помниш] русский язык, да?*
		[Ti pomnish] russkiy yazik, da?
		[You remember] Russian ((language)), *right?*
21	Sasha:	*Ты [пом]ниш*
		Ti [pom]nish
		You [rem]ember
22	Dima:	[yeah].
23	Sasha:	*Py -*
		Ru -
		Ru -
24	Dima:	maybe.
25	Sasha:	*сский язык*
		sskiy yazik.
		ssian language.
26		*Да?*
		Da?
		Right?
27	John:	*Долго мы не говорили вместе по-русский.*
		Dolgo mi ne govorili vmeste po-russkiy.
		We haven't spoken Russian together in a long time.
28	Sasha:	*Dolg mi ni porili deste my sa sa.* ((approximate repetition of John))
29		Hhh.
30	Dima:	Hakunda matata.
31	Sasha:	Hakunda matata.
32		Hhh.
33	Dima:	Hhh.
34	Sasha:	Means no worries.
35	John:	Ok Dima,
36	Dima:	Yes?

37	John:	Six-eighths versus one half.
38		Where's one half?
39		Well let's see.
40	Dima:	There?
41		It's a ha:lf.

The complex processes of language socialization, language learning and identity construction that occur in transnational adoptive families are evident in this short episode. John displays his competence in Russian, which he learned as a means to communicate with his adopted children and to smooth the transition to their new home. This represents an accommodating act on his part. The children, however, demonstrate both that they do not want to speak Russian with John and, to some extent, that they can't replicate his speech (lines 18 and 28). Dima immediately indicates that he doesn't want to speak Russian in line five with a negative, 'uh uh'. Sasha, on the other hand, responds in Russian at first, answering 'Da!' to John's request in line six. Dima resists, at first laughing and then saying 'maybe' he remembers (showing that he understands, but will not speak). Sasha repeats John from lines eight to 28, but ends up breaking into nonsense syllables (line 28). Dima finally responds, 'hakunda matata', a (mispronounced) Swahili phrase popularized in US culture by the Disney film *The Lion King* (Hahn & Allers, 1994), which causes both boys to laugh and effectively stops John's attempts at eliciting Russian. In conclusion of the episode, John changes the topic to Dima's math homework.

This pattern of resistance, and particularly Dima's refusal to participate in the parent-directed interaction, is a type of agency that I examine more thoroughly in Chapter 4. Here Dima's strategies, as well as Sasha's humorous attempts to speak Russian, subvert John's attempts to record the family speaking Russian on the audiotape. Dima's reference to the Disney film and song 'Hakuna Matata', further position him as an English-speaking, US child who is fluent in American pop culture and not a Russian-speaking adoptee (further drawing on ideologies of language, and the rather narrow use of languages other than English, in US popular culture). Thus two competing family identities, the father's vision of a bilingual Russian–English speaking adoptive family and the boys' positions as competent English-speaking, US kids, collide in this excerpt and demonstrate the influence the two children have in interaction over their father.

It is exactly the kinds of interactional control that children, in this case transnational adoptees, have over their parents and the effects of such control or influence that I examine in this book. I take a longitudinal perspective on how children socialize parents and other family members into specific narrative, metalinguistic and code choice practices through the use of resistance strategies seen here as well as other forms of agency such as participation and negotiation. What is key to these processes is the children's achievement of agency in interaction with their parents. In all of these cases, parents accommodate to children's strategies. Negotiations of language practices, language choice and language competence in intercultural communication are potentially tied to the negotiation of power relations and interactional roles that correlate with larger scale identities. As in the excerpt provided above, language choice, language competence and individual identities are negotiated simultaneously, suggesting that the cognitive and social aspects of language learning and language use are inextricably tied.

While a large body of research on transnational adoptees focuses on adoptee identities and adoptive family cultures (Grovetant *et al.*, 2007; Jacobson, 2008; Stryker, 2010; Volkman *et al.*, 2005; Yngvesson, 2010), few studies have looked carefully at the role of language in adoptee identity construction. Concomitantly, the adoptive family, like other transnational families in which members have unequal access to linguistic resources (Canagarajah, 2008; Fogle & King, in press), provides a unique opportunity to investigate processes of second language socialization in the family sphere. This book follows three transnational adoptive families in the early stages of their lives together. In each family, I examine how language is used and learned both by parents and children. I show how establishing different roles, relationships and identities coincide with linguistic practices in the family sphere. In addition, I discuss how the local context, in concert with parental ideologies, shapes not only parental strategies, but also the strategies children use to meet their interactional needs.

Conclusion

To sum up, I have two main goals in this book. The first is to examine the social worlds of young second language learners (i.e. transnational adoptees) outside of the classroom and probe the notion of learner agency as an explanatory construct for second language learning. To do this, I show how different types of agency – resistance, participation and negotiation – emerge out of the different family contexts and relate to language learning processes in each family. At the end of the book (Chapter 7), I will discuss in more detail why participation in a community of practice such as an adoptive family might lead to greater acceptance of certain types of learner agency (such as resistance) deemed counterproductive in most classroom or educational settings. The types of resistance and negotiation of experts' (i.e.

parents') practices found in this study will lead to a better understanding of the micro processes associated with cultural transformation and change. This discussion also contributes to the newly emerging importance of affect in second language socialization and a consideration of aspects of long-term identity construction for second language learners who experience disruptions and change in their life trajectories (Duff, 2011; Lapkin *et al.*, 2010).

A second major goal for this book is to look at daily life in the transnational adoptive family and provide accurate and realistic representations of the processes that occur in interactions in such families. Adoption is a well-researched social institution, and adoptive parents and adoptees are perhaps scrutinized more thoroughly than other families, as I will discuss further in Chapter 3. However, few research studies have attempted to collect data from everyday life in the adoptive family. Such an approach is important for understanding how adopted children both take on and negotiate the family norms held by their parents and to understand how family relationships and identities are constructed in daily interactions. In this book I connect these social processes with learning processes to better understand the unique social and educational needs of transnational adoptees and, potentially, a wider group of transnational children who reside in fluid and changing family environments.

The book is organized around three main analysis chapters that showcase each of the three participating adoptive families individually. In Chapter 2 and Chapter 3, I will contextualize the families and the goals of the study by introducing the language socialization paradigm and the recent phenomenon of transnational adoption in the West respectively. Chapter 4 introduces the first family, the Sondermans, a single father and two sons who consistently resist their father's routine attempts to engage them in talk about the day. Chapter 5 presents the second, dual-parent family, the Jackson-Wessels, comprised of a young daughter and homeschooled son who repeatedly question their parents to gain turns in the family conversation and elicit talk about language or languaging. Chapter 6 describes the third family, the Goellers, comprised of four prior adoptees and two recent teenage arrivals, and how the use of Russian is negotiated through code-switching amongst family members. Only one of these families, the Goellers, actively used Russian in their daily interactions, although John Sonderman, in the first family, had learned Russian in an intensive university program prior to adopting as discussed above (Excerpt 1.1).

The processes in the first two families are related more closely to acquiring English in the family sphere, while the third family presents the opportunity to analyze how English and Russian were negotiated by family members who were all (including the parents who had taken a Russian

Berlitz course), to some extent, bilingual. The theoretical background and methods for the study as a whole are presented in Chapter 3; however, each analysis chapter also includes some background on the specific area of investigation (i.e. narrative, languaging and code-switching) in order to motivate the data analysis for each chapter. Chapter 7 considers the direct implications of this study for second language learning and the implications for supporting first language maintenance for transnational adoptees. In brief, I argue that the children themselves actively shape the language practices in these three families to meet specific language learning goals and open opportunities for the construction of certain identities. I conclude that learning how to establish such agency in family interactions forms part of the process of socialization into middle-class US families which can play an important role in classroom settings and helps to explain the construct of agency in second language learning. My conclusions suggest a need for a more nuanced and explicit treatment of 'agency' in second language learning research. They also point to ways in which therapists, teachers and others working with adoptive parents can support them in their children's language development.

Notes

(1) All names have been changed to protect the privacy of participants.
(2) From transcript 1Q (see Table 3.1); 5/9/06; Dima, 10; Sasha, eight.

2 Second Language Socialization, Agency and Identity

Second language learning in the late 20th and early 21st centuries has increasingly been depicted in the applied linguistics literature as a phenomenon associated with sociopolitical and sociohistorical processes of globalization, migration, transnationalism and post-colonialism (Block, 2007; Byram, 2008; Duff, 1995, 2008a, 2011, 2012; Heller & Martin-Jones, 2001; King, 2001; Kramsch, 2010; Norton Pierce, 1995; Philips, 1992; Rampton, 1996). At the same time that second language learning has come to be considered more fully within its macro social context, new approaches to second language learning research that emphasize the sociocultural and ecological foundations of learning have emerged (Atkinson, 2011; Block, 2007; Lantolf, 2000; Leather & van Dam, 2003; van Lier, 2004). In these approaches, language learning is constructed as essentially a social phenomenon situated within a complex nexus of sociohistorical processes (e.g. transnationalism and globalization), immediate and long-term goals and intentions of learners, relationships, desires, identities and norms.

As understandings of second language processes have expanded and questions of ideology, identity and policy have begun to take a more central role, new methods and approaches have been proposed for investigating learning processes within the sociocultural context, including ethnography of communication (Duff, 2002), language ecology (van Lier, 2000), identity based approaches (Block, 2007), sociocultural and sociocognitive theories (Atkinson, 2002; Lantolf, 2000; Lantolf & Thorne, 2006) and language socialization (Bayley & Schechter, 2003; Duff, 2012; Rymes, 1997; Watson-Gegeo, 2004). Originally formulated as a way of understanding child first language acquisition, in which the process of language learning was tied to becoming a competent member of a community (Ochs & Schieffelin, 1984), the language socialization paradigm has afforded second language researchers the tools to better understand how second language learning can be conceptualized as a process of participation in and apprenticeship into communities of practice (Duff, 2012; Pavlenko & Lantolf, 2000). This paradigm has most often focused on child language development, and early applications of this approach to second language contexts were primarily in elementary school classrooms (e.g. Poole, 1992; Willett, 1995).

By viewing second language learning as a process of socialization (for both children and adults), researchers have begun to uncover the cultural and ideological underpinnings of language learning processes and to draw connections among interactional contexts, learners' experiences and macrosociolinguistic phenomena. With the interest in both family and classroom settings and, in some cases, the interconnectedness of both, the language socialization paradigm provides a useful framework for understanding the language learning and socialization processes of transnational adoptees. This book contributes to furthering the field of second language socialization by examining child and adolescent second language socialization outside of the classroom setting. The transnational adoptive family represents a context in which mainstream ideologies of language and learning intersect with second language learning processes and a complex negotiation of multiple identities and roles.

Traditionally, first language socialization focused on the reproduction of cultural norms into and through linguistic practices (e.g. Ochs, 1988; Schieffelin, 1990) in which parents' ideologies and beliefs played an influential role in what and how children learned. However, rather than viewing learning as a primarily unidirectional apprenticeship of novices into expert roles (e.g. Lave & Wenger, 1991; Ochs, 1988), the second and bilingual language socialization literature has emphasized a need to understand how negotiations of norms and practices, as well as contradictions in identities and productions of self, characterize second language learning processes and complicate notions of expert-directed socialization processes (Luykx, 2003, 2005). Taking a bidirectional perspective on language socialization allows for understanding of cultural and linguistic change (see Garrett & Baquedano-Lopéz, 2002) and is particularly relevant in contexts of learning such as the transnational adoptive family where negotiation among family members is key to language learning processes.

From Cultural Reproduction to Transformation

Early language socialization research integrated two larger fields in the social sciences, the sociological and anthropological study of socialization with psycholinguistic or linguistic analyses of (first) language acquisition and development, primarily through ethnographic research. The foundational tenets for this work were that: (a) the process of acquiring a language is affected by the process of becoming a competent member of a society, and

(b) the process of becoming a competent member of society is realized through language by acquiring knowledge of its functions, social distribution and interpretations in and across socially defined situations (i.e. through exchanges of language in particular social situations) (Ochs & Schieffelin, 1984: 277). Early work in this field demonstrated that processes of language acquisition were culturally determined and, importantly, factors thought to be universal and necessary for child language acquisition, such as child-directed speech, were in fact culture-specific (Ochs, 1988; Schieffelin, 1990; Watson-Gegeo & Gegeo, 1986).

Following the foundational work by researchers Elinor Ochs and Bambi Schieffelin, others applied the interest in connections between culture and language development to the learning experiences of older children. One avenue of research focused on the acquisition of literacy and school-related discourses (Heath, 1982, 1983; Michaels, 1981). Heath's (1983) study of language socialization in three different communities in the Piedmont Carolinas, for example, pointed to differences in home socialization across ethnic and socioeconomic lines and demonstrated the ways in which mainstream schooling practices marginalized working-class children. Other studies of school-age children's discourse competencies have found that cultural patterns of socialization play a role in children's readiness to conform to mainstream school norms and practices (Michaels, 1981; Philips, 1992; Scollon & Scollon, 1981). Further, studies of middle-class Anglo-American family socialization practices have found that the discourse practices in these families (such as problem-solving narratives and metalinguistic discourse) coincided with discourse practices associated with schooling (Ely et al., 2001; Ochs et al., 1992). In addition, foundational work in bilingual language socialization explored the maintenance of a minority language in the home (Lanza, 1997/2004; Zentella, 1997). Many of these studies brought to light inherent culture and class biases in traditional schooling and the role of social factors in explaining educational outcomes for different populations of students in the United States.

It is important to note, however, that these early language socialization studies generally focused on language socialization as cultural reproduction, as mentioned earlier. Cultural reproduction refers to the transmission of cultural norms from generation to generation (Bourdieu & Passeron, 1977). As a construct, cultural reproduction helps to explain how positions of power or privilege are maintained across generations and how mainstream education has often functioned to preserve social inequities, particularly in terms of social class. The studies of literacy socialization and schooling discussed above, for the most part, do not examine the reverse process when school-age children bring socialization from school or the wider community into the home or how children develop their own practices and beliefs outside of the family sphere. In cases where family ideologies conflict with value systems external to the family (such as those of the wider society or the education system), processes of cultural transformation occur. This process of change in language practices is most apparent in studies of language shift (e.g. Dauenhauer & Dauenhauer, 1998; King, 2000, 2001; Kulick, 1997), and can be considered an integral part of second language learning processes (Donato, 2001; Duff, 2012).

More recent research in language socialization, and specifically socialization studies that begin to look at how children socialize or influence their parents, have suggested revisions to original notions of communicative competence emphasized in early language socialization studies by drawing on related theories of learning that focus on participation and, subsequently, negotiation. Garrett and Baquedano-Lopéz (2002) outlined the ways in which children can socialize their parents into the use of a majority language in the home or through the use of other modalities such as computer-mediated communication. They concluded that such processes, in which so-called 'novices' take on expert roles, 'call for a notion of competence that takes into account the inherent heterogeneity of culture and cross-cutting dimensions of power and identity that partially structure and organize that heterogeneity' (2002: 346). Gafaranga (2010) further found that such heterogeneity is accomplished within the family unit through talk-in-interaction. In Gafaranga's (2010: 241) study, interactional strategies such as children's medium requests were found to 'talk language shift into being'.

Further, processes involving conflict, negotiation and even 'failure' are potentially more common and salient in second language socialization, as Duff (2012: 567) writes:

> In addition to the possibility of high levels of [second language] L2 achievement and acculturation, outcomes and attitudes might include ambivalence, defiance, resistance to or rejection of the target language, culture, or community (or aspects thereof), or prematurely terminated or suspended L2 learning ... Such syncretic processes and outcomes exist in L1 socialization as well (e.g., Garrett & Baquedano-Lopez, 2002; Kulick & Schieffelin, 2004) but may be especially salient in the context of globalization, migration, multilingualism, transnationalism, and lingua franca use in which the language learners or users may affiliate to different degrees with the non-primary languages and communities they are connected with and those affiliations and allegiances may change radically, frequently, and unpredictably over time for social, economic, political and other, more personal, reasons.

These processes are related to learner agency, or more specifically in this case, learner resistance (although this is only one form of agency as will be discussed in greater detail below). Agency, negotiation and conflict then are key constructs for understanding second language socialization. As Donato (2001: 46) writes, 'A central concern in sociocultural theory is that learners actively transform their world and do not merely conform to it'. It is the processes of the emergence of learner agency in interactions, the strategies learners use to achieve agency and the resulting transformation within the family context that I examine in this book in order to inform understandings of second language socialization.

Studies of language shift in the home environment have examined how children influence parents and other family members to shift toward a majority language. Kulick (1993), for example, examined cultural beliefs about the agency (or self will) of children along with socioeconomic changes in a community experiencing language shift in Papua New Guinea. He found that parents in the village interpreted vocalizations of children over the age of one as being produced in Tok Pisin, and not the local (parents') language, Taiap. This interpretation, along with the belief that Tok Pisin was an easier language than Taiap and therefore better suited for use with small children, led to parents' suppression of Taiap in interaction with children in the community. Kulick's findings reinterpreted notions of language socialization as a process through which children acquired communicative competence in a language from parents and pointed to the fact that competence, and the sociocultural norms for language use that go along with it, are negotiated in interactions between experts and novices and mediated by parental ideologies. Corsaro (2004: 18) further argued that processes of child socialization involved not only 'adaptation and internalization' by children, but also 'appropriation, reinvention, and reproduction'. The children in the current study, who are older than the children discussed in Kulick's study, have potentially greater resources for negotiating their parents' interpretations and strategies because of their older ages and engagement with peer groups outside of the home, as well as their prior socialization into a different (Russian) language and culture.

In her study of bilingual language socialization in Aymara households in the Bolivian town of Huatajata, Luykx (2003: 40) concluded that language socialization was better viewed not 'as a one-way process' but as a 'dynamic network of mutual family influences'. Luykx (2005: 1409) identified three ways in which children can influence parents' language practices: (a) they can resist parental preferences of language choice and thereby 'challenge or ignore aspects of the parents' desired "family language policy"', (b) they can influence parents in contexts of immigration to adapt their language to 'promote desired linguistic competencies in their children' – when these adaptations persist, parents' linguistic development can be affected, and (c) 'parents may actually learn new varieties', or elements thereof, from their children (during homework sessions in particular). These findings suggest that children not only form youth cultures that instigate language change across generations (e.g. Eckert, 1988), but that they influence the adults with whom they interact on a daily basis, causing change within the family sphere. Gafaranga's (2010) study of language shift in Rwandan families in Belgium further concluded that children played an agentive role in this process as their medium requests toward French were accommodated by parents and demonstrated how these role reversals in language socialization can occur with regard to language choice. The micro interactions in these families were both influenced by and constructed the macrosociolinguistic phenomena in the greater community. This bidirectional effect is found in transnational adoptive families, and a shift to the higher status language, English, is assumed to take place even in families where Russian is used by parents.

The home environment connects in important ways with outcomes for young bilingual children in formal schooling (King *et al.*, 2008), but what are the implications for these connections if children are influential actors affecting socialization processes? On the one hand, in bilingual families the introduction of a majority language to the home environment has been known to be driven by school-age children (Gafaranga, 2010; Tuominen, 1999; Wong Fillmore, 2000), and this shift can potentially limit children's access to heritage languages and identities which might become more important as they grow older. Additionally, children in transnational families, where members participate in migratory flows across national boundaries, might assert their needs in interaction with parents and other family members who have greater access to local discourses (Fogle & King, in press). Children can also bring school-related discourses and practices into the home as older children socialize younger children into homework practices and 'schooling' (Hawkins, 2005). Home socialization, then, can shape children's linguistic competencies, identities and even the sense of agency that plays a role in outcomes in school settings.

Few studies have investigated the interactional processes in which children are able to have such a sustained influence over parents and other family members (Gafaranga, 2010). This book begins to fill this gap by looking at children's resistance, questioning and negotiation strategies that are found to have an effect on parents in the home. These are potentially the same strategies that play a role in children's agency and negotiation of identities in school classrooms (e.g. Hawkins, 2005; McKay & Wong, 1996), and here I suggest that the ability to use such strategies emerges across both home and school settings and can be part of culture-specific socialization patterns associated with middle-class parenting. The data presented here provide a unique opportunity to understand three main aspects of child second language learning: (a) what second language learners can do discursively in daily interaction with a caring adult, (b) how learners actively construct opportunities for learning outside of an instructed situation, and (c) how negotiations among transnational family members in which individuals have uneven access to linguistic resources and cultural norms influence both children and adults in terms of language learning and identity construction.

Parent Language Ideologies, Strategies and Child Outcomes

In order to understand how children can influence language practices in the home and the methods by which they do so, it is helpful to consider the different components of parental language policy and use in daily interaction with their children. Following Spolsky (2004), studies in the newly emerging field of family language policy have articulated three main areas of investigation of home language: (a) language ideologies, (b) language practices, and (c) language management (King et al., 2008). Children's language learning in the home environment is mediated by parental ideologies (about language but also about learning and the role of children in society in general) and the strategies parents use in interaction with their children or the linguistic environment (De Houwer, 1999; Fogle, in press; King & Fogle, 2006). One question for this area of research that is to be addressed in the current study is at what point in the process can children have an influence on the construction of family language policies – that is, to what extent can children change parental ideologies of language and learning that will in turn lead to a lasting change in strategies and management?

Language ideologies refer to the 'representations, either explicit or implicit, that construe the intersection of language and human beings in a social world' (Woolard, 1998: 3) and are often thought to be the underlying force in language practices and planning or 'the mediating link between language use and social organization' (King, 2000: 169). Language ideologies then are one aspect of family language policy that link individual families with larger societal processes. More than one language ideology, however, is often at work in a given community (Shohamy, 2006; Spolsky, 2004), and the conflict between competing ideologies is often the genesis of language policies. The family sphere can become a crucible for such ideological conflicts, as has been seen in work on language shift and revitalization. Studies of Indigenous communities' efforts to revitalize or maintain a native language point to tensions that can arise between conflicting explicit and implicit ideologies (Dauenhauer & Dauenhauer, 1998; King, 2000). King (2000), for example, points to how conflict between community members' stated, explicit 'pro-Indigenous' and privately held, implicit 'anti-Indigenous' language ideologies together shaped home language practices toward community language shift. These cases have emphasized both the importance of language ideology in language revitalization efforts and the complex nature of language ideologies themselves. However, few studies have looked at how children can influence policy making from the bottom up.

One ideological aspect of mainstream, middle-class parenting in the US that is relevant to the current study of adoptive families is an emphasis on the linguistic and cognitive development of young children that is achievement-oriented and sometimes fails to lead to meaningful use of two languages (e.g. Pizer et al., 2007). Several studies of bilingual families (Felling, 2007; King & Fogle, 2006) report on middle-class trends toward 'hyper' parenting in which learning another language became an additional extracurricular activity in an already packed family life. Pizer et al. (2007: 387), for example, found that parents' introduction of baby signs ('the use of visual gestural signs between hearing parents and their young hearing children') fit with ideologies of child rearing that emphasized early communication and 'self-lowering' techniques (see Ochs & Schieffelin, 1984) to accommodate the child; however, these early practices quickly disappeared as children gained the ability to speak. Thus, academic and social goals did not align with long-term outcomes for bilingualism or, in this case, bimodal bilingualism.

Adoptive parents, as will be discussed in greater detail in Chapter 3, are potentially influenced by ideologies of mainstream parenting and the 'achievement' culture described above, as well as ideologies of parenting that place children as emotional assets in the home. The desire to bond with children and form families often motivates adoptive parents' parenting practices (Stryker, 2010). In the following chapters I outline the ways in which mainstream ideologies about language and learning influence and connect with the different parents' approaches to communicating and interacting with their older adoptees. These ideologies often intersect and even conflict with ideologies about adoptees that emphasize adoptive parenting as 'risky' and adopted children as potentially 'damaged' (see Melosh, 2002). These perspectives can potentially result in parents withholding educational or linguistic support in an effort to ameliorate stress levels for adoptees. In the analyses of each family in Chapters 4, 5 and 6, I carefully emphasize differences in the families based on factors such as educational background and occupation, as well as the ways in which the local context, and children's participation in particular, affected parents' ideologies or strategies despite prior beliefs. In many cases in these data, the children influenced parents' practices despite firmly held parental beliefs and policies. To better understand how this role reversal is accomplished, we need to turn to the constructs of agency and identity in socialization processes.

Approaches to Agency in Second Language Learning

The importance of agency in second language learning has been noted in classroom studies (e.g. Hawkins, 2005; McKay & Wong, 1996) as well as studies of adults in instructed and non-instructed settings (Lantolf, 2000; Morita, 2004; Norton Pierce, 1995; van Lier, 2007). But what do we mean when we attribute learning success to 'agency', and what forms does it take? Duff (2012: 413) notes that agency and identity are closely tied in second language acquisition research:

> Learners are not simply passive or complicit participants in language learning and use, but can also make informed choices, exert influence, resist (e.g., remain silent, quit courses) or comply, although their social circumstances may constrain their choices. Such actions or displays of agency, which might be as simple as insisting on speaking one language (one's L2) versus another (others' L2) in a conversation with a language exchange partner, can also be considered acts of identity and the site of power dynamics.

Here Duff summarizes the different possibilities for learner agency as: choice, influence, resistance, silence, dropping out and compliance, not all of which lead to the acquisition of language. Studies that have equated agency with learning typically focus on complicit (participatory) or controlling agency (agency of power) (e.g. van Lier, 2007). These approaches to agency, while acknowledging the co-constructed nature of agency, emphasize the importance of the learner's intentions, will and autonomy.

Pavlenko and Lantolf (2000: 169), for example, attribute ultimate attainment in a second language to the individual's agency, which, in this quote, is tied to the learner's decision and choice to engage in a process of identity transformation:

> We would like to argue that the ultimate attainment in second language learning relies on one's agency ... While the first language and subjectivities are an indisputable given, the new ones are arrived at by choice. Agency is crucial at the point where the individuals must not just start memorizing a dozen new words and expressions but have to decide on whether to initiate a long, painful, inexhaustive and, for some, never-ending process of self-translation.

Van Lier (2007: 46) also sees agency as closely linked to learner autonomy and motivation, 'the focus in second language studies has gradually shifted from linguistic inputs and mental information processing to the things that learners do and say while engaged in meaningful activity'. These studies emphasize participation as a metaphor for second language learning. However, not all learners, and especially the children and the transnational adoptees in this study, have access to such 'choices' about their language learning or identity transformations (many transnational adoptees, for example, find it necessary to call themselves by new names upon adoption because of their parents' choices). Thus, there is general consensus that such assertions of agency are not simply achieved by free will or an individual's choice. The possibility for individual agency and the opportunity for choice are shaped by multiple forces on multiple layers. The questions that arise in these and the studies of school-age learners discussed below entail understanding why some learners are able to achieve agency and others aren't, and why some types of agency are acknowledged while others aren't. To answer these questions, it is useful to turn to the studies of young learners in classroom settings in which agency and identity have played an important role.

Agency and Identity in Classroom Second Language Socialization

Learning, in Lave and Wenger's (1991) approach, is a process of identity formation in which apprentices become legitimate members of a community of practice. A small set of studies have shown important links between establishing a 'good student identity' or affiliative identity toward schooling through both participation in classroom activities and home socialization that influenced language learning and academic outcomes for the children (Hawkins, 2005; Norton & Toohey, 2001; Toohey, 2000; Willett, 1995). The good student identity, according to Hawkins, is one that is ascribed onto the student by the structures of the school, but it is also one that the children construct for themselves through active participation that resonates with the teachers' and school's idea of success.

Along the same lines, identity construction through participation in classroom routines has been found to benefit young second language learners. For instance, Willett (1995: 494) conducted a yearlong ethnographic study of a mainstream first grade classroom that consisted of four English language learners (three girls and one boy). She found that, over the course of the year, the three girls collaborated in the daily seatwork routine and were able to acquire grammar skills as they developed in other areas as well, such as literacy. The group of three girls was able to move from the appearance of competent participation in phonics seatwork (through stringing together linguistic chunks used by more competent members of the class) to using syntax for meaning, interpreting meaning from written symbols, acquiring academic norms and constructing identities as competent students. However, although he received more feedback from teachers and aides, the English language-learning boy in the class did not reach the same level of language competence because of his lack of access to the collaborative interactional routines of the girls. Willett's study explicated the ways in which larger contextual structures (i.e. gender, classroom seating arrangements and routine discourse) can organize linguistic development for individual learners and showed how agency in the classroom setting is achieved through the participation and collaboration that entails identity construction as a good learner.

In a comparison of two English language learners in a mainstream kindergarten classroom, Hawkins (2005) found that one child (Anton) was more successful at constructing a 'good learner' identity in the classroom than a second child from a higher social class and subsequently had greater linguistic and academic gains at the end of the school year. More specifically, Hawkins found that Anton's proactive strategies to recruit other students in interactions provided him access to language practice, scaffolding and affiliations with school and schooling (three routes to English language development and learning identified in the study). Hawkins (2005: 78) concluded that these strategies were engendered in home interactions between Anton and his sister, who was more familiar with the practices of schooling:

> The tools and experiences that Anton brought, together with his agency – [his] actions stemming from his understandings of this space and who he could (and wanted to) be within it – resonated with institutional views of successful learners and enabled him to claim an identity as a learner.

Children's agency in Hawkins' study turned out to be an important part of the learning process and one that, importantly, seemed to be cultivated at home. Anton's home situation was not exactly parallel to the middle-class families described in this study, but Hawkins determined from home visits and interviews with his mother that his sister was primarily responsible for his socialization into school practices. These findings once again reinforce the notion that children bring external socialization to the home sphere and, taken together with the findings from the current study, that middle-class values are reproduced in schooling structures (Heath, 1983; Michaels, 1981). That is, values Anton inherited from his sister, which were passed from the school environment to the home by his sister, helped him develop interactional and learning strategies that assisted him in his own classroom.

However, establishing a good learner identity does not always result in actual learning. Rymes and Pash (2001: 279) argued that taking on a good learner identity could compromise actual learning: 'Becoming an "expert as a learner" without learning "the performance and skills themselves" is a conundrum . . .'. Toohey (2000) further showed how classroom practices, child identities and larger discursive and socialization processes intersected to afford some students success in the classroom while limiting others. Most studies of 'good learner' identities have investigated how learners fit into preexisting classroom structures and norms, but one question that Toohey poses and one that arises in other work (e.g. McKay & Wong, 1996), is how young learners display identities and exercise forms of agency that do not fit with the possibilities offered by formal schooling (see Lin, 2007). One child in McKay and Wong's study, for example, resisted the teacher's limitations by conforming to the *form* of the assignment (e.g. telling a story or writing a narrative), but included transgressive or subversive content (e.g. telling a story about going to a Chinese brothel). In Chapter 4 of this book, I further explore one adopted child's similar exploitation of a parent-directed narrative game in which he conforms to the routine, but includes transgressive content that challenges his father. I focus on what effect these children's strategies have on parents' own communication patterns and how such displays of child agency coincide with developing and constructing alternative identities outside of those previously imagined by parents and/or children. These findings further suggest a need to view agency as multiple and complex, as I discuss in the following sections.

Agency is Socioculturally Mediated

The study of agency has a long history in the social sciences and here I will focus primarily on work that has emphasized a need for examining the relationship between language and agency. The first way to begin to address these questions is to see agency as 'socioculturally mediated', which implies that accepted forms of agency for different actors and agents will vary across cultures and contexts. Ahearn (2001) notes that individuals vary and adapt the way they conceive of their own and others' actions, attributing agency to different entities (e.g. individuals, fate, deities) over time or place. For instance, researchers have found that middle-class parents in the US tend to encourage young children's individual agency through the use of accommodation strategies that 'lower' their own speech to the child's level and simultaneously 'raise' or expand the child's speech (Ochs & Schieffelin, 1984; Zentella, 2005). Ochs and Schieffelin (1984: 287–288) summarized the ways in which Anglo-American middle-class parents accommodate to their children: by simplifying speech in a child-directed register, by richly interpreting child utterances and by expanding on or paraphrasing child utterances. These strategies socialize children into practices involving ambiguity (that utterances can have more than one meaning), authority (that some interlocutors are in positions to interpret meanings of utterances) and negotiation (that the child has a right to agree or disagree). However, as has been well established in the literature, such patterns are not universal (Goodwin, 1997); in many contexts, children are not treated as conversational partners and their utterances are not taken to be communicative (Ochs & Schieffelin, 1984). This self-lowering pattern of middle-class parenting is particularly relevant to the current study where children are accommodated to and allowed agency in ways that, in some cases, might not be accepted in other contexts, such as the classroom, and in other cases might facilitate the transition to the US classroom.

Teachers and other experts are also subject to a myriad of sociohistorical processes that determine their own agency in helping students in their classrooms. S. Scollon (2005), for example, analyzed how an English language teacher (and member of the Chinese American community) exercised individual agency by helping students fill out census forms to assist in obtaining resources for the community, and how this agency was influenced by 'historical layers' of census taking and globalization at multiple layers with multiple actors. S. Scollon argued that agency was distributed over participants, times, mediational means and discourses. In this sense, agency was a product of other historical processes that afforded individual will to the teacher, and not the students, who for various reasons, such as access to linguistic resources and prior socialization into cultures in which census taking was not trusted, did not feel empowered to fill out the forms. The strong interplay of historical cycles with the momentary action leads Norris (2005: 195) to conclude that 'agency and free will appear to be deeply embedded within society and the communities of practice which the individual belongs to, so that we need to question whether we can speak of agency and free will at all'. Thus processes of socialization and individuals' experiences are central to the achievement of agency.

In the analysis in the coming chapters, I show over time how children are allowed to exercise control over their parents in day-to-day interactions as parents increasingly accommodate to their interactional strategies. These accommodations not only lead to learning opportunities for the children, but also in some cases to dramatic changes in the possibilities for identity construction and roles and relationships in the family sphere. Negotiation of linguistic practices, learning opportunities, agency and identities in these data go hand-in-hand.

Agency is Achieved in Interaction

As all of these studies suggest, agency does not reside within the individual, or in this case, the learner. Agency itself is both socioculturally and interactionally mediated (Al Zidjaly, 2009). Ahearn (2001: 118) argues that theories of agency need to account for social transformation and change at the same time as they explain cultural reproduction. Linguistic approaches to identity in interaction have, as Bucholtz and Hall (2005) summarize, helped to disperse the artificial dichotomy between structure and agency debated in the social sciences and to reconceptualize human agency as not simply the intentionality of the individual, but also as socioculturally mediated. As Norris and Jones (2005: 170) argue, agency is 'always something that is negotiated between individuals and their social worlds'. As an example of the negotiated nature of agency, Ahearn (2001: 129) provides the following example from McDermott and Tylbor (1995/1983):

> Rosa, a first-grade student who cannot read, constantly calls out for a turn at reading aloud – and yet on close examination, Rosa, her classmates, and the teacher all seem to be colluding through the use of subtle gestures and timing cues in order not to give Rosa chance to read aloud.

In this case the learner and student, Rosa, can bid for the opportunity to act, but is not granted that possibility by the other members of her classroom community. Thus Ahearn (2001: 112) defines agency as the 'socioculturally mediated capacity to act'. In keeping with Bucholtz and Hall's (2005) approach, Al Zidjaly (2009) expands on this definition by concluding that this mediation is accomplished through *linguistic* meditational means. In her study of conjoint action in which multiple participants author a letter together, Al Zidjaly demonstrates how interactional strategies such as asking questions, rejecting assistance from an interactant and constructing an expert identity, lead to the achievement of agency in interaction. The interactional achievement of agency is also clearly presented in Gafaranga's (2010) study of language shift in which children used a particular interactional strategy (i.e. the medium request) to negotiate code choice with their parents. In this study I contribute to an understanding of the strategies used by learners to achieve agency by examining three different types of strategies that develop in the three different interactional contexts of the adoptive families: resistance strategies and non-responses, questions and elicitations of talk and code negotiations such as the medium request.

One limitation of the treatment of agency in second language studies thus far has been an over attention to one type of agency (i.e. complicit or participatory agency) in which learners find ways to work within established norms for the community of practice in which they are entering and are able to establish a degree of autonomy and control that leads to learning. Learner resistance and rejection of target language and cultural norms are also forms of learner agency; although, in many cases, these forms of agency are seen as constraining or lead to problematic outcomes such as trouble at school, dropping out and not learning (e.g. Harklau, 2000; McKay & Wong, 1996). The success of some types of agency at facilitating learning and the relative failure of other types of agency in doing so has to do with the interpretation of and accommodation to learners' actions by so-called experts in interaction. Jones and Norris (2005: 170) conclude that analyzing agency includes not only the individual's discursive self-construction, but also the interpretation of such actions: 'Thus, any analysis of agency must focus on the tension between the way agency is constructed by individuals in their discourse, and the way it is interpreted by others as actions unfold.' It is the responsive stance of others that shapes the possibilities for agency and learning in different contexts, and this is one of the big differences between second language learning in the classroom and the adoptive family home, as I will show.

Examples of the negotiated and varied nature of agency in second language studies include Morita's (2004) study of Japanese women in Canadian university classrooms and McKay and Wong's (1996) earlier study of middle school English language learners. Morita discussed the nuanced nature of learner agency in second language socialization settings. In this study, Japanese students' silence was intended to have different meanings by learners and was interpreted in different ways by university instructors.

These processes led to different outcomes in terms of learner agency and acceptance to the classroom communities of practice. Morita showed that the ways in which learners' actions are interpreted, evaluated and accommodated to will influence how they achieve agency in interaction and their learning processes. McKay and Wong (1996), further, discussed the 'curtailment' of learner agency as an outcome of racist discourses on immigration that led to teacher-centered practices that controlled the output of students and did not acknowledge or make use of student's prior knowledge. Agency for the English language-learning students in this study was limited by macro-level ideologies and expectations that were enacted in micro-level interactions that involved power relations between teacher and student. Some of the children in the McKay and Wong study most affected by such negative processes found ways to reclaim their agency through resistance and reclamation of other identities (although these did not always coincide with educational processes).

To sum up, in order to understand agency in second language socialization we need to start with three main ideas. First, conceptions of individual agency emerge through socialization – a child learns how to be agentive in interaction with parents, other caregivers and peers. Second, agency takes many forms and in many cases is multiple and complex (thus an action might at once be both resistant and compliant). Third, the interpretation (or recognition) of agency by others is one key to the achievement of agency in interaction. By examining these different aspects of agency in interaction, we can see that agency is not a product of an interaction or a set of ideologies or norms, but rather a constant process of negotiation, achievement and revision.

Types of Agency

As discussed above, in second language socialization research, the focus has typically been on agency that leads to participation and legitimate membership in the new community of practice. However, agency can take many forms and functions. As Ahearn (2001: 130) notes,

> One fruitful direction for future research may be to begin to distinguish among types of agency – oppositional agency, complicit agency, agency of power, agency of intention, etc. – while also recognizing that multiple types are exercised in any given action. By doing this, we might gain a more thorough understanding of the 'complex and ambiguous agency' (MacLeod 1992) that always surrounds us.

In her analysis of Muslim women's practices, for example, MacLeod (1992) showed how women's choices to wear the traditional veil, or some type of covering, related not only to patriarchal values, but also to new positions of women working outside of the home in urban Cairo. Thus the practice of veiling was at once complicit in reproducing cultural norms at the same time that it was resistant and transformative of those norms as women took on new roles and positions in society. Gallagher (2007) built on MacLeod's analysis to show that power, in terms of patriarchal male control, does not negate women's agency within familial relationships in the Middle East. In these two studies, agency is construed as layered, complex and at times contradictory. This approach to agency is particularly relevant to the transnational adoptive family where the newness of the institution and consciousness of the participants in the creation of a new type of family lend themselves to both participation and resistance in shaping new norms and practices. As we will see in the analysis of the family interactions that follow, these negotiations depend on the relationships that are formed and affect bonding among the family members, which I discuss in greater detail in the conclusion of the book (Chapter 7).

In the following chapters, I investigate three main strategies that lead to the achievement of children's agency in the participating families. By examining the achievement of agency from a language socialization perspective, I also show how 'the capacity to act' affects the interactional context of the family and parents' strategies and beliefs over time. In this way, learner agency leads to transformation and change within the community of practice. For such change to occur, the agency of the children must be recognized as such, and the adults must accommodate to it. These processes depend on subtle negotiations of the children's strategies and the parents' policies.

Constructionist Approaches to Identity

Agency is closely linked to the construct of identity. Because of the importance of identity to language learning processes, and the apparent value of establishing an agentive good learner identity for succeeding in the classroom, as discussed in the previous section, it seems important to consider in more detail what we mean by identity. In this book I will take a constructivist approach to identity, which involves the examination of identities emerging in interaction and discourse (Bucholtz & Hall, 2005; De Fina et al., 2006). Discourse analysts working on social constructionist approaches to identity have drawn on a wide set of methods and theoretical perspectives, including interactional sociolinguistics, positioning theory, membership categorization and critical discourse analysis (De Fina et al.,

2006). These perspectives on identity take a socially constructed point of view in which identities are not seen as innate, inherent or otherwise essential to the individual, but rather as created and built from discursive resources through which particular actions and stances (Ochs, 1988) are, as Gee (2000) notes, interpretable as 'being a certain kind of person'.

In proposing a sociocultural linguistics, Bucholtz and Hall (2005: 585) delineate five principles (Emergence, Positionality, Indexicality, Relationality and Partialness) derived from empirical research on identity and interaction. These principles respectively state that identities: (a) are socially and culturally constructed, (b) are constructed by both macro- and micro-level processes, (c) may be linguistically indexed, (d) are relationally constructed through the relationship of self and other, and (e) are both conscious and unconscious. In short, identities are multiple, complex, expressed through language and contextually sensitive.

As an example, in an analysis of interactional sequences taken from group meetings of a university physics team, Jacoby and Gonzales (1991: 174) used conversation analysis and ethnomethodology to demonstrate how 'macro' roles (such as tenured professor, doctoral student, etc.) do not always determine expert–novice relationships. The micro interactions them-selves revealed that 'participants negotiate who is more or less knowing at particular interactional moments'. This conceptualization of expert–novice (i.e. as locally produced), according to Jacoby and Gonzales (1991: 174), not only accounts for the bidirectionality of language socialization but also for 'change and innovation in communities of practice'. In relation to the adoptive family, I see this process of negotiating expert–novice roles as key to the ways in which parents and children establish intersubjectivity and collaboratively construct a family unit.

These perspectives on identity are important for understanding a myriad of social problems and social change, such as the creation of new families and kinship through the transnational adoptive families involved in this study (which will be discussed further in Chapter 3). They also help us to understand processes of learning. As individuals negotiate new roles, relationships and identities they are also learning about the ways in which to do so. The learning processes associated with socialization and identity construction become more salient in second language settings where competences are uneven and power relationships potentially have greater asymmetry. Thus as the children in this study learn English through the interactional routines of the new families, they take on new identities as competent members of the family community. The surprising aspect of this process is that as the parents enact their parenting role, primarily by accommodating to the children, they allow the children to shape and transform their own preferred practices and policies. This bidirectional socialization allows the children agency in the family interactions, not only to act but also to effect change in the context of the family.

A further way to understand identity construction in relation to learning processes is to consider these phenomena in relation to time. Lemke (2010: 24) points out that momentary actions themselves do not lead to long-term identities. Rather, it is the repetition and recurrence of actions and stances, as shown in studies of family language socialization, which construct an individual's larger identity on a long-term timescale.

> But the longer term aspects of our identities are not determined by a single performance. They constitute patterns across time across situations, even across clusters of situation types (e.g., all the types of situation in which acting the 'good father' make sense).

In the current study, the family members are represented as 'adoptive parents' and 'adoptees', 'Russian speakers' or 'English speakers', 'children' and 'parents'. What we will see in the analysis is that the expectations for each of these larger identities (e.g. that parents teach and socialize children, that Russian adoptees speak Russian and their parents speak English) and the behaviors commonly ascribed to 'good parents' (e.g. to set boundaries or to accommodate to children's needs) and 'good children' (e.g. to be cooperative or independent) in middle-class, US families are not always what occur in everyday interaction, and new identities form in interactional processes. In this study I utilize the concept of the timescale in the study of adoptive family discourse in three main ways: (a) to examine how repetitions of interactional roles (i.e. questioner, resistor, etc.) come to represent a speaker identity for individuals in the family conversations, (b) to show how repetitions of these speaker roles over time lead to more persistent identities (such as unwilling participant in family interactions), and (c) to examine examples where family members make reference to longer timescales, usually through narratives or parts of narratives about the distant past in order to share knowledge and experiences about a time (i.e. pre-adoption time) in which the family was not together and subsequently co-construct identities of themselves as adoptees, children, parents and families.

Research Questions

In light of these current trends and gaps in the field of second language socialization, the current study examines three main questions:

(1) What language socialization processes emerge in transnational adoptive family interactions?

(2) What role do school-age adoptees play in shaping language socialization processes in family interactions?

(3) How can processes of language learning and language socialization be (re)conceptualized in light of the findings from questions one and two above?

Conclusion

In this chapter I have outlined the field of second language socialization and have highlighted the constructs of agency and identity as integral to the understanding of both individual language learning and larger cultural transformation processes. As agency is one construct that has potentially been under-theorized in second language studies, I have made an effort here to represent agency as both socioculturally and linguistically mediated, as well as complex and layered. How learner agency emerges in interaction in the transnational adoptive family, the types of agency available to child learners in that setting and the processes of learning that the achievement of agency engenders in these families will be the subject of Chapters 4, 5 and 6 in which I focus on each of the three participating adoptive families. In the next chapter, Chapter 3, I look more closely at transnational adoption and language and the role language and language learning potentially play in forming the family.

3 Transnational Adoption and Language: An Overview

In the previous chapter, I outlined the ways in which language socialization in the family could lead to the reproduction of cultural norms (Ochs & Schieffelin, 1984). I also argued that bi- or multilingual and transnational families offer opportunities to examine in more detail processes of cultural transformation as children who participate in communities of practice outside of the family setting, for example at school or in other contexts of care (orphanages, extended families, etc.), can influence their parents' and other adults' language practices and ideologies (Garrett & Baquedano-Lopéz, 2002). In this chapter I focus on the role of language in constructing family membership and identity as well as belonging. Examining these processes in transnational adoptive families with older adoptees, such as the ones who participated in this study, can further contribute to our understanding of how families *become* family and how kinship ties are formed discursively in daily interactions. The language(s) a family speaks, the way that families talk about language and the interactional roles and processes involved in family communication all play a role in constructing family membership and identity (see Blum-Kulka, 1997; Tannen et al., 2007; Zentella, 1997). At the same time, in transnational adoptive families, and particularly those with children adopted at older ages, linguistic difference and second language learning take an integral role in family socialization processes, as learning a second language (for children and potentially parents) becomes a part of forming relationships and identities, and language competence is intimately tied with belonging in the family.

Linguists have studied the language development and attrition of transnational adoptees to better understand second language and bilingual acquisition processes (e.g. Nicoladis & Grabois, 2002; Sato, 1990). One line of this research has sought to understand how to meet the language learning needs of transnational adoptees by comparing them to monolingual norms for speech-language therapy (e.g. Glennen & Bright, 2005; Pollock & Price, 2005). A second line of research has been interested in linguistic theory building and understanding how much of adoptees' first language is lost after an abrupt transition in dominant languages. In this chapter I argue that these clinical and psycholinguistic perspectives do not reach far enough for understanding the socially complex ways in which transnational adoptees learn and use language. I further suggest ways that a sociocultural approach can broaden our understanding of adoptees' learning processes.

The Phenomenon of Transnational Adoption

In a recent study of adoption trends in the US, Vandivere *et al.* (2009: 1) note that while adoptees (both domestic and international) represent a small number of all children in the US, they are of particular concern because of the role the government plays in adoption policy making and the vulnerability of adoptees:

> While adopted children comprise only a small portion of the overall U.S. child population – about 2 percent – their absolute numbers are sizable, numbering nearly 1.8 million. This group of children is of particular concern to policy makers and the public both due to the government's role in establishing adoptive parent-child relationships as well as the potential vulnerabilities of some segments of this population.

Both international and domestic adoptions have been credited with transforming US society and notions of kinship. These processes have both been facilitated by and have also contributed to a growing multiculturalism in the US in the late 1990s (Esposito & Biafora, 2007; Pertman, 2001). Adoption has also overwhelmingly been noted to be a successful intervention for children in need (van Ijzendoorn & Juffer, 2005). However, adoption as an institution has also been criticized and problematized for a variety of reasons. In transnational adoption, the inherently uneven economic and power differentials that make some nations senders of children and others predominately receivers of children have been questioned. In these contexts children are constructed as 'resources', and the desires of adoptive parents for family are bolstered in a way that potentially creates unrealistic expectations for the adopted child (Stryker, 2004, 2010). New approaches to adoption research seek to better understand the experiences of adoptees post-placement and situate adoptees' differences in more ethnographically informed understandings of family and culture (Stryker, 2011). These studies promise new approaches to post-placement interventions that take into consideration cultural, ethnic and racial differences for adoptees, their parents and the national contexts in which they belong. In this chapter I add to this mix an examination of linguistic difference and the role language plays in both adoptive family and adoptee identity formation.

Transnational adoption entails positions of power on the macro level of government policies and relationships between sender and receiver nations that further inform micro-level processes within the transnational adoptive family (Yngevesson, 2010). World events such as the end of the Cold War and the fall of the Soviet Union contributed to the transnational flow of children as restrictions were loosened and US parents also found a philanthropic purpose in adopting children in need from abroad (Melosh, 2002). Yngvesson (2010: 29) notes that sender nations are created by crisis; the fall of the Soviet Union created internal turmoil and uneven relations between countries such as Russia and Ukraine and the West:

> The shifting patterns of sending and receiving nations highlight the complex forces shaping the movement of children in transnational adoption . . . The specifics differ from case to case, but always there is a combination of conditions that are simultaneously local and global and have the effect of placing certain categories of children at risk of becoming a liability in one location even as they become objects of desire in another.

In these situations adoptable children become resources for both sender and receiver nations.

At the same time that these events affect relationships and assumptions within the family, phenomena within transnational adoptive families also serve to construct these macro-level processes themselves. In the data presented in the following chapters, parents place interactional demands and set up interactional contexts that, for the most part, replicate predominate middle-class norms in US families. Such practices include routines for talking about the day at mealtime, talking about language or engaging in metalinguistic discourse and using English as a family language. In some ways these types of discursive practices are what make up *being and doing* a family in these settings. The socialization of adopted children into these practices constructs the parents as socializers of children into the dominant cultural practices and norms of the receiving nation. This process, however, can be filled with conflict, negotiation and disruption (Stryker, 2010; Yngvesson, 2010), and adoptees themselves can resist such socialization. In the chapters that follow, I show how such resistance and negotiations take place linguistically and discursively in the family setting and how adoptees develop discursive strategies that shape socialization processes in the adoptive family and negotiate their parents' linguistic practices.

Transnational Adoption Trends

From 1990 to 2004, when this study began, the adoption of foreign-born children by US citizens more than tripled from 7093 international adoptions reported in 1990 to over 24,000 in 2004 (Office of Immigration Statistics, 2004). Researchers and authors interested in adoption issues often cite both domestic and foreign social and political factors to account for this trend. In the United States, overall increases in maternal age have caused parents to look for alternative ways to build families. In addition, fewer numbers of infants available for adoption and other social and cultural considerations, including the increased prevalence of open adoptions in which birth mothers maintain connections to their children, have led some US parents to seek adoptions from abroad.

Until 2005, China was the largest sender of children to the US, with Russia in second place. In recent years, however, these numbers have changed as countries from the former Soviet Union and China have slowed some adoptions due to concerns about both the eventual outcomes for the children and other social factors. In general, the years 2005 to 2008 have seen a slight decline in international adoptions overall, with 17,438 adopted children entering the US in 2008 (US Department of Homeland Security, 2009). The data for the study at hand were collected during the period between 2004 and 2008 when the rates had just begun to fall.

While these statistics also show that most transnational adoptees arrive in the US as infants, one aspect of the transnational adoption trend has been an increase in the number of school-age (five years or older for the purposes of this study) adoptees arriving in the US each year. The phenomenon of adopting older or school-age children from abroad is one that is confined largely to Russia and other countries of the former Soviet Union (e.g. Ukraine, Kazakhstan, etc.). About 20% (1016) of the total number of children adopted by US parents from Russia in 2003 were over the age of five at the time of arrival, whereas only 1% (~100) of children from China were of comparable age. In 2004, 1095 children from Russia and Ukraine combined were adopted at ages five to nine compared to 133 from China and 118 from Guatemala and 87 out of 277 in total from Ethiopia. These numbers have declined. Russia and Ukraine combined sent 726 children in the five and older group in 2009 compared to 367 from China, 77 from Guatemala and 536 from Ethiopia; however, in 2007 Russia and Ukraine combined still sent about one-quarter of all children five years and older adopted by US parents (Yearbook of Immigration Statistics, 2009).

Culture Keeping and Language Maintenance

Examining the post-placement experiences and language socialization of children adopted at older ages from the former Soviet Union can provide valuable perspectives on the transnational adoption phenomenon and how parent ideologies, language practices and identity construction coincide. Russian-speaking adoptees are typically, though not always, White, and share phenotypical features with their adoptive parents. This racial similarity can influence parenting practices, according to Jacobson (2008), who found that racial difference led to more efforts on the part of Chinese adoptive mothers versus Russian adoptive mothers to practice 'culture keeping' and keep their adopted children in touch with their cultural origins. Because Russian children 'blend in' to the middle-class, White US adopting family, their perceived difference, and therefore the perceived need to maintain past cultural ties, was minimized in parenting practices.

Adopting older Russian children from abroad, however, entails linguistic and cultural differences that are potentially overlooked by parents, teachers and clinicians, as racial similarity masks these differences and enhances the sense of belonging. (In general, East European children are often described as privileged immigrants who face an easier time adapting to US schools [e.g. McKay & Wong, 1996], although there is little empirical data to support this assumption [see Shohamy, 2006 for discussion of Russian immigrants in the Israeli context and Watson, 2006 in the US].) These similarities potentially increase others' sense of the Russian adoptive family as an 'as if' family (Yngvesson, 2010) where parents and children appear to be a biological family, and the presupposed belonging of the adopted children and adoptive parents obscures difference. The actual linguistic and cultural differences that potentially go unaddressed, however, and the desire for sameness that obscures difference might cause long-term disruptions in adoptive family life.

As an example of how these undetected differences play out in family life and post-placement interventions, Stryker (2004, 2010), for example, found that adoptive parents (and the adoption agencies and therapists who work with them) expected adoptees to enter the home as 'emotional assets' for family members who contribute to the loving environment and familiness of the group. This expectation conflicted, however, with adoptees' socialization in cultures of care outside of the nuclear family and adoptees' expectations for different types of relationships and roles. Stryker (2000) further reported on data finding that peer networks in Russian orphanages were emphasized over caregiver–child relationships. Bonding with an adult was not common or encouraged in that setting, while bonding with and learning from older children was. The expectation of US adoptive parents that Russian adoptees enter the home as emotional assets, then, led to disappointment and a sense of failure when children did not respond and this conflict was related to assessments of reactive attachment disorder and the therapies parents chose (Stryker, 2010), as some of the parents in this study also note. The invisible cultural differences that Russian children brought to their new families and the ideologies of children and childhood held by US adoptive parents, therefore, affected the perceptions of success at forming a family that adoptive parents felt.

These processes are evident most clearly in the third family presented in this book in which two teenage girls are adopted into a family comprised of four younger Russian adoptees. The arrival of the teenagers leads to replication of some of the patterns of participation common in Russian orphanages as discussed by Stryker (2000), which causes disruption in the family relationships. The language negotiations over code choice (i.e. Russian vs English), which occur in that family, seem related not only to the children's language competencies but also the construction of family roles and power relations. These processes warrant greater attention to language as a mediating tool in family formation and establishing affect among family members.

How parents' motives for adopting intersect with language use and language learning in the family sphere is not clear. The widespread view of adoptees or children as emotional assets for parents could potentially affect the expectations parents have for children's participation in discursive routines, particularly ones associated with family bonding such as mealtime talk or story times. In addition, added stress over language learning, literacy and schooling, often noted to be problems for older adoptees, could lead to a sense of failure if children do not perform the expected emotional role and, in addition, do not seem to do well in school. In this way the adoptee becomes a burden rather than an asset to the family and only parents with realistic expectations (such as the parents in all three families who participated in this study who were well educated and experienced in adoption processes and outcomes) seem to know what to do when problems arise or how to avoid problems in the first place. In Chapter 7 of this book I offer some advice to adoptive parents and therapists regarding language and education planning for older adoptees.

In Chapter 2, I referenced seminal work in language socialization which concluded that Western, English-speaking parents used 'self-lowering' techniques such as child-directed speech to accommodate to pre-lingual infants. I argued that adoptive parents also take an accommodating stance toward adoptees that is informed both by this style of parenting as well as ideologies of risk that surround adoptees. One way that adoptive parents have been found to accommodate to their transnationally adopted children is through the practice of culture keeping. Culture keeping is a term coined by Jacobson (2008) to describe practices of transnational adoptive parents who actively promote the maintenance of and engagement with an adoptee's birth culture once the child is living in the US home. Culture keeping is promoted by adoption agencies and, as Jacobson finds, is an integral part of adoptive family life. It can involve serving ethnic foods at home, decorating the house with artifacts from the birth culture, participating in culture days sponsored by adoption agencies, enrolling children in dance or music classes, language classes and even taking heritage trips back to the home country. Volkman (2005) specifically points to the ways in which culture keeping 'transforms' culture through these transnational practices, and these practices make it possible for white adoptive mothers, for example, to claim hybrid identities such as Asian American.

One aspect of culture keeping that is generally not discussed in great detail is the maintenance of the adoptees' first language and the acquisition of the child's first language by adoptive parents. While first language maintenance is often viewed as 'impractical' by adoption professionals or even tied to trauma and negative experiences (e.g. Gindis, 2005), as is discussed below, some of the parents in my studies (e.g. Fogle, in press) have reported learning a child's first language and even using that language exclusively in the initial periods after adopting. While first language maintenance for adoptees can be related to helping children maintain ties to their birth culture and even extended family members and friends in places of origin, it was also tied, at least for one parent in this study (John Sonderman), to reducing the stress of adoption and diminishing the differences in the initial period (discussed in Chapter 4). This linguistic accommodation on the part of parents, as well as the negotiations over language choice that necessarily accompany it, are related to the collaborative nature of language socialization and the role the child plays in socialization processes. These processes are similar to the ones described by Stryker (2010) in which family members negotiate 'alternative family roles, power relations, and structure' (abstract).

Language and Belonging

Linguistic difference can play a role in an adoptee's sense of belonging to both the birth culture and the adoptive culture. For older adoptees, learning the dominant language of their parents and the adoptive society at large might seem integral to becoming a new member of family and society.

Unlike the racial differences of Korean, Chinese, Ethiopian and other adoptees, for East European adoptees linguistic differences might be the only perceptible marker or identification of 'non-belonging' to the outside world. Russian adoptees who assimilate fully to the linguistic norms of the new (English-speaking) community are able to achieve an 'erasure' of past belongings. However, this erasure can be further complicated by loss of the heritage language and, with it, ties to family members in the sending nation. The single father in the Sonderman family who participated in this study, for example, noted that he had stopped making phone calls to the boys' biological grandmother in Ukraine because the boys could not (or refused to) communicate with her in Ukrainian or Russian. Adoptees' success in school and socialization into US discourse norms is intimately tied to their 'in-between' status and belonging in two nations, cultures and networks of caring (including families and orphanages).

In the chapters that follow I examine these linguistic processes in everyday interactions between adoptive parents and adoptees. I look specifically at microinteractional processes that make up family roles and identities. I show how families themselves create the narratives that tell the children's stories of adoption and their place of belonging, and in doing so both reproduce and transform macro-level discourses. I examine language learning as a complex process that involves both the socialization of children into language practices as well as the accommodation of adults to children's competencies and practices, which is inextricably tied to the process of becoming a family and establishing new identities in the new time and place.

There are three linguistic processes in particular that are relevant to the situation of older transnational adoptees: (a) the process of learning the dominant language of parents and the community, (b) participating in family discourse practices that make up the social world of families (e.g. narrative events in family conversations or metalinguistic talk), and (c) maintaining heritage languages that enable adoptees to maintain a sense of past identities and connections to past worlds. While almost all researchers would agree that the first two of these points are vital to adoptees so that they might succeed in the English-speaking family and school environment, the third point still seems to be an open question in adoption research as clinicians have argued that it might be impractical for adoptees to maintain 'birth' languages, or even harmful if they have painful associations to their past. These perspectives place the transnational adoptee as essentially different from other immigrant children whose parents are first language users of the minority or heritage language. Indeed, ethnographic studies have found that adoptees themselves are uncertain of their status as immigrants

(Yngvesson, 2010) and current approaches to linguistic interventions for adoptees in the US school system see adoptees as non-immigrants despite the fact that they are English language learners, which I will discuss in greater detail below. Thus cultural and ideological perspectives on kinship and adoption shape the way these children are educated and taught in school settings (Fogle, in press).

In the data I present in the following chapters, I show that while adoptees do learn English in the family settings, these processes are by no means straightforward and simple. Learning English in the transnational adoptive family entails a complex negotiation of norms and expectations on the part of parents and children that intersect with educational processes in the school and attention to literacy and first language maintenance at home. These findings coincide with current perspectives on other bilingual immigrants and heritage language learners. While the transnational adoptive family provides a context of learning that is fundamentally different from other immigrant and bilingual families (where parents and children share linguistic and cultural backgrounds), it is not so different from other transnational families – in which children and birth parents might be separated by migration for long periods and reunited multiple times – that are just beginning to receive attention in the research literature (Boehm, 2008; Fogle & King, in press). These families imply negotiation of linguistic competencies and norms as part of the family formation process and both draw on and contribute to school and educational processes in new ways. While children in these families might present a conundrum to schoolteachers, therapists and administrators when compared to monolingual and 'mononational' norms, they also present new possibilities for imagining multiple competencies and multiple selves in a globalizing society.

Discursive Constructions of Family

Tannen, Kendall and Gordon's (2007) volume on family talk takes as a starting point the notion that family identities, roles and relationships are constructed in everyday interactions. Language in the family, according to Kendall (2007), is used to manage power and solidarity in family relationships, negotiate gender and family identities and co-construct family belief systems and values. In addition, specific language practices, such as the use of diminutives in Spanish-speaking families or other types of evaluative talk, have been found to play a role in building affect in parent–child interactions (e.g. King & Gallagher, 2008) and thus facilitate emotional bonding. As discussed in detail in Chapter 2, the family environment contributes to language learning and parents' ideologies about language as well as their interactional strategies, which shape children's linguistic outcomes. There are two main ways, then, that family formation and belonging in the transnational adoptive family intersect with language use and language learning: (a) family language practices and parent–child interactions serve to construct family identities, relationships and values (e.g. adoptees' narratives of their own adoptions most likely originate in parent–child interactions), and (b) for transnational adoptees adopted at older ages, learning the dominant language of the family becomes a means for establishing membership and belonging. In this section I review these phenomena in relation to recent perspectives on adoption and current findings regarding the language development of transnational adoptees, with an interest in bringing together research on transnational adoptees' language learning and identities.

Stryker (2010) notes that some parents understand the adoptive family to be exceptional in its ability to adapt and negotiate differences in novel ways. Volkman (2005) also points to an acknowledgement on the part of adoptive parents of the family as 'socially constructed' and 'hybrid' rather than essentialized. The conceptualization of the adoptive family as an 'other' type of family that does not conform to conventional norms could also be enacted discursively in family interactions and deserves further attention. In taking a language socialization approach to this process and looking carefully at how adoptees shape discourse practices in the family environment (and eventually have a socializing effect on parents), this book attempts to demonstrate how the adoptive family is a negotiated family in interaction where children become agents of change in interactional patterns and the learning environment. Taking such an approach also helps to better understand the strategies that adoptive parents can use to facilitate family integration (such as first language maintenance) and promoting adoptees' sense of belonging in the family.

Adoption and Risk: Focusing on Language

Adoptive families differ from biological families in several main ways: (a) adoptive parents tend to be older than biological parents, (b) more adopted children live above the poverty line than biological children, and (c) adoptive parents behave in different ways from biological parents for a variety of reasons including their demographics (age, socioeconomic status and educational backgrounds) and their knowledge about adoptees (Vandivere et al., 2009). In a study of census data from 13,000 households with first-graders in the family, Hamilton et al. (2007) found that adoptive parents spent more money on their children and invested more time on activities such as reading to them, eating together and talking with them about their problems, even after controlling for factors such as parental income, education and maternal age. These findings suggest that adoptees are actively socialized into middle-class discourse and literacy practices in the adoptive family, such as mealtime talk about the day, which I discuss in greater detail in the following chapters. For children adopted at older ages, and specifically those adopted from different linguistic backgrounds, these practices might not line up with their prior expectations for family sociability and what the parents take for granted in terms of what is 'normal' family interaction (e.g. sharing stories about the day or talking about emotions) could potentially seem inappropriate or troublesome to adoptees who are not accustomed to bonding with adults in this way (see Stryker, 2000).

Further, Melosh (2002) argues that the lack of genealogical heredity between adoptive parents and adoptees has historically led to a perception of risk in the adoptive family relationship. Indeed, adopted children are diagnosed with psychological and emotional disorders at higher rates than non-adopted peers. Miller *et al.* (2000) analyzed data from over 20,000 middle school students who participated in the National Longitudinal Study of Adolescent Health. This study found that adoption status alone was a greater predictor of receipt of psychological counseling than adolescents' self-reported problems (along with other factors such as race, parental education and health insurance coverage). These findings confirmed previous studies that found a lower threshold for referral by adoptive parents versus biological parents (Warren, 1992). Brodzinsky (1993: 162) argues that research on adoptees' psychological and academic problems needs to consider the problem more holistically, considering not only the pre-placement history of the child (i.e. time in foster care or institution and early trauma), but also the 'societal, interpersonal, and familial factors in children's adoption adjustment' that are tied to the child's identity. Stryker's (2011) recent proposals for intervention with transnational adoptees diagnosed with reactive attachment disorder, for example, emphasizes a need for a more child-centered, phenomenological approach that considers the children's point of view and strategies for negotiating narratives of belonging including both the birth and the adoptive family. In this chapter I further argue that language problems for transnational adoptees, like psychological and emotional disorders, are potentially over-diagnosed based on misinformation and a parent-centered approach. In addition, language in and of itself is a key way in which family members negotiate what it means to be an adoptive family, with language learning playing an important role in this process.

The Problems with a Deficit Approach

The discourses of adoption and risk have pervaded and influenced considerations of the language development of transnational adoptees. A central question of language-related research (primarily in the field of speech-language pathology) with adoptees thus far has been at what rate and to what extent do transnational adoptees measure up to monolingual, English-speaking norms. As transnational adoptees are most often expected to fit into the monolingual English-speaking family and attend English-medium schools, early initiatives to understand language-learning processes for transnational adoptees focused on comparing linguistic development for these children in relation to their monolingual peers. This practice, however, has been largely critiqued and discounted for other populations of bilingual children in the field of linguistics, as well as speech-language pathology (Kritikos, 2003; Mennen & Stansfield, 2006). Studies with adoptees primarily examined development processes for younger children (infant to preschool ages) and were based in what most linguists would consider to be deficit-oriented approaches, in which the first language was seen as a problem that would potentially cause delay or problems with (second) language acquisition.

The early adoption and language studies made two main assumptions about transnational adoptees as language learners that need to be critiqued: (a) that adoptees will not maintain (or even be exposed to) their first languages in the new environment, and (b) that the rapid shift from the first language to the new language for older adoptees would cause potential cognitive and academic delays for adoptees (e.g. Gindis, 2005; Glennen, 2002). These assumptions both fit in with and help to construct ideologies of normativity for adoptees and add to the assumptions of risk that older adoptees in particular might face. They do not take into account the vast amount of research on bi- and multilingual children's language and literacy development that clearly points out different developmental processes for multilingual children (e.g. Cummins et al., 2001). They also do not acknowledge decades of critique and rejection of concepts of cognitive deficit by researchers who study young bilinguals, which I will review below. I will first overview a set of language and adoption studies from the past decade and then argue for why other approaches are needed.

Two studies, spaced five years apart, investigated the language development and school performance of a group of infants and toddlers adopted from Eastern Europe. Glennen and Masters (2002: 432) surveyed at regular intervals (every three to six months) the parents of 130 infants and toddlers (36 months or younger) adopted from Eastern Europe from the time of adoption until the children reached age 36–40 months. This study concluded that transnationally adopted infants and toddlers learning an adopted first language mirror developmental growth patterns for non-adopted English-speaking children. For children adopted at younger ages, English first words and two-word phrases emerged at the expected ages. Furthermore, children in the study that were adopted at older ages (but were still under three years) began speaking English immediately and made rapid gains in development soon after coming to the new home. Thus adoptees met monolingual language-learning norms. This study did not mention first language maintenance as a possibility for young adoptees.

Pollock and Price (2005) found that children aged 15–33 months adopted from China rapidly caught up to monolingual English-speaking norms in phonology. These authors concluded that children who had been in their English-speaking homes for two years or more could be assessed using the same phonological inventories as monolingual toddlers, and therefore might be considered first language learners of English. Snedeker *et al.* (2007) investigated the language development of a group of 14 preschoolers (ages three and four) adopted from Eastern Europe and also found that they met monolingual milestones on the same trajectory. These studies suggest that infants, toddlers and even preschool-age adoptees develop English skills in a manner similar to monolingual, non-adopted children who learn English as a mother tongue.

Glennen and Bright (2005), in the follow-up study to Glennen and Masters (2002), suggested that differences might emerge for children adopted at young ages when they started school because the need to 'talk to learn' would uncover subtle delays or deficiencies in linguistic and possibly cognitive functioning. This study followed 46 of the original participants adopted as infant/toddler (under 30 months) from Eastern Europe of the Glennen and Masters' (2002) study. The 2005 study found a decrease over time in speech and language delays or disorders, developmental delay and sensory integration disorder. However, Glennen and Masters found an increase over time in ADD/ADHD, learning disabilities, poor vision and visual processing disorder diagnoses. The most commonly received support service for this cohort was speech and language services (23.9%) compared to about 8–10% of children in the general population (AHSA, n.d.). Overall, adoptees scored lower on inventories of pragmatic skills (standardized tests administered to the participants in the study) than monolingual norms, and the authors concluded that this could be attributed to subtle delays associated with institutionalization that become evident only in the school context. However, the study also found that the length of time in the orphanage for the 46 children was not significantly correlated with the delays noted in the results of the inventories, suggesting that other factors such as the family language environment or individual differences in language acquisition must play a role.

Language socialization in the home environment, including parent–child interaction and access to literacy socialization, therefore, could play a role in the outcomes of such quantitative measures. In sum, these studies conclude, prematurely in my opinion, that it is appropriate to compare younger transnational adoptees to their monolingual counterparts in terms of language development, and that any observable problems in language or literacy development can be attributed to inherent cognitive deficits associated with being adopted. Although these findings related to younger children, these constructs set up dangerous assumptions in which normal second language learning is potentially considered by parents and therapists to be evidence of problematic development. In addition, because adoptees are not seen as bilingual, important first language support is not offered to them to assist in language learning or developing academic skills, and this is true for older adoptees as well.

Warnings of cognitive deficits or language disabilities associated with institutionalization and language attrition are echoed in a number of publications aimed at adoptive parents, including popular adoption magazines, support group websites and literature from regional TESOL organizations (e.g. Gindis, 2000; Glennen, n.d.; Magady, 2004), even though such terms and constructs have been rejected by linguists and researchers in bilingualism as politically and ideologically, rather than linguistically, motivated (MacSwan, 2000; Martin-Jones & Romaine, 1986; Peal & Lambert, 1962; Valadez et al., 2000). These assumptions are loosely based on theoretical frameworks which suggest that below age-appropriate levels of competence in both of a bilingual child's languages, along with lack of support (i.e. development of literacy and academic skills) in a bilingual child's L1, can result in what has been characterized as cognitive delays (Cummins, 2001). Although these ideas provide some means of understanding why bilingual children from minority language backgrounds have been found to lag academically in comparison to children from majority language backgrounds in bilingual immersion programs (Cummins, 2001), these concepts have been criticized for being poorly defined and potentially damaging to language minority students (MacSwan, 2000; Valadez et al., 2000).

For example, Valadez et al. (2000) studied a group of children labeled as 'non proficient' in both of their languages (Spanish and English) to determine if quantitative differences did exist in language proficiency for these children compared to Spanish–English bilingual children who were considered proficient. This study found that no differences existed in linguistic competence (i.e. lexical and morphosyntactic proficiency), but that differences did exist in the children's reading and writing skills. Difference in exposure to literacy and development of reading and writing skills, therefore, might account for what has previously been characterized as language proficiency. The point to take away from this is that fears of language and learning disabilities or cognitive deficits based on the switch in languages that adoptees face are potentially misguided. Multiple factors play a role in a child's language development, literacy learning and academic performance (Hornberger, 2003), but we don't have a clear picture of what those factors are for older transnationally adopted children. The second language-learning and school experiences of transnational adoptees might be different than those of other bilingual populations, and contextual aspects such as inclusion in a language majority household, exposure to literacy in the home environment and access to extra academic support, such as tutors and extra classes, could give adoptive children an extra edge in getting ready for school. In short, we do not know how transnational adoptees to the US, nearly all of whom become members of English-speaking families, adapt to school in a second language. Further, some evidence suggests that expert opinions promoting a 'deficit' view of transnational adoptees' cognitive abilities can influence parents and the formation of kinship relations in the adoptive family (Stryker, 2010).

One of the ways that adoptive parents 'legitimize' their children as language learners and English speakers is through an ideology of first language acquisition. Just as Norwegian parents sometimes claimed a 'rebirth' of their adopted child in the airport upon arrival, US parents sometimes talk about their transnational adoptees being first language learners of English even though they have arrived speaking another language (Fogle, in press). This erasure of a past language, and the cultural and social identity that goes along with it, gives the child claim to authenticity and belonging in the US family. Unfortunately it also leaves her or him with little to help reconstruct a sense of belonging to the past. This ideology also impedes access to current thinking on the care of bilingual children, which includes first language education and maintenance (Baker, 2000). Howell (2007) further argues that psychological models of child development trickle down into adoptive parents' parenting practices. In an interview study with adoptive parents, I also found that ideologies about deficits in language acquisition were repeated and used to explain parenting decisions regarding transnational adoptees (Fogle, in press). While the psychological perspective might seem useful to parents trying to understand their children's learning and developmental processes, which were very different from their own, it presents an obstacle to other ways of understanding and hinders parents' access to actual research on bilingual children, language acquisition and academic language. In order to better understand these aspects of adoptees' language use and learning, we need to ask different kinds of questions.

Academic Literacies and Adoptive Families

Empirical studies investigating the language and academic development of transnational adoptees have concluded that these children test lower than age expectations on a variety of standardized language and communication skills measures and are likely to be diagnosed with learning disabilities such as attention deficit disorder/attention deficit hyperactivity disorder (ADD/ADHD) (Glennen & Bright, 2005; Hough, 2006). However, as noted above, Glennen and Bright (2005: 99) concluded that 'longer institutionalization did not impact school age language skills or related behaviors'. Further, Hough (2005) found that time in institution, age of adoption and time in the US did not correlate with standardized measures of receptive and expressive language, but did correlate for reading and non-word repetition scores. These results suggest that the language and learning difficulties that show up with transnational adoptees on standardized tests may, as with other bilingual children, be related to literacy and early schooling in the first language (Cummins, 2001; Genesee, 2004) rather than the cognitive deficits that fill the popular adoption literature. In addition, the higher rates of diagnosis for language and learning disabilities found by Glennen and Bright may actually be related to adoptive parents' higher rates of referral for such services rather than children's actual problems, as discussed above.

In addition to the erroneously assumed problems of switching languages, some studies claim that adoptees do not have access to adequate first language acquisition in the orphanage. When applied generally to all transnational adoptees, this hypothesis is problematic for two main reasons. First of all, not all adoptees live exclusively in an orphanage for their whole childhood. Some of the children in the current study, for example, had maintained ties with biological grandparents with whom they had lived and had also lived with their biological parents and other family members at different times before or in between time in the orphanages. Second, peer networks are complex sites of socialization for children in orphanages. Stryker (2000) found that younger children in Russian orphanages were encouraged to bond with older peers, and this social organization shaped the way adoptees saw their new family environments. Such networks influence language development. Famous cases of language acquisition point to the ability of children in institutional settings to construct their own language when input from adults was lacking (Polich, 2005). The idea that older adoptees arrive with 'no language' is related to a parent-oriented approach that prioritizes the Western culture and new family as crucial to the child's development and emphasizes an erasure of prior ties and knowledge.

Do Adoptees Maintain Their Birth Languages?

Although there are no comprehensive data, to my knowledge, collected about the languages adoptees speak post-placement (even the USA adoption survey [Vandivere et al., 2009] fails to report on first language maintenance for transnational adoptees), a review of studies seems to indicate that transnational adoptees to the US typically have English-dominant parents and attend English-medium schools. For instance, in a study of 130 children adopted from Eastern Europe before the age of 36 months, Glennen and Masters (2002: 419) found that only one adoptive parent, a first language (L1) speaker of Russian, used that language above the level of 'simple words and phrases'. Isurin (2000) further documented the language attrition process of a nine-year-old girl adopted from Russia over the first year after her arrival in the US and concluded that the child experienced a process of first language 'forgetting' that was associated with related gains in second language acquisition. Nicoladis and Grabois (2002: 441), in a study of a one-year-old Chinese adoptee's acquisition of English, also noted that the child's loss of Chinese and acquisition of English were 'remarkably fast', a finding that the authors attribute to the already established social and communicative processes of the child. Studies with Korean adoptees have had slightly different findings due to the Korean adoptees in question returning back to Korea as adults.

Heritage Language Learning as Belonging

Recent work with adoptees as heritage language learners has focused primarily on Korean adoptees. Higgins and Stoker (2011) investigated a population of Korean adoptee-returnees to Korea. The goal of this study was to understand how learning Korean as a heritage language facilitated social inclusion and belonging to Korean culture. All of these adoptees had chosen to return to Korea as adults. While this community had not felt fully integrated or accepted into Korean society, they had been able to establish a third or hybrid community of adoptee-returnees. Lo and Kim (2011) further investigated how two Korean celebrities, both heritage language learners of Korean and one of whom is an adoptee, are evaluated based on their language competence in Korean public discourse. They link these metaprag-matic framings to racialized representations of the two men and focus on their legitimacy as Korean in the public discourse. Finally, Shin (2011) presents results suggesting the heritage language programs for adoptees are a viable form of culture keeping in some regions of the US. These studies have looked in depth at individual cases of adoptees' belonging and heritage language learning. They point to the very complex social aspects of lan-guage learning and social integration that adoptees face. This research is relatively new, however, and contrasts with the psychologically based models that have been in use over the past decade for understanding transnational adoption and learning.

In short, we don't know much about children who immigrate to the US as adoptees at school age and enter the US school system as English language learners in relation to other bilingual children who arrive with members of their biological families. While many studies such as the ones described above are based on a belief that adoptees by their very nature will possess learning delays and disabilities, these constructs are often contextualized within a specific sociocultural perspective that emphasizes normativity (Gee, 2000). In addition, the basic assumptions that are made about adoptive families could be wrong. In two of the case studies presented here, for example, the adoptive parents spoke Russian with their children on a daily basis, and in the third family Russian was maintained to some extent through supplementary classes. In addition, we don't know how home socialization plays a role in the transition and assimilation process for adop-tees. On the one hand, the transition to the new culture and educational system could be easier for adoptees as they are potentially exposed to socialization at home that matches that of schooling; on the other hand, this transition could be more difficult as they experience changes in both their external, public lives and their private home lives. Many of the findings of this study connect with academic and literacy socialization and the role that children play in gaining access to these discourses.

Doing Adoption Research

Adoption research and research investigating problems of adoptees have cycled through a series of iterations from a psychopathological approach that emphasized the risk of adopting and potential cognitive, emotional and mental problems associated with adoptees, to literature arguing against this approach, which claims that adoption is a 'natural' and successful way to protect children and facilitate development (van Ijzendoorn & Juffer, 2005). While much of the adoption research is situated in these two paradigms (i.e. focused on the deficits or benefits of adoption for children), recent research has begun to take more critical approaches that problematize the adoption industry, parents' reasons for adopting and the underlying ideologies of much of the research that has come before. These studies see adoptive families, and all families for that matter, as socially constructed and contextualized (Brodzinsky & Palacios, 2005; Howell, 2007; Stryker, 2000). In this approach, adoption can be successful and is seen as a viable means of family formation, but the extent to which parents and children negotiate differences and see themselves as a family are key.

In much the same way that the phenomenon of adoption has changed over the past century and adoptive families have gained in status as 'normal' (albeit nontraditional) families (Palacios & Brodzinsky, 2005), adoption research has changed focus to keep up with changing times. Several researchers argue for approaches that emphasize examination of the post-placement environment of adopted children and focus on understanding 'resilience factors' that protect children from early adversities (Palacios & Brodzinsky, 2005: 262). Further, a better understanding of how the adoptive family changes and evolves to incorporate different concepts of family and different affective stances can help in determining appropriate interventions (Stryker, 2011). Moreover, transnational adoptive families help us to understand processes of transnationalism and the negotiation of norms and identities that language contact and language learning in micro settings entail.

In this chapter I have argued for the importance of a focus on language and discourse in understanding the construction of family and the unique case of older transnational adoptees. By taking a language socialization approach (outlined in Chapter 2), we can closely examine the ways that establishing roles and patterns of interaction in the newly formed family as well as the construction of group family identities contributes to and informs language-learning processes. Negotiation of language choice and negotiation for meaning in terms of creating a context for communication between parents and children are important factors in the processes that lead to children taking on agency in interactions with their parents in order to take part in family conversations. I discuss these processes in detail in the analysis chapters that follow, focusing on three main family discourse practices: narrative talk about the day (Chapter 4), languaging or metalinguistic talk (Chapter 5) and English–Russian code-switching (Chapter 6).

Methodological Perspectives and Concerns

Many foundational studies in applied linguistics, and SLA specifically, have been case studies of one or two learners (Duff, 2008a), and the study of bilingual development has been informed by case study approaches (Lanza, 1997/2004). The study presented in the following chapters of this book draws heavily on the language socialization paradigm and case study approaches for guiding questions and methodologies (Duff, 2012; Garrett, 2004; Lanza, 1997/2004; Ochs & Schieffelin, 1984). Case studies, which typically focus on an individual language learner, teacher, speaker or writer in applied linguistics (Duff, 2008a), have pointed to variation within groups of learners and can help to explain and understand the inner workings of complex processes. In the current study, data from three adoptive families are presented as a multiple case study in which each family is considered discretely within its own context. Naturally occurring interactions with and among all family members are considered for the analyses. The advantage of this approach is to provide an emic understanding of the language practices of each family in order to better understand the range of variation that can exist across families (although the three families considered here are in some ways exceptional because of their willingness to participate in such an intensive research study). Data consist of naturalistic audio-taped family conversations collected over a period of eight months in three different adoptive families. The recorded data are supplemented with open-ended interviews and some field notes.

There are two main criticisms of this approach: on the one hand, language socialization does not allow for generalizations because of the small number of participants and focus on relativity (Gregg, 2006; see Block, 2007 and Thorne, 2000 for responses to this general critique in the SLA literature); on the other hand, early socialization studies have also been criticized for homogenizing variation in the interest of presenting a coherent picture of a culture (Bayley & Schecter, 2003; Garrett & Baquedano-López, 2002; Luykx, 2005). The families in Ochs's (1988) original Samoan study, for example, were not presented as contextually different but rather as unified exemplars of Samoan society. In this study I present data from three very different transnational adoptive families who share only a few things in common: (a) they can all be considered middle-class based on residency and occupations, and the parents are from European American backgrounds; (b) they all consist of at least one adopted Russian-speaking child who was over the age of five years at the time of arrival; and (c) they all live in the same metropolitan region on the east coast of the United States.

In keeping with Stake's (2000) argument that collective case studies should be treated separately, I resist comparisons of the three families as an analytic tool (though I do refer to the other families in the respective chapters as reminders of what we have seen before). The members of the three participating families are not easily compared because of the contextual differences in each family's experiences. I therefore attempt to present the analyses of these three families' data as 'possibilities' of what *can* happen in transnational adoptive families, but not what *does* happen in all families or what all adoptive families do (see Peräkylä, 1997). In presenting the three very different parenting styles, family makeups and language socialization phenomena, I hope to present a range of possibilities within which other adoptive families might fall; however, without subsequent research it is impossible to know what other possibilities exist.

Researcher's Background

My interest in this project grew out of my service as a Peace Corps Volunteer in Ukraine from 1995 to 1997. As a Peace Corps Volunteer, I experienced second language learning in an uninstructed context, observed the tensions over language planning and policy in post-Soviet life and transformed myself as I was socialized into new ways of acting and doing in my daily life there. I lived with a host family for three months in the western Ukrainian town of Luts'k (near L'viv) and participated in Ukrainian language training. At the start of the school year, I moved to the Russian-speaking city of Mikolayiv (Nikolayev) where I would work as a British and American literature teacher for 10th and 11th grades at an English-specialized school for two years. Over the two years, I learned Russian from coworkers, neighbors, students, vendors at the market and friends. I visited two orphanages in southern Ukraine during that time and worked on a number of development projects in the region. Although Ukrainian was made the official language of Ukraine in 1996 while I was in service, the language I was most exposed to in Mykolaiv during that time was Russian.

While working on my Master's degree in TESOL back in the US after the Peace Corps, I took a tutoring job with a family who had recently adopted two children from Russia. My initial experiences working with those children helped to develop the ideas for the current project and specifically the need for taking a language socialization approach. I returned to Eastern Europe in 2002 to Russia on a Fulbright grant and have continued to study Russian here in the US. My (biological) son was raised for the first two years of his life with the help of a Ukrainian nanny from Crimea, and we spoke only Russian at home during the day while I was working on the data analysis for this project. All of these experiences have informed my understandings of the language socialization of transnational adoptees.

Recruitment and Evolution of the Study

Recruitment notices for this study were distributed in one of four ways: (a) to an online listserv of a popular grass roots family support group for families who have adopted or are planning to adopt from Russia, Ukraine and other countries of the former Soviet Union; (b) to local adoption agencies specializing in transnational adoptions; (c) to a Saturday Russian school that offered programs for Russian adoptees; and (d) to local pediatricians and therapists known to work with transnational adoptees. A representative of the online support group distributed notices on the listserv on my behalf in order to avoid controversy over outside solicitations. In addition, I held several information sessions on raising bilingual children for adoptive and bilingual parents at the Russian Saturday school in 2004–2005. I also presented preliminary findings of this research to therapists at a monthly case meeting on transnational adoptions at a pediatric medical center through which I made some contacts, but my primary recruitment source was the email listserv.

Families were eligible for the study if both parents were native English speakers and at least one child over the age of five had been adopted from Russia or Russian-speaking regions (e.g. Ukraine or Kazakhstan). One parent in each of the first two families (the Sondermans and the Jackson-Wessels) responded to a notice posted on the listserv described above to participate in an interview regarding language learning and transnational adoptees (Fogle, in press; 2009). At the end of the interview, these two families agreed to participate in further research and were contacted later in the year to begin the in-home audio recordings. Out of 11 families who participated in interviews, these two were selected for in-home recording because in both families the fathers were the primary caregivers, the children were close in age, the families were made up of the same number of children (i.e. two adoptees), the parents had no prior children and the four children had arrived within the calendar year about three months apart from one another in each family.

In short, I chose the first two families presented in this book from a pool of 11 families because they were matched closest in terms of the age of the children, the age of arrival, length of residence and family makeup. The Sonderman children attended a public charter school with ESL classes while the older child in the Jackson-Wessels family was homeschooled (for more discussion see Fogle, 2008b). John Sonderman had learned Russian and used it at home with the boys exclusively for the first six months. The Jackson-Wessels, in contrast, reported knowing only a few words of Russian and made the shift to English immediately. These linguistic differences made a difference in the discourse patterns in the family and potentially in the children's language outcomes. At the end of data collection with these two families, I proposed to conduct a second study with participating families in which the makeup of the family and the children themselves were more closely matched for age, arrival time and other factors.

Recruiting participants for this more controlled study of second language acquisition and language socialization was a difficult task. The recruitment criteria required that families begin data collection within the first month after the children's arrival and recruitment fell at a time when adoptions from Russia were beginning to slow (Vandivere *et al.*, 2009). While several families expressed interest in the study, only one family agreed to the weekly family recordings. I think this was for several reasons – the intimate nature of recording one's own mealtimes, the perceived difficulties in the early period after arrival and the fact that I was a stranger who was also not an adoptive parent. In the end what emerged was a collective case study that presents a range of possibilities, as discussed above.

The Goellers were the only family who agreed to participate in the new study after six months of recruiting. It turned out that parents Melanie and Paul had met me in 2004 when I had given a talk to parents at the center that held Saturday language and mathematics courses in Russian. This initial personal contact, I believe, played an important role in their decision to participate in the data collection after their fifth and sixth children arrived. Melanie was also familiar with some of the research conducted with younger adoptees in language learning and was interested in contributing to research done with older adoptees. Finally, I think Melanie also had an interest in providing as much support as possible (and Russian-speaking support) for the teenage girls, and I had included in the announcement that I would meet with the children once a week to talk about their adjustment and schooling. It was these weekly meetings that seemed the most important to Melanie, and perhaps also to the teenagers as they were consistent in scheduling and being home for those events.

A Note on Adoptee Histories

While prior studies have sought to generalize the experience of being an 'adoptee' or 'post-institutionalized' as discussed above, there is much variability in early experiences that may not even be known to adoptive parents (several of the children in this study, for example, had lived with their parents or other family members at different times in their lives and were not raised exclusively in an orphanage). Because of these facts, I focus on the post-placement lives of the children in this study by analyzing strategies and practices that I felt were linked to the local context and situation. I also did not explicitly ask the parents about their motives for adopting (other than what the participants shared in conversation with each other or in interviews). I made these decisions for two reasons: (a) while the parents of course had information about the children's backgrounds, I did not feel confident as a researcher basing my analyses on this knowledge, and (b) as a researcher interested in language learning and bilingualism who was collecting fairly private data over an extended period of time, I did not feel comfortable directly asking about motives for adoption or the children's backgrounds because I did not want to perpetuate stereotypes that circulate about transnational adoptees that might influence the parents' practices. For the most part, in interacting with the parents and children I stuck to understanding the recent interactions or problems from their perspective without imposing the supposed importance of the children's prior lives or the parents' motivations onto the data (see also Stryker, 2010).

The two teenage girls in the Goeller family (Chapter 6) who reintroduced Russian to their adoptive family were my primary inspiration for looking more carefully at how children influence their parents and what implications such processes have for understandings of language socialization. What was a fairly transparent process in the Goeller's interactions (i.e. parents' and other family members' use of Russian to accommodate to the new arrivals) was obscured by the fact that parents and children shared the same language of interaction (English) in the other two families. However, sharing a language of interaction did not mean that the Sonderman or Jackson-Wessels' children did not influence and affect their parents' interactional patterns, as I will discuss in detail in Chapters 4 and 5. In short, while the Goellers, with six children and two adopted teenagers, did not fit into my intended research design, their participation in the project allowed for a new perspective on language socialization that I had not previously imagined.

Participants: Three Families

The Sondermans

The Sonderman family was comprised of a single father and two boys, Dima and Sasha, ages 10 and eight respectively at the start of the study (Table 3.1). The family lived in an urban condominium-style town home within the borders of the city. John was self-employed as a psychotherapist and held two Master's degrees. John was the oldest parent and the only single parent participating in the study (see Table 3.2). I met with John

Table 3.1 Demographics of children arriving between 2004 and 2007

Family	Child	Gender	Age at data collection	Age of Arrival	Grade	First Language
Sonderman	**Dima**	M	10	8	3rd	Russian/Ukrainian
	Sasha	M	8	7	2nd	Russian/Ukrainian
Jackson-Wessels	**Arkadiy**	M	7	5	Home-school	Russian
	Anna	F	4	3	Preschool	Russian
Goeller	**Lena**	F	16	16	9th	Russian
	Lesya	F	15	15	9th	Russian
	Valentina (Valya)	F	10	8	n/a	Russian
	Inna	F	10	7	n/a	Russian
	David	M	9	8	n/a	Russian
	Tolya (T.K.)	M	9	6	n/a	Russian

approximately one month after the boys had arrived. At that time John reported using only Russian with the boys whom he believed were bilingual in Ukrainian and Russian. In the initial interview, John had indicated that he made the decision to use Russian to help the boys deal emotionally with the transition to the new family. He also stated positive attitudes toward having Ukrainian children as opposed to American children; he expressed an

Table 3.2 Parent demographics

Family	Parents	Gender	Age	Education	Occupation	Other languages
Sonderman	John	M	50	MA (2)	Psychotherapist	French, Russian
Jackson-Wessels	Kevin	M	31	JD	Stay-at-home father	none
	Meredith	F	28	JD	Staff attorney	none
Goeller	Melanie	F	49	1 year of college	Senior compensation analyst	French, Russian
	Paul	M	39	BS	IT security architect	Russian

interest in the cultural differences and the processes involved in forming a transnational adoptive family.

As the study progressed, I also found that John had kept in touch with the boys' grandmother with whom they had lived before entering the orphanage, as they talked about writing or calling her on occasion in the mealtime recordings. Although John was a fluent speaker of Russian, when I returned 13 months later to conduct the audio recordings he reported that the whole family had switched to English as the primary means of communication. Dima was reported to have completed one year of schooling in Ukraine, and Sasha had no prior schooling or exposure to literacy. However, John had made a concerted effort to introduce the boys to English literacy from their first meeting by bringing handheld Leapster® toys (multimedia learning systems) to Ukraine that the boys practiced on.

The Jackson-Wessels

The Jackson-Wessels were a dual-parent family with two children, a boy, Arkadiy, and a girl, Anna (ages seven and four respectively), who were biological siblings. Both parents held law degrees; however, Kevin had chosen to be a stay-at-home dad and homeschool teacher. The mother, Meredith, worked as a government attorney. The family resided in a single family home in the suburbs of a major metropolitan area. Neither Arkadiy nor Anna had previous schooling or much exposure to literacy at the time of arrival, according to Kevin. At the beginning of the audiotaping, Arkadiy was being homeschooled by his father and Anna attended a part-time preschool. I first met with Kevin approximately four months after the children's arrival and began audiotaping five months after that first interview. Kevin reported that he and his wife had learned only a few words and basic commands in Russian, such as 'brush your teeth', but could not converse with the children in the language. In the first interview, Kevin noted that an inability to communicate through a common language had been a major source of stress for his wife and even his in-laws in the initial period after the children's arrival because the children would address the adults in Russian despite their inability to understand. At the initiation of the data collection, the children spoke English between themselves and Russian was not used in the home environment (though Arkadiy still had some contact with Russian at a Saturday supplemental school).

The Goellers

The Goellers, were also a dual-parent family, but consisted of four adopted siblings prior to the adoption of the two focal children (Lesya and

Lena) for this study (see Table 3.1). The parents, Melanie and Paul, both worked full-time, with Melanie taking on primary caregiving responsibilities for the children around her work hours. When I started the study, Melanie was on family leave from her full-time job as a Senior Compensation Analyst (in human resources for a government office). Paul worked in information technology. There were six adopted children in the family total, three sets of two siblings that were adopted from 2004 to 2007. Melanie and Paul had taken a Berlitz course in Russian prior to the arrival of their first children, had basic communication skills in the language and reported using Russian with their children, as well as on their trips to Russia. Melanie also often cooked Russian foods and they, as well as the children, had kept in contact with the orphanages from which the children had been adopted.

In many ways, the Goellers incorporated the children's Russian heritage and their own interest in Russian into their daily lives while maintaining the Jewish traditions of Paul's side of the family (through Hebrew school), and to a lesser extent the French Canadian background of Melanie (the boys playing hockey, for example, was noted to be related to Melanie's background). The Goeller children participated in many extracurricular activities including tae kwon do, gymnastics, horseback riding, hockey, Hebrew school and Saturday Russian school (for the first arrivals, but not Lesya and Lena). Such activities were an important part of life for these children and much of dinnertime was spent planning for activities to take place later that evening or week. In addition, Melanie and Paul scrupulously kept up with each child's responsibilities in terms of chores, and chore charts with a list of duties for each child according to the day of the week as well as a large family calendar were posted to the kitchen walls along with examples of Cyrillic, Roman and Hebrew alphabets and other school-related materials. Dinnertime conversations usually ended with a discussion of what chores needed to be done or what activity the children were supposed to attend next.

Lesya and Lena, the newest arrivals to the Goeller family, are the oldest adoptees to participate in the study. Both had attended some high school in Russia and both had some prior exposure to English. Lena had been placed in technical school to learn to be a cook in a restaurant. Her English courses were geared toward preparing her for that job. Lesya was still in general high school courses and had not been tracked in a vocational program; however, she indicated that her English classes were not as good as Lena's prior to arrival. All six children in the family were native speakers of Russian.

Data Collection

Data collection for all three families consisted of in-home audio recordings and regular visits by the researcher for interviews. Because the children in the Sonderman family and the Jackson-Wessels had been in the US for approximately one year and no great changes in language choice or competence were expected, a monthly data collection schedule was implemented in which parents were asked to record at least two mealtimes and two literacy events during one week of each month following methods outlined by previous researchers, including, for example, Tomasello and Stahl (2004). Lesya and Lena, the new arrivals in the Goeller family, were expected to show development in English at a faster rate. The Goellers, therefore, were asked to collect the same types of data on a weekly basis in order to capture changes in language competence and language choice from the first week. Table 3.3 presents the amounts and types of data collected. It is evident that each family had a preference for the type of recording they completed, a fact that is discussed further below.

In addition to recording their home interactions, the parents in all three families and the oldest children in the Goeller family participated in regular interviews. These interviews lasted from about 10 minutes to up to 45 minutes and took place in the participants' homes. I used a mixed method interview format during these sessions. In general, interviews were open-ended and ethnographic in nature in that they sought to capture what was important or meaningful from the participants' perspectives. Topics usually ranged from perceptions or concerns about school performance, communication strategies or changes in family dynamics, language mistakes and correction strategies used by the parents, and reflections on the children's behaviors and alignment with peer groups.

In addition to asking general questions about how things were going or what changes the parents/children had noticed, I also used a modified version of stimulated recall methodology (a popular method used in second language acquisition research [Gass & Mackey, 2000]) to elicit feedback on clips from the family recordings. Parents and the children Lesya and Lena listened to an approximately 30 second clip of one of the family recordings,

Table 3.3 Recording times by family

Family	Dates	Family interactions	Interviews
The Sondermans	October 2005 – July 2006	14 hrs	2.5 hrs
The Jackson-Wessels	October 2005 – July 2006	7.5 hrs	2 hrs
The Goellers	July 2007 – January 2008	4 hrs	4 hrs

which had usually taken place in the month or week prior to the interview. I introduced the clip by asking family members to listen and then tell me what they heard, thus eliciting talk about the speech event. After providing a description of the clip, I usually asked some follow-up questions such as 'Do you know why you said that?' or 'Can you talk a little bit more about that strategy?' I also used these interviews to gain clarification on unintelligible speech (especially in the Jackson-Wessels) and contextual details (e.g. Where were you sitting?).

Doing research with sensitive populations presents additional challenges, as Duff (2008) notes. The fact that adoptive families seemed especially sensitive due to public scrutiny and the role of government policies in forming the family compounded my concerns over controlling the data collection. As the study progressed, the parents and the children played an active role in determining when and where to record, and this is reflected in the data analyses. While the children knew I was audio-recording their conversations and was interested in their language learning, not all of the children wanted to be recorded all of the time. When this happened, parents turned off the recorders, as I had instructed them to do. In some cases (the Goellers in particular) the family would not return data if the children did not feel like being recorded.

Because of these concerns and issues, I did not have as much control over the data collection in this study as in other language socialization research. Most of the language socialization or family based language development research I was familiar with at the time of starting this study had been conducted in other cultures (e.g. Ochs, 1988) or communities bounded by geographic location (Zentella, 1997), in the classroom (Poole, 1992; Willett, 1995), with the children of the researchers (Bongartz & Schneider, 2003; Cruz-Ferreira, 2006), in one-time video recordings in middle-class homes (Ochs et al., 1992) or longitudinal studies where the researcher was present during the audio-recording (Lanza, 1997/2004). While longitudinal studies of middle-class US based families in which parents controlled the data collection were emerging (e.g. King & Logan-Terry, 2008; Tannen & Goodwin, 2006), there were few examples of how to manage data collection with multiple families in the same study over time. In the current study, I selected the main areas of analysis (i.e. narrative, languaging and code-switching) based on practices that seemed both frequent and salient in the data that the parents had chosen to return to me. Thus, the different family contexts shaped the data analysis presented here. That is, rather than organizing the analysis for all three families around a specific aspect of adoptive family talk from the beginning, I drew on what emerged as important in each family's recordings individually.

My presence as a researcher potentially affected the amount of data recorded as well as some of the interactions in the families. John, who had a background in psychology and research methods, kept to a strict schedule and recorded four mealtimes per month. This was more than I had expected and was a challenge for him to do since he worked in the evenings at times (see Chapter 4). Although John indicated that he and the boys did eat meals together, in the end my presence most likely shaped the frequency of family mealtimes and thus the frequency of the bad thing/good thing narrative routine that I analyze in Chapter 4. Another influence I had (along with a second Russian-speaking researcher who assisted in the data collection) was to provide an additional context in which Lesya and Lena Goeller could use and maintain their Russian. Our interactions in that family no doubt provided examples of Russian speakers (and second language learners of Russian) in the US that helped valorize Russian in that environment. This influence potentially affected Lesya and Lena's use of Russian at home. It was not clear to me what influence I had on the family interactions in the Jackson-Wessels, but their recordings were all very different (from different activities with different family members) (Table 5.1), which in the end made it difficult to trace changes in interactions over the course of the study (Chapter 5). Finally, all families were given copies of all the recordings made of their conversations at the end of the study and they listened to parts of the recordings as the study was ongoing. This helped the parents (and Lesya and Lena) to understand the aspects of their conversations that interested me and to reflect on how they communicated as a family. In short, my presence as a researcher influenced each family in a different way and potentially augmented preexisting practices (e.g. narrative activities or code-switching) because of my interest in them.

In the end, the parents in the three families who volunteered for the study had an intense interest in language and their children's learning. All three sets of parents had sought out additional tutors, language support or Russian-speaking environments for their children. They also participated in online forums for adoptive parents and worked with therapists and other professionals in helping their children adjust. Participating in the research was just one of many strategies the parents used to understand their children's learning processes. As far as I can tell, my presence as an observer affected the quantity of data collected by the parents more than it affected the quality of that data. The families still discussed taboo topics, had arguments and went through regular routines without much reference to the presence of the audio-recorders, but they did decide how much to record and what to return.

Conclusion

Second language socialization has emerged as a powerful tool in under-standing the varied social worlds of second language learners and connec-tions between social and cognitive processes associated with second language learning. This field emphasizes the negotiated and sometimes conflicted nature of second language learning as multiple identities, ideolo-gies and contexts interact in the learning process. This book foregrounds these processes by taking the learner's perspective in understanding how language socialization is collaborative and co-constructed. While learners respond to the structures and expectations of the context in which they are learning, they also find ways to affect those contexts to open up spaces for learning and alternative identities. These processes are perhaps most evident in the context of the transnational adoptive family where two concomitant processes make affordances for children's agency. On the one hand, adoptive parents, or at least the ones in this study, are aware of the need to accommodate to their adopted children because of the assumed stress of the adoption process as well as the children's backgrounds. On the other hand, this type of accommodation and allowance of children's agency is characteristic of Western, middle-class parenting styles in which parents use 'self lowering' techniques to encourage young children as conversational partners. Examining how second language-learning adoptees take advantage of their parents' willingness to accommodate allows us a better understand-ing of what young language-learning children can do in interaction with caring adults and how they shape interactional contexts to meet their individual needs.

4 'I Got Nothin'!': Resistance, Routine and Narrative

In this chapter, narrative socialization is considered as a type of second language socialization that constitutes a site of language learning, negotiation and identity construction. There are two types of narrative activities that I examine in the Sondermans' mealtime conversations: routine talk about the day and spontaneous narratives of the children's pre-adoptive lives in Ukraine. I contrast these two types of narratives in relation to the dimensions of tellership, or the ability to establish a role as a teller, and tellability, the understanding of what is a tellable story, on Ochs and Capps' (2001) scale of conversational narrative dimensions. While a parent-directed narrative routine led to conflict between father and sons over events of the day, more spontaneous narratives initiated by the children about their lives in Ukraine led to more fluid, collaborative tellings that represented fragments of an adoption narrative and ways of talking about their transnational selves that involved the family members constructing a joint identity.

In the Sonderman family, children's agency emerges as instantiated resistance. As mentioned in Chapter 2, resistance is one form of agency that has received an extensive amount of attention in research in the social sciences (Ahearn, 2001), and thus resistance seems to be a fitting place to begin for an analysis of learner agency in language socialization. Resistance itself can take many forms – from outward protest and revolt involving large communities to more implicit and individual refusals to act (including refusal to participate and, subsequently, learn) in ways constrained by existing structures (Duff, 2012). Resistance in second language socialization often arises in conflicts between how learners are represented by authority figures or in-group members and their own conceptions of self and desires (Harklau, 2000; McKay & Wong, 1996; Norton Pierce, 1995). Most documented instances of learner resistance in second language socialization lead to missed opportunities or outright rejection of opportunities to learn. Few studies examine resistance that leads to learning opportunities or the actual interactional mechanisms that construct resistance in micro interactions. In this chapter, I will look at how learner resistance, documented in micro interactions, has some alternative outcomes, namely changes in an interactional routine and collaboration in socialization processes. Focusing on children's resistance in particular, and its effect in interaction with adult caregivers, can help to elucidate the co-constructed nature of socialization processes.

Narrative Socialization

Narrative socialization, or the processes through which children or other novices learn both the structure of narratives and important cultural content conveyed through narrative activities, is an extremely robust area of language socialization research. According to Ochs and Capps (2001: 64), narrative socialization can encompass, 'the socialization or acquisition of particular narrative structures as well as the instillation of valued ways of thinking, feeling, and acting'. Garrett and Baquedano-Lopéz (2002: 353) view narrative as 'a primordial tool of socialization', and Ochs and Capps (2001: 2) point to conversational narratives in particular as being specifically important 'to imbue life events with a temporal and logical order, to demystify them and establish coherence across past, present, and as yet unrealized experience'. From this perspective, narrative productions in family interactions take on a role as a primary site of making meaning about daily events. Thus analyzing how stories are told in the adoptive family can provide insight into how family members arrive at shared understandings of their new family and lifeworlds.

Storytelling events, in which participants collaborate in selecting, telling and evaluating narratives, are socializing activities in that they help children and family members construct identities and world views. Narrative, according to De Fina (2003b: 369), 'both reflects social beliefs and relationships and contributes to negotiate and modify them'. Thus constructing stories in interaction provides interlocutors, and more specifically for the purposes of this study, parents and children, an arena to construct mutually shared values and knowledge as well as participant identities. Research in narrative socialization in the family environment has been primarily interested in personal experience narratives that include a problem-solving element (Ochs & Capps, 2001). Problem-solving narratives represent a site of negotiation where participants consider different meanings and moral stances. These negotiations allow children opportunities to learn about what to expect from life events (especially in younger years) and serve to construct world views, moral stances and family histories, as well as to engage in cognitive problem-solving activities associated with academic discourses (Ochs et al., 1992) and thus relate to identity construction.

Prior research in family language socialization has noted the prevalence of one particular type of narrative activity (i.e. talk about the day) in mealtime conversations (Blum-Kulka, 1997; Ochs & Taylor, 1995). Elicitations of such talk from children play a role in their socialization of what to expect from everyday life and how to talk about unexpected events. Talk about the day can also play a role in setting up power relations in family interactions. Ochs and Taylor, for example, show how mothers' introductions of children's stories to fathers serve to construct a 'father knows best' dynamic in middle-class family interaction. Most research on 'talk about the day' and family storytelling in general has focused on parents' elicitations of children's narratives. Few studies have focused on the forms and functions of child-initiated narratives, despite pervasive findings that older children in particular resist parental elicitations and generally do not like to engage in 'talk about the day' (Blum-Kulka, 1997; Ochs & Taylor, 1995). In this chapter I examine how a single father's (John) elicitations of talk about the day that were a part of a mealtime game were met with resistance from his two boys, and how this resistance at once serves to break down the routine at the same time as it serves to open up space for new, more collaborative, discourse activities.

There is ample research on family dinnertime narratives to suggest that families do not need to institute explicit routines to encourage family storytelling – these are already prompted regularly by family members (Ochs & Capps, 2001). However, currents in the popular press, as well as recent academic reports, point to fears of – as well as evidence supporting – a decline in the amount of rich interactions family members have in their times with each other, often attributed to the phenomenon of the dual-income family. Heath (2006) for example, notes that the data presented in two major studies of family interaction (led by Deborah Tannen and Marjorie Harness Goodwin and presented in a recent issue of *Text and Talk* [2006]) show very little of the narrative discourse known to be facilitative in developing children's academic competencies. Other studies have shown that the frequency of family dinners in US families has decreased (Larson *et al.*, 2006), and socialization research has even moved away from the mealtime activity to find other sites of interaction where parents and children are in regular contact. Adler and Adler (1984), for example, focus on carpool to and from school as an important site of socialization. While some of the families in this study did remark that other sites of socialization, such as carpool, were useful to the family, they also all indicated that they met for family meals on a regular basis and, as the data here show, they were rich sites of interaction.

In the data presented below from the Sondermans, there are 19 occurrences in 22 mealtimes of a parent-moderated bad thing/good thing routine in which each family member is prompted (either by another family member or himself) to tell one bad thing and one good thing about the day. This routine, which was inspired by a magazine article that the father, John, had read, was most often initiated (usually with a prompt like 'So Dima, something bad today?') and moderated by John in an effort to raise the two boys to engage in more adult-like discourse and to provide an opportunity for the boys to talk about their feelings, as I discuss in more detail below. In every instance of the routine, at least one boy issues a 'nothing' or other avoidance response. I analyze this pattern of interaction in relation to Ochs and Capps' (2001) narrative dimensions to show how the father is socialized out of the routine by his school-age children and how the talk within the routine contrasts with stories spontaneously told during the family mealtimes. More specifically, I compare how talk about the day embedded in the bad thing/good thing routine differs from narratives told about other times. I show how both the type of story told and the interaction that occurs in the telling (i.e. resistance versus spontaneous initiation) play a role in establishing roles in the family conversations, as well as shared knowledge among the family members that serve to shape a family identity. Finally, I discuss what implications these findings have for transnational adoptees and young second language learners in classroom settings.

John attempted to promote family sharing time through the bad thing/ good thing routine for a variety of reasons (e.g. to control the topic of conversation at mealtime, to encourage the children to share their feelings and to learn about what happened at school that day). The routine facilitated the boys' participation in mealtime conversations (Fogle, 2008b). However, it also provided a site of identity and role negotiation that was conflictual and problematic at times. In examining the development of this routine over the course of the study, we can see how learner or child resistance in tandem with accommodation from a caring adult leads to new forms of talk and narrative that are very different from talk about the day and perform different functions in the family conversations. In this way the boys guide the narrative activity, and socialization processes become collaborative and child-directed.

In the later mealtime conversations, Dima and Sasha initiate other types of spontaneous narratives that do not typically fall within the realm of 'talk about the day' but rather describe and explain events and scenes from other times. This kind of talk has been associated with children's preservation of family memories and potentially the construction of family identities over time (see Nelson, 1990; Ochs & Capps, 2001). For the transnational adoptive family where parents and children do not share early childhood memories with one another, early memories and stories must be reconstructed collaboratively in family interactions to include the new family context and thus construct a sense of belonging across time and space. Ochs and Capps (2001: 40) point out that 'narratives of a lifespan scope are rare in everyday social interaction'. However, it could be that these stories are told in segments in short-term interactions, as with the fragments of narratives that are examined at the end of this chapter, which recur over longer times and gradually begin to construct life stories. In the data below I look at how the two adoptees in this family, Dima and Sasha, guide storytelling about their past lives in Ukraine and the role that such talk plays in the family context.

Narrative as Process versus Product

Sociolinguistic and discourse analytic perspectives on narrative are generally traced back to Labov's (e.g. Labov & Waletsky, 1967) early work on monologic, canonical 'stories with a point' (Johnstone, 2001) that were elicited and told in interview settings. There have been two main developments in narrative research that have expanded on Labov and Waletsky's original work in this area and form the starting point for the narrative analysis in this chapter. The first, arising primarily from analyses of naturally occurring conversations and language socialization work with family interactions, has been a reanalysis of personal narratives from monologic performances to tellings co-constructed among multiple participants (Georgakopoulou, 2007; Ochs & Capps, 2001). In this turn, narrative as text has become reanalyzed as narrative as practice (Georgakopoulou, 2007). Close analysis of how parents and children or other participants elicit, tell and evaluate narratives in interaction with each other shows that narrative activities, and not simply narratives as texts on their own, are rich sites for problem solving, establishing cultural norms and values and negotiating identities.

A second development in narrative research has been an expansion of investigation on narrative structure. Labov and Waletzky (1967) originally proposed the following elements as being essential to the narrative: abstract, orientation, complicating action, evaluation and coda. However, more recent approaches have considered other forms of narrative (e.g. life stories, chronicles, small stories, etc.) that do not always conform to a set structure or foreground one element of the narrative over others. In De Fina's (2003a) chronicles, for example, orientations take on a more important role as a site of negotiation of power and place. Further, in Georgakopoulou's (2007: 2) study of small stories (what she refers to as 'an umbrella term to cover a gamut of under-represented narrative activities'), narratives that occur in conversational interaction do not conform to set structures; instead, structures are emergent and sequentially based. In this conversational or emergent approach, as employed by Georgakopoulou as well as Ochs and Capps (2001), narrative events become a site of identity construction not only by the story told or the discourse used to do so, but also in the interactional mechanisms through which the narrative is elicited, told and evaluated. It is through the analysis of the interactional elements of narrative that microanalysis of storytelling can be connected to larger, macro-scale identities.

Related to expanding narrative approaches, monologic productions of narrative cannot account for the *process* of socialization into narrative practices. Ochs and Capps (2001: 19) offer a model of the conversational narrative in which four interactional moves, questions, clarifications, challenges and speculations, correspond to the four primary elements of narrative structure, description, chronology, evaluation and explanation. By coupling the analysis of narrative in interaction and narrative elements, this model has the potential for examining the narrative as both activity and text. Ochs and Capps (2001) further argue that conversational narratives fall on a continuum of five dimensions: tellership (one versus multiple), tellability (high to low), embeddedness (detached to embedded), linearity (closed temporal and clausal order to open) and moral stance (certain, constant to open, fluid). In these data, the dimensions of tellership and tellability become sites of contention and negotiation among the family members.

Tellership refers to 'the extent and kind of involvement of conversational partners in the actual recounting of a narrative' (Ochs & Capps, 2001: 24). Tellability, according to Ochs and Capps (2001: 33), is 'the extent to which [personal narratives] convey a sequence of reportable events and make a point in a rhetorically effective manner'. The talk about the day routine at once provides a framework in which the boys take on teller roles and learn about what is tellable; however, as the routine progresses and they reach greater competence they find expert ways to resist the routine including not only the 'nothing' response, but also subverting the goals of the game. These practices constitute a manipulation of expectations about tellership and tellability that reshape the narrative activities. As the children find other ways to initiate narratives and stories in the family conversations, tellership becomes more collaborative and fluid and the tellability becomes more open-ended. These processes lead to tellings that fall on timescales outside of the day-to-day and constitute pieces of a long-term identity construction project.

Resistance in Interaction

Research on narrative socialization has focused primarily on the parents' roles in shaping children's narrative productions and the ways in which they elicit and evaluate children's tellings. As mentioned above, few if any studies have examined the impact of children's resistance to storytelling activities and challenges to their parents in eliciting narratives in conversation, although these interactional moves are common, especially for older children, and potentially play a role in collaborative socialization processes. Resistance, according to Ahearn (2001), is one form of agency that occurs in and through discourse, and it is one option within socializing encounters that is open to novices and particularly second language learners (Duff, 2012). In adult second language learning, resistance is constructed as a type of avoidance or deliberate failure to replicate target language norms (e.g. Ohara, 2001; Morita, 2004). As Morita (2004) argues, these forms of resistance are hard to recognize because outsiders (teachers, researchers and other authority figures) can interpret avoidance or passive resistance in other ways (e.g. as an incapability or failure to learn or as passivity and shyness) or mistakenly attribute such behaviors to differing cultural norms. These misinterpretations result in constraining learners' agency in the sense that the intentionality of the actions is missed and learners are marginalized for their failure to participate. The capacity to act or to learn is not granted. Learner resistance in these contexts is typically found to be harmful in educational settings. Harklau (2000), for example, described how young adult students' resistance led to increased confirmation of their deficiency in the eyes of their teachers, and eventually led to students dropping out of the ESOL program in the community college.

What happens when learners or novices use resistance strategies that are easily interpreted as such by experts and authority figures in contexts outside of the classroom? Instantiated resistance such as the 'nothing' response that Dima uses when prompted to talk about their day in these data is easily recognizable in its explicit refusal to participate. In the classroom, this type of resistance would typically be construed as problematic and/or defiant and would not in most cases result in productive learning for the student. In the examples below, however, I find that in interaction with a caring adult, such outward resistance can result in changes in the interactional context that facilitate learning and identity construction processes. John, the father, certainly became frustrated and annoyed by the resistant responses of his children, but he eventually accommodated to the behavior and avoided the specific types of prompts and elicitations that were met with resistance by the children in the routine. This negotiation over the ways in which the family would interact at mealtimes shows how children and second language learners can achieve agency through resistance that leads in some ways to richer and more harmonious interactions. (Although John continued to see Dima as resistant in numerous types of interactions.) These processes can be attributed to the context of the transnational adoptive family in which the need to collaborate and accommodate may be greater, and creating a continuity across disruptions in the adoption process may lead to greater awareness of past and historical identities.

The two boys in this study resist participating in a parent-directed routine in three main ways, with the first and most salient mechanism being used primarily by the older child Dima (age 10 at the time of recordings). This is the 'nothing' response or explicit refusal to participate in the routine when prompted by his father. A second form of resistance is an avoidance tactic used more frequently by Sasha, the younger son, in which he would nominate another speaker when prompted by his father, for example by saying 'you first' or 'Dima hasn't said his yet'. This tactic allows Sasha to appear to be a harmonious participant in the routine event without actually participating in the storytelling activity. Finally, when the 'nothing' response stops working for Dima, a third form of resistance emerges in the routine in which Dima participates in the storytelling by choosing a topic for his 'bad thing', but does so in a way that subtly subverts John's original goals of the routine (e.g. to be able to talk about emotions and bond as a family). In these examples, Dima complains about his father's or other authority figures' actions or discusses potentially taboo events that position Dima as the family member in power and place John in a position of either being defensive or critical of the participation he has actively elicited from Dima. These three forms of instantiated linguistic resistance – explicit refusals to participate with 'nothing' responses to prompts, avoidance by nominating another speaker and subversion through infelicitous participation (i.e. conforming to the form of the routine, but not the overall intentions) – play a role in the family dropping the routine as part of early mealtime conversations.

The Sondermans

The Sonderman family stands out among US families, as well as the adoptive families participating in this study, in two main ways. First, it is a family headed by a single father. In 2006, 9% of all households in the United States were single-parent families, and only one-fifth of those had single fathers (US Census Bureau News, 2007). Second, although Dima (age 10 at the start of the study) and Sasha (age eight) had only been in the United

States for a little over a year (the boys were eight and seven when they arrived) (see Table 3.1), their language production was easily passable to casual interlocutors for native speakers of English. This is remarkable due to the fact that one of the only prior longitudinal studies of transnational adoptees' second language acquisition found that the two brothers adopted from Vietnam in the study had not acquired past tense morphology even after a year in their new home (Sato, 1990). By the end of the study and the second academic year in the US, both Sasha and Dima were well beyond this point and even at or above grade level in reading, according to their father.

The Sondermans' Data

The Sondermans – John, Dima and Sasha – participated in the study for eight months and returned six months of data. In general, John collected mealtime recordings on a regular schedule (four per month) at dinner times when the three family members ate together. He also included literacy events (including homework sessions and reading from magazines, books, flyers from school, etc.) that usually took place at the dinner table immediately after the meal. Table 4.1 shows the recordings returned by the Sondermans.

Three recording sessions involved activities other than dinner. One recording was made in the car on the way home from school (B) and two were of activities at the dinner table, but no meal was served or eaten (the family was planning a trip to Six Flags and playing a card game). Sasha and John were present at all recordings; however, Dima was not present for one dinnertime because he was away at his grandparents' home. John had noted at the start of the study that he and the boys did eat meals together on a regular basis, but also suggested that carpool would be an easier place for him to do the recording. Because of the rich prior research on family mealtimes and language socialization (e.g. Blum-Kulka, 1997; Ochs & Taylor, 1995; Ochs *et al.*, 1992; see also Blum-Kulka, 2008), as well as the fact that the other family (the Jackson-Wessels) participating at the same time was primarily recording mealtimes, I requested that John focus on mealtime recordings if he could, but added that carpool recordings were also fine if they fit his schedule better. In retrospect, allowing the parents to choose the most meaningful context of socialization and place to record to them might have contextualized the analysis even further in relation to the family's everyday routines.

John also participated in monthly interviews with me. During the interviews I asked him open-ended questions about the children's performance

Table 4.1 The Sondermans' recordings

Month	Recording	Date	Time	Activity	Bad thing/ good thing routine occurred?
December 2005	1A	12/7/2005	38:18	Dinner/reading	Yes
	1B	12/8/2005	17:27	Carpool	No
	1C	12/9/2005	28:29	Dinner/reading	Yes
	1D	12/11/2005	28:11	Dinner	Yes
January 2006	1E	1/15/2006	33:34	Dinner/reading	Yes
	1F	1/17/2006	34:18	Dinner	Yes
	1G	1/18/2006	27:57	Dinner	Yes
	1H	1/20/2006	33:00	Dinner/book-reading	Yes
February 2006	1I	2/24/2006	35:39	Dinner	Yes
	1J	2/26/2006	33:05	Dinner/reading	Yes
March 2006	1K	3/1/2006	33:28	Dinner	Yes
	1L	3/3/2006	25:46	Dinner	Yes
	1M	3/26/2006	40:42	Dinner	No
	1N	3/31/2006	26:51	Dinner	Yes
April 2006	1O	4/1/2006	21:08	Dinner	Yes
	1P	4/5/2006	47:13	Dinner	Yes
May 2006	1Q	5/9/2006	28:00	Dinner	No
	1R	5/10/2006	24:24	Dinner/homework	No
	1S	5/14/2006	37:12	Dinner/homework	Yes
	1T	5/2006*	19:32	Dinner/homework	Yes
July 2006	1U	7/2006*	27:08	Dinner	Yes
	1V	7/21/2006	32:43	Dinner/reading	Yes
	1W	7/22/2006	34:08	Game	No
	1X	7/30/2006	58:34	Planning trip/game	No
August 2006	1Y	8/9/2006	31:26	Dinner	Yes
Total			13 hours, 15 minutes		

*Exact day unknown

in school and interaction at home. The interviews also included a modified stimulated recall procedure as described in Chapter 3. As with the interviews with Kevin and Meredith Jackson-Wessels (Chapter 5), the interview data were transcribed and coded using Grounded Theory Protocol (Strauss & Corbin, 1990) in Microsoft Word and Filemaker for major themes for a prior study (Fogle, 2008a). This was not done with interviews with the Goellers (Chapter 6) because they did not participate in the earlier study.

Coding for Narrative Activity

The mealtime conversations were coded initially for the start and end of the bad thing/good thing routine. The types of elicitations, responses and narratives that occurred within its boundaries were then coded to reflect the interactional moves that occurred during participation in the routine (Table 4.2). Excerpts for analysis were selected from five turns above the first elicitation for a bad thing and five turns below the end of the last bad thing, good thing or related 'spinoff' topic in order to examine the sequential emergence and closure of the narrative in the interaction.

In the analyses here, I focus on changes in the bad thing/good thing routine over the course of the study and the emergence of other types of narrative in relation to those changes. This focus emerged both in ongoing analysis of the family's recordings as well as the interviews with John, the father, who stated several times during the study that he was beginning to stop doing the routine because of the children's resistance to it. The children's participation in the routine offered clear instances of resistance to their father's efforts at engaging them in a potentially socializing event, and further, over time, demonstrated the effects of children's resistance on a parent's interactional strategies and attitudes toward a particular discourse event. In order to capture the types of talk that occurred outside of the routine, talk before the first elicitation or mention of the bad thing/good thing routine for transcripts 1K–1Y (see Table 4.1) was coded for type of talk (e.g. metalinguistic talk, language play, negotiation over food, narrative) and the speaker who initiated the talk.

Narratives were considered to be either monologic or multiparty constructions of a past, present or future event which included temporality, a problem or disruption and evaluation (see also Georgakopoulou, 2007). Present time narratives included narrations usually of language play (i.e. announcing a football game with a tomato as a ball, 'He runs with the ball … and he scores!'), while future narrative included planning for imagined and real events (inviting friends to brunch or a child imagining getting caught spying). Narratives in these data included stories, reports and small stories.

Table 4.2 Coding for prompts and responses in bad thing/good thing routine

Type of prompt or response	Explanation	Example
Initiating prompt	First prompt for each bad thing/good thing (up to six total in one transcript)	What was your bad/ good thing?
		Something bad/good?
		How 'bout you?
Repeated prompt	Second and subsequent prompts for bad/good thing	Did you say your bad thing?
Self prompt	Speaker nominates self for bad thing/good thing	My bad thing,
		Something good for me?
Avoidance response – deferral	Speaker selects other speaker instead of taking turn in routine.	You first.
Avoidance response – 'nothing'	Speaker responds to prompt with 'nothing'	Nothin'.
		I don't know.
Other topic nomination	Other speaker nominates a bad/good thing for person prompted.	What about when you. . .
Correction	Correction from other speaker regarding rules of bad thing/ good thing routine.	BAD thing (not good thing).
		I already said mine.
		It's his turn.
Narrative	Response to prompt that included reference to past event, problem, and evaluation	
Clarifications/ Confirmations	Questions aimed at eliciting further information from speaker.	You what?
		You did?
Unrelated topic	Intervening talk within boundaries of bad thing/good thing routine that is not related to bad thing/good thing topics	Talk about food, behavior at the table, or other topics

Background of the Bad Thing/Good Thing Routine

The bad thing/good thing routine in which the Sondermans participated was designed to elicit narratives through which family members would engage in the kinds of problem solving and emotional or moral development discussed in Ochs and Capps (2001). In interviews, John reported that he originally read about the routine in an article in *Parade Magazine* sometime after he brought the boys home in September of 2004. The article was actually published August 15, 2004, around the same date that Sasha and Dima came to the United States and started school. The author of the article, Bruce Feiler, who is a popular writer and not a psychologist or parenting expert, refers to the routine as a 'game' that he links to his own childhood mealtime practices. Feiler's rationale for recommending the bad thing/good thing game is based on a perceived need for family members to learn to talk about the good and the bad and to listen without passing judgment. The 'rules' of the game outlined by Feiler (2004: 1) are as follows:

(1) Designate a moderator. This should be a rotating role, and each member of the family should get a turn at it. The moderator asks each person at the table, 'What happened bad to you today?'
(2) Review the bad stuff first.
(3) Everybody gets a chance to speak, no matter how young.
(4) Respect each answer. You can react to another person's reply, but you can't put it down.
(5) End with the good. In Round Two, the moderator asks each person, 'What happened good to you today?' Everyone gets a chance to reply.

In conclusion, Feiler (2004: 2) states that the benefit of this game for family members is the ability to develop listening skills and deal with difficult conversations in a 'safe' environment:

> The lesson of 'Bad & Good,' I believe, is not just that Mommy and Daddy have problems too. It's that self-awareness begins with articulating the building blocks of what makes us happy and sad. Difficult conversations can be had with people of all ages, often with conflicting points of view. And the key to living in harmony with others is finding time to listen to their hopes and fears – and learning not to knock them.

In an interview where John explains his goals in instituting this routine, he makes similar comments about the value of talking about bad things/good things:

It [bad thing/good thing] was from an article about families uh having a family that actually speaks to each other instead of just goes past each other all the time, ... it's to actually take a moment to let people in on what your experience has been. And we – we start with the bad thing first so we can end with a good thing, and it also let's people uhm, let's people know that uh we assume there's going to be bad stuff and that it's ok to talk about it. And that conversations are open to both possibilities (January 2006).

These goals are not always met by the activity of the routine itself, however, as we see in the analysis below.

The Routineness of the Routine

The Sondermans' participation in the bad thing/good thing game could be considered an interactional routine in the simplest sense of the term simply by its pervasiveness across transcripts (it occurs in all but three dinnertimes). There are also other clues to the game's status as an interactional routine that 'calls forth a set of responses' (Peters & Boggs, 1986: 81). In previous work (Fogle, 2008b) I have shown that Sasha, the younger sibling, used repetition of the initiating turn of the routine (e.g. 'My good thing was ...') to gain or regain turns in the conversation with his father and older brother (who often interrupted Sasha). In the following excerpt Sasha presupposes that John's prompt (line 2) is an opener for the routine:

Excerpt 4.1 So tell me,
(1O, April 1, 2006, Dima – 10, Sasha – eight)
1   John: Um,
2   so tell me,
3   ((pause))
4   Sasha: Something good.
5   John: /Well I was gonna say/, tell me about the movie.
6   Sasha: <burps> Oh, that – that woman who wanted to get,
7   the – all of the dalmatians to make a coat.
((retelling of movie continues))

In this excerpt Sasha anticipates his father's prompt and then completes the initiation of the routine with the phrase 'something good' in line 4, suggesting that the bad thing/good thing game was so routinized that it could be recognized by Sasha simply by the prompt opener that John utters in line 2, 'So tell me'.

There are other routine aspects of the enactment of this game in the family's interaction. Over the eight months of recording, John typically prompts one child, then the other child and then prompts himself for bad things and good things. Further, John selects each boy to go first about equally in the data (excluding two sessions where Dima was not present). Dima is selected nine times and Sasha eight in the recordings where both boys are present. Even in situations when someone else initiates the routine (i.e. Sasha), John still plays the role of moderator.

John also both implicitly and explicitly established a set of rules during the routine. A comprehensive list compiled from the different transcripts included:

(1) Bad things first.
(2) Tellers go in the same order for bad and then good.
(3) The bad thing/good thing had to have happened that day.
(4) The bad thing/good thing had to have happened to you (not another person).
(5) The person selected by John should respond for himself.

These rules to the game functioned to constrain the type of narrative produced in the bad thing/good thing storytelling. In short, in relation to Ochs and Capps' (2001) narrative dimensions, the time and place of the events told were constrained, tellership was tightly controlled and the evaluation of the events told was predetermined in the sense that it was already deemed as a 'bad' or 'good' event although additional evaluation occurred in the telling.

Mothers' elicitations of talk about the day in middle-class families have been interpreted as moves associated with both exerting power in family interactions (Ochs & Taylor, 1995) and showing solidarity (Tannen, 2007). This tension between power and solidarity in story elicitations is also found in John's role as a single father and moderator of the narrative routine. His interest in eliciting stories about bad things and good things in the meal-times is related to his desire to connect with his children, find out about their lives outside of the home (including aspects of school life that might need his intervention or evaluation) and at the same time help them talk about their experiences and feelings, as he states in interviews and explains to Dima during mealtimes when he refuses to participate. The routine also provided a structure for the family conversation through which John could control the type of talk at mealtime and enforce 'polite conversation' as he comments in the interview data and as occurs in recordings where John initiates routine after long pauses, burps, off-color jokes and uncomfortable silences. He talks about his strategies for controlling the children's table talk in this quote:

> John: Uhm, and I've actually started now reading at breakfast ... It's – part of it is self defense, it's like how can we have something that feels like a civil discourse. Instead of, you know fart jokes. (October 2005)

In keeping with John's interest in raising the conversational level of his children, in at least two of the episodes John initiates the bad thing/good thing routine immediately after an audible burp or off-color joke told by one of the children, as in this excerpt:

Excerpt 4.2 Knock-knock joke
(1F, January 17, 2006, Dima – 10; Sasha – eight)

1	Sasha:	Ok.
2		Knock knock,
3		knock knock!
4	Dima:	Who's there?
5	Sasha:	Uhm, bacon.
6		Uh, just say uh, bacon who.
7	John:	Bacon who?
8	Sasha:	Bakin' a DOODIE just for you.
9		hhhh.
10		hhh.
11	John:	Does everything have to be uhm,
12		not nice?
13	Dima:	No.
14		Yeh, like doo doo.
15	John:	Ok, Sasha something bad for you today?
16	Sasha:	Uhm, nothing.
17	John:	Nothing bad?

John's selection of Sasha as first teller in the routine in line 15 follows his explicit disapproval of Sasha's joke. Here we see the narrative routine becomes a means through which John, a single father, can instill some control over the discursive production of his sons and maintain what would be considered more polite dinnertime conversation.

The knock-knock joke told here and reference to 'impolite' or taboo topics (i.e. excrement) could also be seen to be doing other interactional work in the family. Crystal (1986) suggests that swearing and other types of profane talk by adolescents can be used as a type of 'in-group' talk. In addition, Bauman (1977: 1) concluded that children's control of the knock-knock genre (in the ability to control the outcome) 'show the child's acquisition of his ability to control his communicative environment'. Sasha's introduction of the off-color knock-knock joke at dinnertime invites the two other male members of the family (older brother and father) to join in some 'in group' talk and in so doing treats the father John as an equal interactant in eight-year-old boy talk. John reacts to being 'led into' the off-color joke and responds by exerting control over the conversation through protest (echoed by Dima in line 14, 'Yeh, like doo doo') and an elicitation of 'higher' level, polite discourse (i.e. talk about the day through the bad thing elicitation).

The constraints on the types of narratives allowed, as listed above, and John's role as moderator of the routine had implications both for the boys' willingness to participate in the game and the form of narratives told within the routine. These patterns can be found in the following excerpt, taken early in the data collection:

Excerpt 4.3 Something bad today?
(1C, December 9, 2005, Dima – 10, Sasha – eight)

1	John	Uhm, something bad today?
2		Dima?
3	Dima:	Nothing.
4	John:	Nothing bad?
5	Dima:	Uh-huh.
6	Sasha:	Papa,
7	John:	Your fight with Robert?
8	Dima:	Mm?
9		Mm-huh.
10	John:	Was that – just put the salt down.
11		Dima ((quiet)).
12	Sasha:	Papa, something bad to you.
13		((salt shaker makes sound on table))
14	John:	Dima ((whisper)).
15		Uhm, something bad for me.
16		((pause))
17		Mmm, ... my only bad thing is that I have this test on Monday and this project due and,
18		even though we had a snow day, I had to kind of think about that stuff instead of just hanging out with you guys.
19	Dima:	Daddy?

20	John:	That was my bad thing.
21	Dima:	Daddy, this is for you.
22	John:	What's for [me]?
23	Dima:	[Boo]! Hahhhuuhu
24	John:	Was that a snowball? ((referring to food on the plate))
25	Dima:	Mm-hmm.
26	John:	Sasha how 'bout your bad thing?
27	Sasha:	Hmm.
28		<rattling>
29		Uhmm.
30	John:	You wanna break that chair after I glued it back together?
31	Sasha:	No.
32		Hm. Something bad.
33		Uhm, hmm.
34		Hm.
35		((pause))
36		Hm.
37		((pause, eating))
38		Uhm, I forgot what – what my bad thing was.
39	John:	You forgot?
40	Sasha:	Uh-huh <eating>.
41		Dima, something good.
42	John:	Something good, Dima?

In this excerpt, the family members go through a full round of bad things, with both of the boys resisting or avoiding talk about bad things – Dima uses a 'nothing' response and Sasha defers his turn by prompting his father first in line 12, and then prompting Dima in line 41 to pass his turn at a bad thing. The good things are told over another 47 lines of transcript, starting with the first prompt in line 41. Thus, Excerpt 4.3 provides a good example of how the routine was accomplished through John's prompting as well as the type of resistance to talk about the day that both boys showed in slightly different ways (Dima using resistance strategies and Sasha deferring or passing turns by selecting another speaker). In this excerpt only John tells a story about his day (lines 17–20) – the stories that Dima and Sasha tell during the routine are analyzed in the following sections.

Start Times for Bad Thing/Good Thing

There were 19 instances of the bad thing/good thing routine found in the recorded data (25 transcripts total; 22 total dinnertimes). Three of the recordings are not mealtimes (one carpool session [Transcript 1B, December] and two sessions at home where the family is involved in activities such as planning a trip to Six Flags [Transcripts 1W and 1X, July]). Therefore, there are three missed opportunities where the family is eating dinner, but the bad thing/good thing routine did not occur. These missed opportunities occurred near the end of the eight-month study in April (Transcript 1M) and May (Transcripts 1Q and 1R) (Table 4.1).

The regularity of the routine can be measured by the variation in start times (coded as any family member's first prompt for a bad thing) during the meal. On average, the initiating elicitation for the routine was issued in the seventh minute of the dinnertime conversation (the average length of dinnertime recordings, which often included post-dinner homework or reading time, rounded to the nearest minute was 32 minutes); however, over the 19 episodes, start times ranged from 0:05 in May (i.e. within the first minute of recording 1S when Sasha reminds John to do the routine following two dinnertime recordings where the family did not do it), to 21:50 in Recording V (July 2006) when the family members forgot about the routine (Figure 4.1). The average length of the bad thing/good thing episode was eight minutes, which often included intervening conversation or topics that 'spun off' from the bad thing or good thing being discussed. In general then, about one-fifth of the time the family spent at the dinner table together the

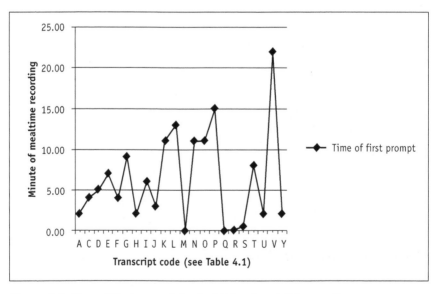

Figure 4.1 Time of first prompt for bad thing/good thing routine

conversation was bound by telling about bad things and good things, and this conversation occurred somewhere in the first half of the dinnertime activities.

By the end of the data collection (Transcripts 1V and 1Y), the routine is initiated at the very end of the mealtime and in the last recording, 1Y, the family tells only bad things because they are distracted by another activity (executing a magic trick from a book). In interviews, John gave two main reasons for the change in start times and growing sporadic nature of the routine over time. On the one hand, he felt that other types of talk had taken the place of the routine telling about the day as seen here:

> John: And, so if I feel like there's conversation going and it – they're sharing about their day or we're kind of wondering about something together, then I may just let it go. Uhm. And I feel like we're doing more of that more – there's more dialogue going on.
> (May 24, 2006)

And on the other hand, John also indicated he felt a sense of failure in the routine and that he was often met with resistance when trying to initiate it.

In the following sections, I discuss both the 'failure' of the routine and the more active dialogue that John refers to above that takes its place. I start by discussing John's role as moderator of the routine and the interactional control he exerts on interaction within its boundaries, I then analyze the two boys' avoidance responses to John's elicitations and how John changes his own strategies. Finally, based on the analysis of start times above, I turn to what types of talk take the place of the bad thing/good thing routine in recordings 1K–1Y, where the routine is not introduced until the second half of mealtime, and show how recent work on life stories and chronicles can help us to better understand narrative socialization in the transnational family.

'Nothing' Responses and Avoiding Participation

One way that John exerted control over the mealtime interactions in general and the boys' telling about the day in particular is through evaluation of the bad thing/good thing narratives. As a single father, John played the role of both initiator and primary recipient of narratives, and like the fathers in Ochs and Taylor's (1995) study, he often passed judgment on the children's reported actions in the narratives. Negative evaluations from John (for good things in addition to bad things, as seen below) can lead the children to 'retract' their narrative and contribute to the avoidance tactics used by Dima especially, as I analyze further below.

In a summary of narrative research and conceptualizations of self, Ochs and Capps (1996) identify minimal responses (one-word responses or no response) as a characteristic of middle-class US children's responses to parental elicitation of narratives. Minimal responses can arise from the child's persistent role as protagonist in narratives at mealtime in this group of families and represent an attempt to avoid scrutiny and evaluation as seen in the above excerpt (Ochs & Taylor, 1995). Nothing responses, which usually took the form of 'nothing' or 'I don't know', to bad thing/good thing prompts were present in almost all of the routines present in these data. Sasha and Dima offer this response about equally (this includes repetitions of 'nothing' in the same turn-prompt sequence). However, Dima is a little more consistent with the response (there is only one transcript where he doesn't use the nothing response compared to Sasha who has four episodes where he doesn't use it and one where he uses it seven times in a sort of language play – 'I got nothin'!') In addition, John reacts negatively to Dima's use of the nothing response (saying it is not acceptable or to find another answer), whereas when Sasha uses the nothing response John usually responds with a move on tactic ('Nothing? Ok.') or mock disbelief ('Nothing bad all day?'). For these two reasons I focus primarily on Dima's use of the nothing response, although both boys used it as a way to avoid the routine. However, the pattern of children's turns in the routine point to larger family identities and conflictual relationships between the two boys, which I discuss below.

In the following excerpt, Sasha finishes up his good thing about doing well in dance class and then elicits a good thing from Dima.

Excerpt 4.4 Kissed by a girl
(1E, January 15, 2006, Dima – 10, Sasha – eight)
1	Sasha:	And uh, we got to go in front of the line
2		First, . . . and uh,
3		\<chewing\>
4		and uh, we – we were doin' a GOOD JOB, so we, we uh, but we didn't get a snack.
5		Ok?
6		Dima, something good \<cough\>.
7		Yeh.
8		\<cough\>
9		Dima, something good.

10		\<cough\>
11	Dima:	That I got kissed by a girl today.
12	John:	Kissed by a girl ((falling)).
13	Dima:	Uh-huh.
14	John:	Ah, when did this happen?
15	Dima:	No time at all.
16	John:	Oh.
17	Dima:	Mm,
18		Aw, what did happen good?
19		There's lots of red on that picture.

In lines 1–5 Sasha tells a story about an undetermined event at school that is both positively and negatively evaluated: 'we were doing a good job, but we didn't get snack' (for more about Sasha's narratives within the routine, see Fogle, 2008b). Sasha seems eager to turn the floor over to Dima, suggested by his question 'Ok?' in line 5 and prompting of his brother, 'Dima something good'.

Dima then suggests a one-line good thing – 'that I got kissed by a girl today' – that potentially serves as an abstract to a story. John repeats the statement with a falling tone that functions to negatively evaluate the event in line 12. John then follows up by eliciting more of the narrative, starting with details of the setting, 'Ah, when did this happen?' in line 14. The intonation of this utterance also suggests a negative evaluation on the part of John, and Dima then retracts the narrative by negating the orientation in response, 'No time at all'. He then prompts himself to select another good thing (line 18) and finally changes the topic (line 19). The fact that this narrative is originally elicited by Dima's brother, Sasha, and not his father, might have played a role in Dima's willingness to respond and to test the waters with a potentially taboo topic (i.e. romantic activity with a girl). His father's evaluative elicitations, however, put a damper on the narrative activity, suggesting that while storytelling is one aim of the bad thing/good thing routine, certain stories are more legitimate than others. As it turns out, Dima begins to capitalize on telling transgressive or borderline stories that help him to appear to be participating in the storytelling routine while at the same time subverting its goals as a family solidarity building activity, as we see below.

Dima's 'Nothing' Response

Dima is fairly consistent in his use of the nothing response, and there is little change seen over the eight months of data collection in the frequency of 'nothing' or 'I don't know' in response to his father's prompts. What does change over time is how John himself responds to the 'nothing' response.

In the first four mealtime transcripts (1A–1E, December–January), John typically offers a topic suggestion for a bad thing when Dima gives a nothing response as seen in Excerpt 4.5.

Excerpt 4.5 Homework
(1A, December 7, 2005, Dima – 10, Sasha – eight)

1	John:	Now what's your bad thing for today?
2	Dima:	Nothin'.
3	John:	Nothing bad today?
4	Dima:	Mm-mm.
5	John:	All day long?
6	Dima:	Hm-mm.
7	John:	What about homework?
8	Dima:	Hm-mm.
9	John:	That wasn't bad?
10		So why were you:,
11		screamin' and hollerin'?
12	Dima:	I don't know.

In the first four transcripts where bad thing/good thing occurs, John used this tactic (i.e. suggesting a bad or good thing) three times in three different transcripts, and explicitly rejected Dima's response by saying, 'find a different answer' only once. For the most part during this period, John accepts Dima's 'nothing' response by using repeated elicitations and suggesting topics to open a narrative. Thus Dima is not granted agency in resisting the routine or telling his own story.

The narrative produced here (primarily by John) takes the form of a small story with a mention of a shared past event that does not include much complicating action or actual telling of the event. The evaluation of the event is embedded in the bad thing prompt. Later, Dima recycles this story and suggests it for his father's bad thing, 'me, screamin' and hollerin','' further indicating Dima's sensitivity to the evaluation and critique that is part of the routine. John suggests a fight between himself and Dima as a bad thing for Dima, but Dima then turns the tables and suggests it as a bad thing for John.

The last transcript of this series in which John nominated topics for Dima is 1E, which takes place in January and is discussed above in Excerpt 4.4 (Kissed by a girl). In the following three transcripts (1F–1H, January 17, 18 and 20), John responded to Dima's nothing response in a slightly different way – instead of offering a topic for Dima, he makes explicit comments about Dima's non-participation ('Give it some thought', 'You always say that' and 'This is a chance to think about your day'). These strategies, which are less accommodating in that they explicitly comment on Dima's unwillingness to participate and require Dima to respond by choosing to participate or not (and not having John participate for him), do result in more active storytelling by Dima. These narratives begin to challenge John in certain ways by telling about transgressions at school or complaining about wrongdoings directed at Dima. We see this in a series of narratives told about a girl in school, Jill, in Transcript 1H, January 20.

Excerpt 4.6 Jill got hit
(1H, January 20, 2005, Dima – 10, Sasha – eight)

1	John:	How bout you?
2	Dima:	Ah.
3		Uh.
4		((pause, eating))
5	John:	Hmm?
6	Dima:	N – nothing.
7	Sasha:	Something bad for me?
8	John:	Dima, . . . try.
9	Dima:	Nothing!
10	John:	Nothing at all happened today that you would – you were frustrated with or would change
11	Dima:	Ok, ok.
12	John:	This is a chance to think back through your day,
13		((pause))
14	Dima:	Jill got hit!
15	John:	Mmm.
16		With?
17	Dima:	By:.
18	John:	By?
19	Sasha:	You.
20	Dima:	Huh-uh.
21	John:	By a person?
22	Dima:	N-gah.
23	John:	On purpose?
24	Dima:	Uh-huh.
25	John:	Somebody hit Jill on purpose?
26	Dima:	Yeh-huh.
27	John:	Why? Who?

28	Dima:	I do NOT know.
29		I mean, somebody got hurt, not Jill.
30		I don't know who.
31	John:	Hhh.
32	Dima:	But some of the girls that I like.
33		I know it's some of the girls that I like.
34		Jill or Marisol.
35	John:	Did you hear about this?
36	Dima:	Yeh.
37	John:	Mm.
38		Well it would be upsetting if a friend of yours . . . got hurt.

In lines 1–13 John attempts to elicit a bad thing narrative from Dima, who responds with the 'nothing' response as usual. John does not suggest a topic in this excerpt, but rather puts more pressure on Dima to participate, 'this is a chance to think about your day. . .'. Dima responds to this prompt with an abstract (a similar strategy to the one we saw above in the 'kissed by a girl' excerpt), 'Jill got hit'. The one-line abstract, which also functions as an unexpected turn in the narrative, then leads to further elicitations from John to build the narrative starting with a negotiation over prepositions, 'with' (line 16), to which Dima responds, 'by'. Sasha's contribution, 'you', suggests that the agent was a person, not a thing, to which John asks, 'by a person?', 'on purpose?', 'somebody hit Jill on purpose?' (lines 21–25), receiving backchannels from Dima. Up until this point Dima has not told the story himself, but rather guided John's questions primarily with yes/no responses to build up a narrative to explain how Jill got hit. The bad thing prompt seems to lend itself to this kind of 'slow disclosure' (Ochs & Capps, 2001) of the narrative where the abstract is given and then further details elicited (and this also occurs in the examples above). In line 29, Dima starts over with the narrative, 'I mean somebody got hurt, not Jill', suggesting that the original abstract had been an overstatement of what he knew, but was perhaps more tellable than the actual story. At this point Dima provides the orientation for the narrative (lines 30 to 34) in which it is clear he is not sure who got hit or what happened. John then questions Dima's authority or role as the teller of the story, 'did you hear about this?', provides a coda, 'well it would be upsetting. . .', and moves on.

There are four things that happen here that are relevant to the current analysis. The first is that Dima has responded to John's more demanding strategies for enforcing the routine by telling a story with a point. The second is that even though Dima initiates and 'tells' the story, he gets John to play the role of narrator for most of it by having him guess at what happened, suggesting that Dima is countering John's control in this narrative activity. Third, Dima is evaluated not only for his actions within the storyworld (as in the kissed by a girl episode), but also for his actions as storyteller (i.e. for telling a story that was not 'his' or about events he himself had not witnessed). Finally, Dima has begun to use the bad thing/good thing routine to introduce narratives of unexpected events to challenge his father and to subvert the goal of the routine. In sum, although John has control over Dima's tellership, Dima can counter that control by conforming to the rules of the game but placing John in the uncomfortable situation of negatively evaluating Dima's actions at school and thereby criticizing him for participating as he is called to do.

This trend continues in the following excerpt when Dima uses the bad thing prompt to initiate a complaint narrative directed at his father.

Excerpt 4.7 You kept me waiting
(1T, May 2006, Dima – 10, Sasha – eight)

1	John:	How 'bout you Dima?
2	Dima:	That you were /???/, that I was in the Pre-K class too long.
3	John:	You were in the pre-K class too long?
4	Dima:	Yeh.
5		I mean, I had, uh you kept me waiting.
6	John:	I kept you waiting?
7	Dima:	Mhm.
8	John:	Oh, goodness.
9	Dima:	Plus there's nothing to do.
10	John:	Mhm.
11	Sasha:	/Me too/.
12	John:	So the bad thing was that you had to be there longer than you wanted to be?
13	Dima:	Yeh.
14	John:	Mhm.
15	John:	Was that part of why you're mad?
16	Dima:	Mhm.
17		Plus the kids /???/.

In this excerpt, Dima does not avoid participation or defer his turn; rather, he is ready with a bad thing that is directed as a complaint at John. In line 2 he provides some orientation with negative evaluation, 'I was in the pre-K class too long'. John repeats this with a question intonation, and Dima revises as an abstract to the story, making his complaint more specific, 'I mean . . . you kept me waiting', using the personal pronoun 'you' and 'me' to implicate John as responsible for the wrongdoing. He then provides some further orientation that explains the problem, 'there's nothing to do there'. John evaluates the telling using a mocking tone, 'oh, goodness' and then retells the narrative, 'so the bad thing was you had to be there longer than you wanted to be' and provides a coda in line 15, 'is that part of why you are mad?'.

In this narrative Dima is not only telling about a bad thing, he is complaining about his father's actions and in doing so taking on the roles of both teller and evaluator of his father (rather than holding himself up for evaluation). This puts John, who later in the conversation explains that he was late because of work, on the defensive. A similar storytelling event occurs in transcript 1N where Dima responds to the bad thing elicitation that the whole day was bad and then initiates narrative, 'Because Ms. Lisa even disobeys her own rules', describing an event where he was not recognized in class even though his hand was raised. These are the final narratives Dima tells in these recordings before the routine drops out of the family mealtimes.

In sum, the above examples of the bad thing/good thing routine in the Sonderman family have illustrated how John, the father, responded to his son Dima's consistent avoidance of participating through a series of different strategies. In the first four mealtimes collected for this study (transcripts 1A, 1C, 1D and 1E), John responded to Dima's nothing responses by accepting 'nothing' or prompting Dima again by suggesting a topic for him. In transcripts 1F–1H (January 17–January 20) John stopped providing suggestions for Dima's bad and good things and instead made explicit comments about Dima's non-participation in the routine. These strategies (over the three dinnertimes in four days) worked in the sense that Dima began to tell more stories in response to the elicitations, but the stories he told were typically about his growing relationships with girls and transgressions in the classroom on their behalf. These stories were met with negative evaluation from John (as seen in the 'I got kissed by a girl' episode), and the undercurrent of tension around the routine remains. When the routine was initiated in the later transcripts (1K–1V), Dima told more elaborated or storylike narratives, but used the opportunity to lodge complaints about others' (his father's or teachers') actions toward him. These strategies effectively socialize John out of the routine.

The change in interactional roles that occurred over eight months in the Sonderman family in this conversational routine are emblematic to some extent of the ways in which macro roles such as 'father' and 'child' can be reconfigured in local interactions, as John maintained the parental role of initiator and evaluator of talk about the day narratives, but Dima used the narrative activity to both push the work of storytelling onto his father and challenge his father with uncomfortable content and even his evaluation of his father's own actions. The constraints on narrative form imposed by the 'rules' of the routine also played a role in this process. In the early stages when Dima refused to participate, the embedded evaluation and constraints on time and place of the bad thing narratives allowed for minimal tellings like the one John proposes in Excerpt 4.5 ('What about homework?'). As John demanded more participation from Dima, we saw how the bad thing prompt could lead to an abstract that then placed the burden of 'guessing' the story on the other interlocutor (i.e. John). The interactional roles, content and story forms that emerged in talk about the day in the Sonderman family were markedly different from those found in spontaneous narratives in other parts of the data.

Revising the First Eight Minutes

As the bad thing/good thing routine fell apart in the mealtime interactions, transcripts 1K–1Y (recorded between February and July), different types of talk took the place of the initiating prompt for a bad thing in the first eight minutes of the mealtime conversation. These types of talk included not only narratives, but also language play (both metalinguistic and fantasy), metalinguistic talk and academic discourse (i.e. recounting items on a geography quiz or talking through math problems), some of which took the form of or are embedded in narratives (for example, Sasha initiates an imaginary game of football with a tomato in which his father is the announcer for the game and Sasha the protagonist). They also included retellings of movie plots, newspaper articles, comic book episodes and other works of fiction.

Spontaneous Narratives

While the interactions within the boundaries of the bad thing/good thing routine for the most part were constrained by the rules of the game and John's elicitations, prompts and evaluations, the narratives that were told spontaneously in the data by both the children and John functioned more as a site of long-term identity construction (rather than negotiation of interactional roles). In these stories we see not only talk about the day, but talk about events in the distant past, plans for the future and generalizations about the world that take the form of narratives. For example, John initiated talk about hosting a brunch in the future by asking the boys what they would serve (constructing the three members of the family as 'hosts' to imagined 'guests'), he talked about his own past acting in a drama troupe in college and meeting the actress Glenn Close and he engaged in a good bit of future talk about the next school year, new teachers and so on, all of which contained elements of narrative.

Of all the spontaneous narratives that emerged in the first eight minutes of mealtime conversation, one type of child-initiated narrative that functioned as 'the way things were' talk or what life was like in Ukraine seemed particularly relevant to the role of spontaneous narratives in adoptive family conversations. This talk, which was primarily child directed, allowed the boys to connect discourse occurring on the short-term timescales of the school year or their new time in the US (e.g. academic discourse acquired recently at school or an event that happened at recess in the recent past) to events and scenes that occurred in the more distant past as children in Ukraine in a different language and time. Narrative studies have focused on retellings of the same story to show how narratives are contextualized in the environment of the telling. Retellings of the same story have led to important understandings of the construction of identity in narrative and the formation of a 'master' narrative (Georgakopoulou, 2007). Temporality in the Sondermans' data, however, falls on a different type of continuum. In these data, and especially in the second extract presented here, narratives from the more recent past are connected to thematically related events that occurred in the more distant past. This movement in time presents the opportunity for the boys to literally translate their experiences from one language and culture to another, with their father acting as facilitator in this process. It also represents a construction of self and family identities across timescales that creates continuity in the children's histories from 'who we were' to 'who we are now'.

These narratives about the more distant past did not always include a 'problem solving' element, but they still functioned as a socializing activity where the family members discussed ways of talking about experiences and negotiated the important elements of the scenes and stories. This type of narrative activity is especially relevant for the context of the transnational family where disruption or displacement has occurred in the children's lives and one of the new 'problems' to be solved is how to construct a shared history and family identity – to make sense of daily events, but also to construct a sense of self then and now, and a sense of family connectedness across past and present. In Excerpt 4.8, John, Dima and Sasha engage in a description of the boys' home in Ukraine that is similar to an orientation sequence or setting for a more tellable narrative, although a tellable event does not actually emerge in the interaction here. This narrative sequence about Ukraine emerges out of pseudo-academic history lesson about wooden legs (lines 4–20), a metalinguistic discussion about the word 'combine' and, finally, a description of life on the farm in Ukraine.

Excerpt 4.8 We live right next to the field
(1N, March 3, 2006, Dima – 10, Sasha – eight)

1	John:	So, soccer game's tomorrow, hopefully,
2		((pause rattling))
3	Sasha:	Pshoo. Pshoo. Pshoo, pshoo, pshoo, pshoo, pshoo.
4	Dima:	Daddy, do woman usually have wooden legs or men?
5	John:	Hh <exhale>.
6	Dima:	When their leg is broken off?
7	John:	Nowadays?
8	Dima:	Uh-huh.
9	John:	Nobody has wooden legs anymore.
10	Dima:	I mean, in the olden times.
11	John:	It would have been the same.
12		They used what they had.
13		You know, it depends on what the technology was.
14	Dima:	I mean like – like those pirates with one leg
15	John:	Yeh?
16		I – ah – I would GUESS that women didn't lose their legs as often as men did,
17	Dima:	Huhh.
18	John:	'cause men would have been more likely to get their legs shot off or,
19		eaten by sharks,
20		or, caught in a combine, or somethin' like that.
21	Sasha:	[/caught in/]
22	Dima:	[I know] what that is.
23	John:	Mhm.
24	Dima:	They have a lot of them in Ukraine because we leave – live right next to the fe – field.
25	John:	<cough> And did you see combines going back and forth and [harvesting wheat]?
26	Dima:	[Oh yeh.]
27	John:	<cough>
28	Sasha:	/And we got/ – and we got – we could have a lot of bread,
29		and uh, we had a lot of bread, and a lot of /those sees/ to – uh -seeds to feed to the chickens.

30	John:	Did the chickens go walking in the field or did your grandma go get the seeds and bring 'em back?
31	Dima:	[Uh-huh]
32	Sasha:	[No], but we had this big case, and it was almost full of seeds.
33		Uh, those kind and, she – uh – put them in a pan and /???/ and throw it out.
34	John:	Here chicky, chicky, chicky.
35		What did she say?
36		What – how – what do they – how do they say
37	Sasha:	/Here chicken/.
38	John:	In Ukrainian what do they say?
39	Sasha:	I don't know.
40	Dima:	I don't – /I forgot/.
41	John:	What's the word for chicken?
42	Sasha:	Chicken.
43		Here chicken.
44		((chewing))
45	Dima:	Hoooo, coot a coot a coot a coo. Hooo, coot a coot a,

The narrative in this excerpt about life in Ukraine (lines 24–45) is primarily made up of an orientation sequence that describes life on the farm. Such orientations, or descriptions of places, have garnered increased attention in recent narrative analysis as important aspects of the narrative activity. Ochs and Capps (2001: 156), for example, view the descriptions of orientations as possible foreshadowers of events in the narrative: 'the pivotal role of settings in explaining the significance of such events. Even when recounted after the unexpected event, settings can contain information that, paradoxically, anticipates a break in life as usual.' In this excerpt, however, the description of the setting does not set up an unexpected event around which the narratives described by Ochs and Capps are organized, but rather describes a place and time that in and of itself are unexpected and different from the current place and time. In telling, John, Dima and Sasha collaborate to talk about life on the farm in Ukraine and bring the past place and time into the present.

Identities are constructed in this sequence through Dima's use of pronouns. Dima initiates the narrative with an orientation clause (line 22) as evidence for his knowledge of the word 'combine', 'I know what that is … they have a lot of them in Ukraine, because we … live right next to the field.' Here Dima moves from a more general statement about Ukraine with a third person plural pronoun 'they', to a more particular, personalized statement using first person plural 'we' that locates himself and his family on a farm in Ukraine. Contrasts in pronoun usage have been shown to connect with different identities constructed in narratives (De Fina, 2003b; Schiffrin, 2002). Here the shift functions in two main ways: the first to establish Dima's authority – that he personally knows what a combine is because he saw them in the fields near his house – and in the second to represent Dima as both a member of a group that sees Ukrainians as the other 'them', as well as being part of that group himself 'we'. Thus as the telling continues and the narrative moves further back in time (from 'I know what a combine is now', to 'we used to see them'), Dima's personal identity shifts from 'outsider' to 'member' of that community and time and place. Thus this description of life in Ukraine allows Dima to construct membership in two communities and time-spaces or places.

Another aspect of this telling that involves collaborative identity construction is in the metalinguistic talk and translations that take place during the orientation sequence. John takes on the role of elicitor in this activity, but the boys (and particularly Sasha) actively participate in co-constructing the place. Rather than evaluating the children's tellings as in the bad thing/ good thing routine, here John takes on a different role as an audience member learning about what life was like in Ukraine and his sons' past histories. His questions contribute to the unfolding of this narrative as he prompts the boys to tell him more about the setting and habitual events on the farm rather than working out the details of a specific deed or event at school. Interestingly, the initiation of this orientation sequence is metalinguistic in nature (i.e. Dima introduces talk about life in Ukraine to explain how he knows what the English word 'combine' means), and it closes with metalinguistic talk as John asks, 'what's the word for chicken?'. Sasha answers in English, avoiding his father's positioning of him as an authority on Ukrainian or Russian and maintaining his in-group, English-speaking status as I outlined in discussion of the *Hakuna Matata* episode (Excerpt 1.1) in the introduction to the book. In some sense this blending of description and semi-narration seems to be the first step in constructing a piece of a larger life story in which the family members collaborate on ways to talk about the children's past lives, construct their knowledge of farm life from prior experiences and figure out how to tell about these experiences in a new language and within a new cultural context.

A second narrative sequence about Ukraine also emerges later in the data collection in the Sonderman family:

Excerpt 4.9 Kidneys
(1K, March 1, 2006, Dima – 10, Sasha – eight)

1	John:	Let's see, my good thing,
2	Dima:	Hmm[hhh].
3	Sasha:	[Yucko]
4	Dima:	Hmh.
5	John:	Let's see what's my good thing?
6		Um,
7	Sasha:	Ahh hhh <inhale, eating>
8	Dima:	Can I call – call Patrick after dinner?
9	John:	My good thing,
10	Sasha:	<slurping>
11	Dima:	Can I?
12	John:	Was, going downtown, and picking up my children,
13		and having a nice conversation with them on the way home.
14		About kidney stones,
15	Sasha:	Oooo!
16	Dima:	That really hurt.
17	John:	You remember.
18	Sasha:	<inhale> I'm done /???/.
19	John:	What do you remember the – about the kidneys?
20		What do they do?
21	Dima:	Th[ey],
22	Sasha:	[They ss -]
23	Dima:	[Suck up all the] bad stuff from your liquids.
24	Sasha:	[get uhm – uh -]
25		Yeh.
26	Dima:	That you drink.
27	Sasha:	Yeh.
28	Dima:	And then they /to/ pee, pee it all out.
29		That's why – hey, Elijah when we were in Fitness,
30		we usually sit – uh – sit on the stairs on the back uh stairway,
31		and – and we uh usually talk about our bodies and stuff.
32		And – and – and once we were talking about the kidneys,
33		and Elijah said, 'My pee comes out green.'
34		Hhh.
35	Sasha:	Hahhahhhh.
36	John:	Hmm, that must mean his kidneys aren't doing their job.
37	Dima:	Once my poop was red.

38	Sasha:	[Oh, uh,]
39	John:	[/???/]
40	Dima:	[You know] why, 'cause I ate a – a lot of, what is it called?
41	John:	Be[ets].
42	Dima:	[Beets]!
43	Sasha:	Once uh I ate a lot of – a lot of beets too,
44		and it was eh – and my friend uh – uh – uh – in Ukraine, he a – ate a lot of beets.
45		Uh, he was going to the bathroom, he like pghhh.
46		Let me look at my poop.
47		Ooo, it's red, [ah]!
48	John:	[Oo hoo].
49	Sasha:	Blood is [coming out, ah].
50	Dima:	[Look, daddy].
51	Dima:	Look, look, look, daddy.
52		((topic changes))

This sequence represents a kind of narrative chain in which four tellable events are introduced (Table 4.3). Each of these narratives is related to bodily functions (the kidneys) and each becomes closer to a canonical story form as they move further back in time.

After telling his good thing, John prompts the boys to recount what they know about the kidneys. Dima offers a definition, and in line 29 he introduces an explanatory narrative (prompted by the metalinguistic talk), 'hey, that's why ...' that begins with general orientation statements in the simple present, 'we usually sit ...' 'we usually talk ...'. This moves into a more canonical narrative with one tellable event in line 32 when Dima introduces the event, 'and once ...', and in line 33 the resolution 'my pee comes out green'. John then provides a kind of coda and evaluation, 'his kidneys must not have been doing their job'.

At this point, the boys introduce a string of narratives about bodily functions (and unexpected bodily events) using abstracts, 'once my poop was red', 'once I ate a lot of beets too ... or my friend ate a lot of beets'. The

Table 4.3 Narrative times

	Lines	First utterance	Time/place
1	1–14	John's good thing	Today in the car
2	29–36	Hey – Elijah, when we were in fitness	Recent past at school
3	37–42	Once my poop was red	More distant past in Ukraine
4	43–50	Once I ate a lot of beets too	More distant past in Ukraine

timeline for these narratives has moved from today at carpool (John's good thing), to everyday at school (Dima and his friends), to one time in a non-specified location, to a specific time in Ukraine. Although Dima does not provide orientation for his narrative about having red poop, the incident itself and the way Dima tells it contain some orienting information for two reasons: (a) beets are not a common part of the US diet and eating them in excess would be unusual in most communities in the US, but they are a regular part of the Ukrainian diet in dishes such as 'borscht', and (b) Dima can't remember the word for the vegetable, suggesting that this is an event he has not talked about frequently in English. In this collaborative storytelling, the boys have been able to connect the talk about novel topics (i.e. the function of the kidneys) and unexpected events (pee turning green) from the current context (i.e. school life in the US) to similar events in the more distant past. Telling these stories entails two phenomena: (a) making sense of unexpected events, and (b) learning how to talk about these events. Dima, for example, needs assistance in finding the word for beets, and the story in the US context does not make sense until this word is found. John plays almost no role in facilitating the telling of these stories.

In both of these narratives, metalinguistic questions become a central part of the narration and key to making the point. Talk about the distant past is related to finding ways to talk about the past and reconstructing the events of the past in a new language – culture specific episodes (i.e. watching combines harvesting wheat or eating too many beets) need some translation and refiguring in the new linguistic and cultural environment. As the boys work through retelling the past in Ukraine with their father who is familiar with the setting and can assist in reconstructing the narratives, the boys are learning how to represent their prior experiences in relation to the new place, time and language. The boys find ways to engage in narrative activities that are meaningful to them and serve to solve longer-term problems such as reconstructing their past lives in their new environment and establishing identities across timescales.

Conclusions

In this chapter I have taken a closer look at learner agency in the form of instantiated resistance within a parent-directed interactional routine in one transnational adoptive family. This type of explicit resistance in interaction is not often reported in studies of second language socialization where resistance is more likely documented as a reason or explanation for failure to acquire certain linguistic features (e.g. Ohara, 2001) or for actively participating in a new learning community (e.g. Harklau, 2000; Morita, 2004). In these studies resistance is implicit and difficult to observe. Alternatively, some studies have shown how learners resist classroom practices by actively subverting teacher-led activities or becoming the 'class clown' (Duff, 2012; McKay & Wong, 1996). In the data from this family, Dima and Sasha resist their father's prompts in a routine by answering 'nothing', selecting other speakers and subverting the goals of the routine through negotiation of what is a 'tellable' story. In interviews John stated that he has stopped initiating the routine to avoid the resistance, and as the study progressed the routine occurred more irregularly in the family mealtime conversations.

The outward resistance to participating in the parent-directed routine then led to a change in the family interactions that opened up the mealtime conversation to talk that was less controlled and more fluid in terms of who controlled the floor and the topics of conversation. During this more fluid time, different types of narratives emerged, and, specifically, the two boys told stories about Ukraine with their father playing the role of recipient and facilitator instead of evaluator. Thus agency in the form of resistance, in this context, led to new learning opportunities and opportunities for work toward long-term identity construction for the boys individually and the family as a whole. John's role as a caring father led to greater accommodation than would most likely occur in a classroom. In these storytelling activities, tellership and tellability are manipulated and result in fluctuations in power dynamics, solidarity and opportunities for identity construction. The long-term narratives open up opportunities for language learning that are associated with learning new words and ways of talking about the past. It is the affective bond that the family members are working on achieving that shapes these processes.

In these data I discussed two aspects of the spontaneous, child-initiated narratives that emerged in the interactions: an orientation sequence that functioned as a 'way things were' narrative that helped the children refigure their past in the present, and a chain of narratives by different tellers that moved from the present to the more distant past and helped to connect old events to new knowledge and circumstances. Fragments such as these were connected to building a longer life story in which the different ways of talking about events and scenes were hammered out in interaction as a family and the experiences of the children's past became shared with the father through the storytelling event. These processes construct the activity of language learning across multiple timescales as long-term events become matters for consideration and shape the interactional moment. The involvement of John, the father, in these tellings make events or scenes from the boys' prior lives become part of their joint family history as they work together to find legitimate ways to talk about pre-adoption places and times. This constitutes family formation. Here the children play an active role not only in choosing the stories they want to tell, but also in shaping their interactional roles and relationships amongst the three of them. Thus the agency that Dima and Sasha achieve in these conversations is twofold – the resistance to parent-led routines leads to new opportunities for participation through initiating new types of narratives.

In conclusion there are three main points to take away from the narrative processes in the Sondermans' mealtimes. The first is that so-called expert advice is not always a one-size-fits-all solution. What works for one family might not work for another, and family interactions grow and change over time. What might have continued as a fruitful and useful interactional routine in another family became a site of conflict and frustration for John and his boys. Second, John's dual strategies of scaffolding the boys' productions through the routine and accommodating over time to their resistance to the routine resulted in the construction of new interactional spaces in which the boys could participate. Finally, what might be considered 'negative' agency (i.e. resistance), can lead to change in a community of practice that has positive outcomes. This process, however, is dependent on accommodation of those in power. In this context, concern for establishing a father–son bond shaped the achievement of the children's agency and possibilities for learning.

5 'But Now We're Your Daughter and Son!': Participation, Questions and Languaging

Agency takes many forms, as discussed in Chapter 2. In this chapter we turn from the older children's linguistic acts of resistance to a pair of younger children's agentive participation in family talk. In this chapter I examine how the two children, Anna and Arkadiy, in the Jackson-Wessels family, play a leading role in obtaining comprehensible input and negotiating the communicative environment with their parents through the use of questions that initiate language-related episodes (LREs) (Swain & Lapkin, 1998) or, to use the updated and more socioculturally informed term, languaging (Swain, 2006) in the family discourse. These elicitations, which most often take the form of what-questions, serve to establish intersubjectivity or the 'cognitive, social, and emotional interchange' that results in a 'sharing of purpose and focus among individuals' (Rogoff, 1990: 9) between the parents and the children in this family. These questions also open up opportunities to talk about events and issues of importance to the children that relate to longer-term identity construction as found in the previous chapter. For the Jackson-Wessels children, Anna and Arkadiy, asking questions is a way to learn language and participate in and control the family conversations, which also ultimately serves as a way to shape the family's understanding of daily life and longer-term events such as the adoption itself. Thus the micro processes of language learning are embedded in a larger context that occurs on multiple timescales.

In the conclusion of her seminal work on language socialization, Ochs (1988: 224) considered the different ways in which socialization processes can potentially be bidirectional, with children influencing parents in much the same way that parents influence children. She surmised that children's use of questions might be one important strategy that has an effect on adults' (in this case teachers') practices:

> In this sense, caregivers may be socialized by the children they are socializing. Teachers as well may be socialized by the students they are

inducting into some area of expertise. Their understanding of the subject matter may be transformed by the responses and questions of students.

In this chapter I focus closely on how particular types of child questions (i.e. what-questions such as 'What is this?' or 'What is that called?') are ratified as legitimate contributions to the ongoing family talk and how they give rise to languaging episodes in the family discourse that meet both language learning and identity construction aims. In the following sections I first review prior research on the functions of questions in parent–child interactions and then look at how languaging occurs in family discourse. Finally, I examine the role LREs and languaging have been found to play in second language learning. Ultimately in this chapter, to better understand second language-learning processes in the adoptive family, I integrate perspectives from three strands of research: (a) family talk about language or explicit metalinguistic discourse in parent–child interaction, (b) the role of what-questions in parent–child interaction and early literacy development, and (c) languaging and LREs in the study of second language acquisition.

Agency as Participation and Control

It is commonly accepted in practice-oriented approaches to language and agency that personal or individual agency emerges in response to or in interaction with the social structures of the local context (Ahearn, 2001; Morita, 2004). Thus actions that are agentive in one classroom or family would not be so in another context or would, at least, not have the same effect across contexts. The resistance tactics employed by Dima in Chapter 4 are a good example of agency that is successful in reshaping and transforming the family dynamic in productive ways in a specific interactional routine but most likely would not be productive, even though they would still be agentive, in the classroom. In the focal family for the current chapter, agency takes the form of participation in the family conversations in a way that also represents control. Anna and Anton exercise the type of agency – by recruiting assistance and seeking out language-learning opportunities – that has been related to learning success in school settings (Hawkins, 2005; Willett, 1995). The use of questions as an interactional strategy legitimizes Arkadiy and Anna's participation in the family conversation and establishes them as cooperating, and sometimes even controlling, members of the family.

However, this sort of agency relies on accommodation from the other participants, in this case the parents. The children's bids for turns are recognized by the parents and serve to redirect the family talk. An unintended effect of such control on the part of the children is an implicit annoyance by the parents that supports their stated beliefs that the children are sometimes overly talkative and headstrong. However, the children's strategies lead to learning opportunities and discussion about family identity and everyday life that were unlikely to have occurred had they not asked questions.

Metalanguage in Family Language Socialization

Explicit metalinguistic and metapragmatic talk in family conversations is an obvious site of language socialization because of the ways in which both the language code and language use become the focus of attention during such talk. Studies of explicit metalanguage in family contexts have emphasized the ways in which early language development is intimately tied to the sociocultural context and ideologies of parents. In one of the earliest studies on this topic, Schieffelin (1990), for example, found that Kaluli mothers' use of direct instruction through the directive 'ɛlɛma' or 'say it like this' were associated with the Kaluli belief that children must be 'shown how to speak' (Schieffelin & Ochs, 1986: 292). Further, several quantitative studies have pointed to significant cross-cultural differences in the amount of metapragmatic talk and metalanguage in families (Blum-Kulka, 1997; De Geer et al., 2002; Ely et al., 2001). These studies all suggest that language acquisition in the family environment is related to cultural values and norms and that comments about language serve both acquisitional and social functions.

Several studies have singled out metalinguistic talk, or talk about the language code, as a practice that is different from metapragmatic talk, or talk about language use, in family discourse. Studies that have examined these differences have concluded that metalinguistic talk does not play as great of a role in socialization processes, but rather is associated with a family 'pastime' or particular family style (Blum-Kulka, 1997; Ely et al., 2001). Ely et al. (2001: 369–370), for example, found no age effects for metalinguistic talk in 22 middle-class, predominately monolingual,[1] families, contrary to their hypothesis that more metalinguistic talk would be directed to older children and thereby related to development. These authors concluded that 'the degree to which families talk about language is more a matter of family style ... the rates with which speakers focus (or do not focus) on different aspects of language may reflect enduring individual and family styles rather than typical developmental patterns'. However, there may be reasons why some families talk about language more than others, including family bilingualism and potentially, as I discuss below in relation to the Jackson-Wessels, parental education and occupations.

Higher rates of metalinguistic talk have been found to occur in bi- and multilingual families in comparison to monolingual families. In Blum-Kulka's (1997) comparison of Jewish American, Israeli American and Israeli families, Jewish American families used more metapragmatic comments regarding discourse management (e.g. turn taking) and maxim violations (e.g. telling lies); Israeli families used more metalinguistic comments (talk about word meanings and comments topicalizing language); and American Israelis used the second most metalinguistic comments. Blum-Kulka attributed these findings to a variety of cultural and linguistic factors. In particular, and of relevance to the current study, is the finding that the higher number of metalinguistic comments in American Israeli families could be attributed to the reality of second language learning for the recent immigrants. In Israeli families, the language ecology of the multilingual environment was also seen to affect the amount of metalinguistic discourse produced. Further, Blum-Kulka characterized explaining word meanings to children to be a 'favorite pastime' in the multilingual environment of the Israeli family, suggesting that such types of talk were not only related to the cultural and linguistic background of the family, but also to discourse activities in which family members engaged in a type of language play or discourse practice aimed at building rapport and providing entertainment for the family members.

In a similar study, De Geer et al. (2002) examined pragmatic socialization in 100 families residing in Estonia, Finland and Sweden (including bilingual Estonian and Finnish families in Sweden). This study focused on the use of 'comments' (defined as utterances with the explicit or implicit aim of influencing a conversational partner to behave or speak in a certain way [De Geer et al., 2002: 1757]) in mealtime conversations. Comparisons were made between the cultural groups' use of comments about table manners, moral and ethical behavior and linguistic behavior (including turn regulation, maxim violations or metalinguistic comments). De Geer et al. (1997: 1772) found that non-linguistic behavior (table manners, moral and ethical behavior, prudential and other behavior) was more in focus than linguistic behavior. However, like Blum-Kulka (1997), this study found that most metalinguistic comments (defined here as concerning language and language use, word meanings, dialects, cross-linguistic comparison, etc.) occurred in the bilingual/bicultural family conversations and were provided by parents in order to correct or enrich children's language use. The few metalinguistic comments produced in monolingual families were mainly provided by the children asking for word meanings either in their own language or in foreign languages. These findings suggest that bilingual families spend more time talking about language in family interactions; however, it is unclear if this type of talk is related to quantitative gains in language development for young children. At the very least, metalinguistic talk in the family sphere represents a type of leisure activity or language play that builds rapport and solidarity among family members; although, in some cases, as in the current situation, it might also represent an annoying distraction from the family activities. Further, the frequency of metalinguistic talk in multilingual families might also prepare children for the task of recruiting interactional and linguistic assistance in other contexts outside of the home.[2] Thus as Anna and Arkadiy develop these strategies in interaction with their parents, they potentially learn how to participate in classroom interactions in agentive ways.

Languaging and Language-Related Episodes in Language Development

In the study of *second* language development, metalinguistic talk has also been studied from a sociocultural point of view as a way of mediating the language-learning process. Learners who talk about language and do so in more complex forms tend to learn more and show greater development in language-learning tasks (Swain & Lapkin, 1998). As with other constructs in SLA, the study of metalanguage in learner talk has moved from a primarily product-oriented approach to a more process-oriented approach. Early work centered on chunks of talk in which linguistic problem solving took place, or 'language-related episodes' (LREs). From a psycholinguistic perspective, LREs were related to learner output and opportunities for noticing gaps in linguistic competency. From a more sociocultural perspective, LREs have been reconceptualized as a process of languaging in which learners mediate the learning process through language (Swain, 2000, 2006).

Swain (2006: 98) defines this type of languaging as 'the process of making meaning and shaping knowledge and experience through language . . . In [languaging], we can observe learners operating on linguistic data and coming to an understanding of previously less well understood material. In languaging, we can see learning taking place.' This view, primarily inspired by Vygotsky's understanding of mediated cognition, grew out of Swain's original work on the output hypothesis in SLA and the observed benefits of producing language on the learning process. In a 2000 article, Swain laid the foundation for expanding the understanding of output and, more specifically, LREs or talk about language in the learning process. In more recent research, languaging has been related to learner agency and affect in the learning process, concepts which are both relevant to the current study. This research has further made the important point that learners can learn in interaction with one another, typically in task-based activities.

Swain (2006), for example, provides an example of an adult learner, Ken, who asserts his agency by rejecting a form suggested by a more competent target language speaker (the reformulator, or person who corrected his writing sample). He does this through languaging and discursively formulating a rule that supports his own production. Eventually, however, he notices the problem spot and changes what he had written based on the reformulator's correction. Swain points out how Ken's prior learning and languaging come together to assert his agency in the interaction. Thus languaging, or talking about language, is an interactional strategy that learners can use to assert authority and agency in the learning process. Ken's strategies coincided with Al Zidjaly's (2009) finding that the assertion of past agentive selves was a way of achieving agency in interaction and further show how such achievement plays a role in second language learning.

Naturalistic settings such as mealtimes in a family environment are not usually structured around a predetermined language-learning task. In SLA research, such tasks are designed to elicit languaging as a pedagogical tool. In everyday conversations, languaging such as that described by Swain and colleagues does occur, but how it is initiated and to what extent different language forms and functions are discussed still remains to be studied in detail. In the data presented here, as mentioned above, children's questions play an agentive role in initiating languaging episodes. In this chapter, I show how languaging about lexical items connects with both cognitive processes of learning and the sociocultural context that shapes and is shaped by the family's discussion of what a word means. Thus the children in this study initiate languaging through questions, and the languaging itself constructs opportunities for learning that go beyond linguistic features to include world views and cultural models.

Along these lines, learners' talk about language has been found to serve important identity construction functions, which in turn relate to the types of learner-directed language socialization processes that are the focus of this book. King and Ganuza (2005), for example, found that bilingual Chilean-Swedish adolescents' talk about their language and language use pointed to how they positioned themselves as 'outsiders' in Swedish society. Similarly, Zilles and King (2005) also linked participants' metalinguistic discourse (e.g. about which languages they spoke better) to the ways in which they presented themselves and constructed individual identities during sociolinguistic interviews. Further, Rampton's (1996: 327) study of Panjabi adolescent learners' talk about their second language outside of the classroom points to the important ways in which metalinguistic discourse in everyday interactions can fulfill both social and acquisitional goals and, more importantly, is oriented toward 'social relations of difference'. These studies suggest that metalanguistic talk can be used strategically by bilinguals and second language learners to position themselves and others as part of different ethnolinguistic groups with different identities. Gee (2008: 78) further argues that word meanings themselves are 'ultimately rooted in communities' and are related to community cultural models or 'simplified world[s] in which . . . prototypical events unfold'. In this chapter I extend this analysis to show how talk about English words and word meanings in adoptive family conversations helps the children to understand new cultural content (about holidays, relationships and family) and further construct new identities as intersubjectivity is established and learning occurs.

Questions and the Initiation of Languaging Episodes

As in the narrative discourse discussed in the Sonderman family's data, interactional processes are at play with regards to who initiates metalinguistic talk or languaging, and in what ways that can provide insight into the ways in which learners are socialized into discourse practices such as talking about language. Questions directed to children by parents in English-speaking cultures play a role in establishing young children as conversational partners, developing early language skills around naming and describing objects (Choi & Gopnik, 1995; Hart & Risley, 1999; Keenan et al., 1976; Ninio & Bruner, 1976), and building early literacy skills (Heath, 1982). Parents' use of 'What is X?' (e.g. What is that?) questions in particular have been related to the development of English-speaking children's naming practices, acquisition of book-reading and literacy practices and discourse level structures (such as topic-comment). In a detailed report on children's development of naming, Ninio and Bruner (1976: 15) concluded that reference, or naming objects, 'is dependent not only on mastering a relationship between sign and significate, but on an understanding of social rules for achieving dialogue in which that relationship can be realized'. The practice of talking about language, then, is tied to the social situation in which it occurs. I first discuss how question–answer patterns develop in parent–child interaction and then turn to the relationships of such patterns to literacy socialization and language learning.

In terms of general patterns for parents' questions, in a longitudinal study of 42 monolingual, English-speaking children across social classes in the US, Hart and Risley (1999) found that the amount of talk produced by children increased as the number of questions (or prompts) directed to the children by parents decreased. In addition, the amount of talk in general addressed *to* children declined sharply after children began speaking as much as their parents (at about 28 months). In other words, as children became more competent conversational partners, parents began to speak to them less. Hart and Risley documented the following factors to account for the rapid decline (and this apparent paradox): (a) parents reported that children were defying and resisting, (b) mothers were often pregnant and there seemed to be a 'societal consensus' that two-year-olds no longer needed close minding, and (c) children began to ignore or discourage parental prompts by saying 'no' and, in short, showed greater independence. These findings point to a process in which children's growing competence, and agency, socialize parents out of early routines (and this occurred in mainstream, monolingual homes).

A related finding in Hart and Risley's (1999: 288) study, and one of importance to this chapter, was that the number of parent questions increased in frequency nearly every month until the children in the study were 24–25 months old. At that point children began holding the floor and, as Hart and Risley described it, 'answering before they were asked', suggesting that children had become socialized into participation patterns and types of talk they should engage in. In the data from the adoptive family I examine here, I find evidence for a reverse trend in which the older adoptees ask more questions to the parents than the parents ask of them. This difference, I argue, is based on a need for the parents in this family to come to understand what their second language-learning children know and what they can do in family interactions. As the parents become better attuned to the children's needs, and the children develop linguistically, the parents change their strategies to anticipate problems in the family discourse.

Such questions and labeling routines have also been linked to early literacy socialization. In analyzing family bedtime book-reading routines, Heath (1982) identified the what-question and noted its similarity to the initiation-response-evaluation (IRE) sequence found in classroom discourse (Mehan, 1979). Heath concluded that children from middle-class families were socialized into these discourse patterns before the age of two in interactions with their parents and were thereby potentially better prepared for school practices than their working-class peers. In a discussion of this work, Gee (2008) also added that higher-level academic tasks such as outlining and writing reports emulate the what-question format, and children who have learned these patterns early on will be better equipped to engage in and accomplish such school tasks.

Finally, information requests in general can also function in interaction to place one speaker in a position of power over another. In speech act theory, information requests have been noted to function as directives, where asking about something (e.g. Is it hot in here?) implies that something should be done (i.e. the heat turned off). Jones (2005) noted that questions play a role in forming discourse identities by placing the questioner in a position of power that requires the one being questioned to respond. When children direct what-questions to parents, they take on the role of 'seekers of information' or 'language learners' who also control the flow of conversation and turn-taking patterns through the use of such questions. In the data presented in this chapter, information requests in the form of what-questions construct the children's agency as both legitimate participation in family conversations and as a type of control or power that transforms the conversation momentarily and leads to longer-term identity construction projects (such as talking about what it means to be a family or remembering past times).

In the analysis below I look specifically at patterns of what-questions in the Jackson-Wessels' interactions to demonstrate a relationship between the context of interaction (i.e. homeschool, book-reading and mealtime activities) and speaker. I then turn to a qualitative analysis of the languaging episodes in the family discourse that are guided by children's what-questions. I argue that such questions, and the resulting metalinguistic talk that they initiate, play cognitive, interactional and social functions in the family conversations. In conclusion, I argue that these patterns attest to the collaborative and co-constructed nature of language socialization.

The Jackson-Wessels

Brother and sister, Arkadiy and Anna Jackson-Wessels, were ages five and three when they arrived in the US on December 24, 2004. I met their father, Kevin, for an initial interview (Fogle, in press) in the summer of 2005 and started the in-home data collection for the current study in November of the same year (see Table 5.1). The family's recordings captured benchmark events in their lives together such as the children's first Thanksgiving and preparations to start school. Anna and Arkadiy arrived in their new

Table 5.1 The Jackson-Wessels' recordings

	Recording	Date	Length	Activity	Participants
November 2005	2A	11/18/2005	27:27	Homeschool	Kevin (K), Arkadiy (Ar)
	2B	11/18/2005	7:36	Book reading	K, Anna (An)
	2C	11/23/2005	20:29	Mealtime	K, Meredith (M), Ar, An
	2D	11/27/2005	21:32	Mealtime	K, M, Ar, An
December 2005	2E	12/14/2005	60:00	Book reading	M, Ar
	2F	12/20/2005	19:03	Mealtime	K, M, Ar, An
January 2006	2G	1/26/2006	25:57	Homeschool	K, Ar
	2H	1/30/2006	17:05	Homeschool	K, Ar
	2I	1/30/2006	13:40	Mealtime	K, Ar, An
February 2006	2J	2/25/2006	21:19	Book reading	K, An
	2K	2/27/2006	22:01	Homeschool	K, Ar
	2L	2/28/2006	53:02	Mealtime	K, Ar, An
March 2006	2M	3/26/2006	16:42	Book reading	K, M, Ar, An
April 2006	2N	4/1/2006	20:40	Other	K, Ar, An
	2O	4/19/2006	9:16	Other	K, Ar, An
	2P	4/21/2006	14:00	Book reading	K, Ar, An
May 2006	2Q	5/30/2006	21:12	Book reading	M, Ar, An
June 2006	2R	6/1/2006	21:25	Mealtime	K, M, An
	2S	6/1/2006	3:35	Book reading	K, M, Ar, An
	2T	6/13/2006	24:53	Mealtime	K, Ar, An

home with very little knowledge of English, and in the initial interview Kevin suggested that the children's continual use of Russian between themselves and to the parents and grandparents had been stressful and disconcerting for the family. The children were perceived by the adults (parents and grandparents) to not realize or care that the adults did not understand Russian, and this created a tension in the household immediately after their initial arrival.

By the time of the first interview (about six months after the children's arrival), however, both children spoke English exclusively with their parents and each other. When the in-home recordings began a few months later, Arkadiy demonstrated maintenance of some Russian through a Saturday Russian language program that catered to the bilingual population and had special programs for transnational adoptees where he took supplemental math classes. Kevin and Meredith were the only parents in this study who did not have a functional knowledge of Russian at the time of the adoption, and when asked at the end of the initial interview what advice he would give to prospective adoptive parents, Kevin noted that learning as much Russian as possible would be helpful.

The Jackson-Wessels were unique among the adoptive parents in this study owing to their choice to homeschool their oldest son Arkadiy (Anna attended a part-time preschool). While homeschooling might be a more common practice in the US than in other countries, the Jackson-Wessels were part of a minority of families who choose this option. Princiotta and Bielick (2006) report that only about 2.2% of all students in the United States were homeschooled in 2003. Adoptive families, however, and particularly those with older adopted children, make up an active subsection of the homeschooling population as is evident on listservs and blogs devoted to the topic in addition to online articles discussing the benefits of homeschooling for older adoptees (Greko-Akerman, 2006; Wilson, 2007). Parents of older adoptees sometimes prefer homeschooling because it provides a way for parents to address the assumed psychological and emotional issues associated with post-institutionalization (Greko-Akerman, 2006).

Like John Sonderman in Chapter 4, Kevin Jackson-Wessels played the role of primary caregiver; however, unlike John, who was self-employed full-time, Kevin was a stay-at-home homeschool teacher. One of the daily challenges in the Jackson-Wessels at the time of recording was finding ways for parents and children to communicate with each other. Because there was little outside influence on the children's language learning in the form of ESOL classes or Russian-language tutors, for example, language teaching and learning were centered in family interactions. The family members negotiated meaning in their conversations through the use of specific communication strategies that centered on the negotiation of lexical items. This negotiation of the conversational level is particularly salient in this family, unlike the Sondermans or the Goellers, because little to no Russian was used between parents and children, as discussed above.

The Jackson-Wessels' Data

Recording in the Jackson-Wessels family took place over an eight-month period (November 2005 to July 2006). The types of recordings returned

Table 5.2 Total recordings in hours:minutes by activity

Book reading	Homeschool	Mealtime	Total
2:24	2:56	2:58	8:18

by the Jackson-Wessels family fell into three main categories: book-reading sessions (for pleasure), homeschool lessons and mealtimes. The Jackson-Wessels family recorded more book-reading and homeschool sessions than mealtimes. Table 5.1 shows the recordings returned by the Jackson-Wessels family.

Several recording sessions did not fit neatly into one of the three categories: mealtime, book-reading or homeschool lesson. These included two sessions in which Arkadiy was reading a book with his father, but the focus was on reading skills – sounding out words and reading aloud – rather than reading for pleasure. These sessions were counted as homeschool lessons. In addition, two recordings involved other activities: making thank-you notes with oil pastels and practicing a skit to perform for their mother. These two sessions were omitted from the quantitative analysis of the data because the activities generated a different interactional pattern in terms of question–answer sequences. The total amount of time recorded in each activity is shown in Table 5.2.

Not all family members were present at all recording sessions, as shown in Table 5.1. Meredith was the least frequent family member to participate in the recording sessions because of her work responsibilities. Kevin managed most of the recording times, often noting when he was beginning and ending recording sessions out loud to the other family members.

Data Coding and Analysis

All data were transcribed as in the other chapters using the conventions in Tannen et al. (2007). A subset of the transcripts was transcribed by a native English-speaking assistant who did not know Russian, and the transcripts were verified by the researcher. The analysis of the data presented below is primarily qualitative in order to understand and explain how languaging in this family connected to the family's social life and construction of a family world view and identity. In addition, to better understand how this languaging originated in the family discourse and the role that children played in initiating metalinguistic talk in the family, a quantitative analysis of what-questions was conducted based on preliminary findings that such questions led to languaging episodes in this family's interactions.

Languaging

As discussed above, languaging can take multiple forms and functions and is best defined as 'the process of making meaning and shaping knowledge and experience through language' (Swain, 2006: 98). For this study, languaging primarily includes explicit metalinguistic talk about what things are called and what words mean including types of talk that have been addressed in previous studies as: lexical LREs (Fortune, 2005; Fortune & Thorp, 2001), meaning based LREs (Kowal & Swain, 1994), explanatory discourse (Ninio & Snow, 1996), labeling (Ely et al., 2001), defining (Snow et al., 1987) and lexical negotiation (Cotterill, 2004).

What-questions

Questions were coded as what-questions if they took that exact form or one of several closely related forms ('What does X mean?' 'What kind/type of X is that?' 'What is that/this/it called?'). Because of the difficulty in determining if the question is about a concept or event (e.g. 'What is that??!' stated with disbelief or excitement), rather than specifically about language, all questions that took this form were coded as what-questions unless some expressive intonation and the broader conversational context clearly marked the question as serving a different function. Interrater reliability for what-questions was established at a high-level (Cohen's kappa = 0.85).

Interview Data and Analysis

Kevin agreed to meet for regular interviews within one week after the recordings for each month were conducted, and Meredith participated in one of these monthly interviews. I asked general questions about the children's language learning as well as Kevin's own strategies for communicating, and then asked Kevin to respond to two to three short prompts from that month's recordings. Overall, about two hours worth of interview data were collected and analyzed for this study (three interviews were lost due to problems with the recording equipment). As with the interviews with John Sonderman, the interviews with Kevin and Meredith were transcribed and coded using Grounded Theory Protocol (Strauss & Corbin, 1990) in Microsoft Word and Filemaker for major themes (e.g. deficits in language learning, offering correction, offering prompts) for a prior study comparing the different parenting styles of the fathers (Fogle, 2008a). In the interviews, Kevin offered perspectives on at least three aspects of interaction with his children: explicit error correction, expansion of child utterances and the nature of the overall family discourse. He also discussed the decision to homeschool and his perspectives on that process over the course of the academic year. Taken together, attitudes on these themes pointed to a specific orientation that Kevin took regarding his role in his interactions with his children.

Kevin and Meredith's Parenting Style

Kevin and Meredith were more explicitly oriented in interviews toward being 'language models' for their children than facilitators (Fogle, 2008b), although there is evidence in the interactional data that they used implicit strategies for providing feedback to their children. In interviews, Kevin and Meredith indicated that they focused on providing a rich linguistic environment as a model for the children, as can be seen in the following quote:

Excerpt 5.1 They're in a controlled environment
(June 7, 2005)
> Kevin: They [other children] had things like 'bestest' and stuff like this, six-year-old speak, and we were like, my god, you know our kids don't use this because they're in a controlled environment you know and their language is good.

Choosing to homeschool and center language learning in the home, then, reflected Kevin and Meredith's beliefs that they could provide the best linguistic environment for Arkadiy and Anna.

Kevin and Meredith also suggested that they had negative feelings toward explicit correction, but, as is evident below, they did indicate that they used implicit negative feedback such as recasts.

Excerpt 5.2 They'll pick it up
(March 23, 2006)
> Kevin: But I never liked the idea of correcting people's grammar . . .
> Meredith: . . . I really never stop them and say, . . . the pronouns should be like this. I would just rephrase it back. You know she says, 'Us – us are going to the store.' I would say, 'Yes, we're going to the store now'. . .
> Kevin: Yeah, they'll pick it up, they'll pick it up.

In the following sections I discuss how this orientation relates to the metalinguistic talk that occurs in the Jackson-Wessels' interactions.

Languaging in the Jackson-Wessels Family's Talk

The frequency of what-questions produced by Arkadiy and Anna in the conversational data were similar to those produced by younger children in monolingual English-speaking families, as discussed above. Because Anna and Arkadiy could not use their first language in conversation with their parents, they needed to find a way to negotiate the high-level of discourse. What-questions were an effective strategy for doing so because they functioned as interruptions and bids for attention at the same time as they fulfilled language-learning needs in initiating languaging with their parents. While Kevin and Meredith complied with and accommodated to the children's requests for information, they also sometimes showed annoyance with the interruptions and competitions for the floor. Anna and Arkadiy were then allowed interactional agency and control of the conversation at times, but not without affecting their identities in the family as both 'talkative' and 'controlling' at times.

Out of 12,339 total utterances in these recordings, 1433 (or about 12%) were coded as talk pertaining to words, word meanings, what to call things, what people were named or how to refer to abstract concepts (such as telling time or recognizing words on a page). Broken down by activity, about 20% of the talk during homeschool lessons was coded as languaging, mainly attributable to the high frequency of what-question and response sequences that made up the teacher–student interactional pattern between Kevin and Arkadiy. Mealtimes and book reading shared more similar frequencies with 9% and 8% respectively of each activity type devoted to languaging. These numbers represent the amount of time the family broke from other discourse activities such as reading from a book, telling stories about the day or planning for events in the future to discuss language, and in particular, words.

The Use of What-Questions

There were 272 total what-questions produced by all speakers (Meredith, Kevin, Arkadiy and Anna) across the 20 transcripts (Table 5.3). Most of these questions were found during the homeschool interactions between Kevin and Arkadiy and were part of an Initiation-Response-Evaluation (IRE) sequence that has been described as a common pattern in classroom discourse (Mehan, 1979). Of particular interest to the analysis in this study is the finding that book-reading and mealtime interactions had roughly the same percentages of what-questions despite findings in other studies that what-questions are in some ways characteristic of or particular to parent–child interaction in book reading (e.g. Ninio & Bruner, 1976) (Table 5.3).

Although there is no real way in these data to prove what came first (and I can't account for any patterns from the children's first language

Table 5.3 Total what-questions by activity type

	Book-reading	Homeschool	Mealtime	Total
'What is X?'	43	174	55	272
Total utterances	3290	3260	5129	11,679
Percentage of utterances	1%	5%	1%	2%

socialization in Russian), it is possible that Anna and Arkadiy learned the questioning strategy from their parents' extensive use of questions in the homeschool context. Other studies have found that children's use of interrogatives is shaped by their parents' use. Vaidyanathan (1988: 533), in a longitudinal study of two children acquiring Tamil as a first language, also concluded that children 'model the usage of interrogatives on the adult behaviour patterns to which they have been exposed, both in terms of form and function'. Young children develop certain uses of questions (i.e. to engage an adult in conversation) before others (to request information) and these functions correspond to the development of forms (i.e. yes/no versus what-questions) (Barnes, 2006). Further, relationships between second language-learning children's development of form and function of interrogatives and adults' (not parents) use have also been found. Hatch *et al.* (1979) note that correlations between the child's development of question forms and question forms used by adults were found in the language production of a young English learner.

The differences in frequency of what-questions across the three contexts can be explained by an analysis of who actually asked the what-questions. In comparing the use of what-questions by parents versus children, it appears that context of interaction plays a role. In the homeschool interactions where Kevin prompted Arkadiy to answer questions based on the teaching material, he was the more frequent user of what-questions. However, in the more conversational contexts of mealtime and book reading, Arkadiy and Anna were the predominate users of these types of questions (Figure 5.1).

These findings suggest that what-questions were a way that Arkadkiy and Anna negotiated potentially challenging interactional environments and participated in conversations with their parents outside of the instructional context. A qualitative analysis of the data helps to explain these results and to show the connections of what-questions to the languaging episodes found in this family's talk.

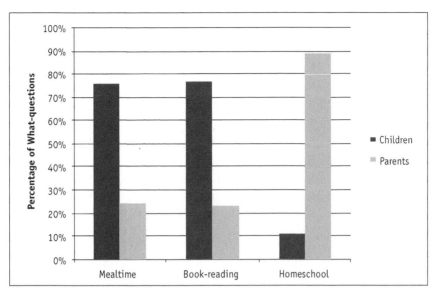

Figure 5.1 Percentage of all utterances that were what-questions for parents and children

Evidence for Language Learning

What-questions redirected the flow of the family conversation and opened up opportunities for languaging or metalinguistic talk that facilitated the children's learning of new words and word meanings. In the following two excerpts Arkadiy and Anna repeat or recycle the term they have queried, allowing them to at least temporarily learn a new word and use it in subsequent interaction. In the first example, Excerpt 5.3, Arkadiy asks for the name of an object in the immediate environment that is related to the topic of conversation (the Christmas decorations the family had put around the house the day before).

Excerpt 5.3 Hot pads
(2D, November 27, 2005, Arkadiy – six, Anna – four)
1   Arkadiy: Mom, what do you call for cooking that thing?
2   Meredith: Hot pads.
3   Arkadiy: Yeh.

4	Anna:	[Mm]?
5	Arkadiy:	[The] Christmas ones.
6	Anna:	Hm?
7	Arkadiy:	Hot pads.

In the same mealtime conversation, Anna queries her mother's use of the word 'wreath'.

Excerpt 5.4 Wreath

(2D, November 27, 2005, Arkadiy – six, Anna – four)

1	Meredith:	No we don't put the – these decorations outside
2		for the outside door. We have to make a wreath.
3		Which is something else we have to do this afternoon.
4	Anna:	What is wr –
5	Kevin:	Oh we're going to make one this year?
6	Meredith:	Mhmm.
7	Anna:	What is wreath?
8	Meredith:	Making a handprint wreath.
9	Anna:	What is wreath?
10	Meredith:	A wreath is a – .. a circular decoration that goes –
11		/???/ hang from doors during the Christmas season.
12	Anna:	Uh huh.
13		Mhm.
14		Yeh.
15		Mama?
16	Kevin:	<laughs softly>

Anna is able to appropriate the new word 'wreath' from her mother's previous utterance (line 2) and then recycle it in the form of a question in line 7, 'What is wreath?'. In these two examples, then, we see that what-questions afford some learning opportunities for the two children in acquiring new lexical items. The chuckling from Kevin, however, introduces a parental evaluation of this event in which he comments on Anna's understanding of the dialogue and her participation as a competent conversational partner, 'Mhm. Yeh.' (lines 13 and 14) without exhibiting real understanding of the new word.

In addition to repeating or recycling lexical items, repetitions of chunks of parents' discourse are also found in these data (see also Fogle, 2008b). In Excerpt 5.5, taken from a homeschool lesson, Arkadiy elicits a definition of the word 'flashcards' from his father in line 5. (This is the second time Kevin has defined the word 'flashcards' in this transcript.)

Excerpt 5.5 What is flashcard?
(2A, November 18, 2005, Arkadiy – six)

1	Kevin:	If you knew how to read, [then we wouldn't have to teach ya].
2	Arkadiy:	[but, papa, /when – why/ you gonna put a this]?
3		You said you gonna put
4	Kevin:	Well, I think /you know/ next week I'm gonna do flash-cards and some key words.
5	Arkadiy:	What is flashcard?
6	Kevin:	Flashcards is I'll hold up a card,
7		and it'll have a word on it that you'll have to know,
8		and you have to /be able to read it/, ok?

In a homeschool lesson some months later, Arkadiy appropriates (and approximates) this definition to explain why he is having trouble with the reading task in line 5.

Excerpt 5.6 Square card and pick it up thing
(2H, January 30, 2006, Arkadiy – six)

1	Arkadiy:	And
2	Kevin:	In
3	Arkadiy:	In
4		But you – but remember you haven't yet did
5		some letters I don't know, you haven't put it in a square card and pick it up thing?
6	Kevin:	You're fine, big guy, what's this word?
7	Arkadiy:	Remember you said [you were going to]?
8	Kevin:	[Yes, and we have] done it.
9		Now come on, what's this one?

In this set of examples, Arkadiy in Excerpt 5.5, line 5, requests a definition of a word from Kevin and then recycles the definition in a later conversation as a type of communication strategy because he cannot remember, or chooses not to use, the word 'flashcard'. This appropriation suggests that these types of languaging episodes are opportunities for learning not only the names of things or new lexical items but also larger discourse level practices such as defining. This approximation also serves a further discourse function (i.e. to complain about the lesson activities). Languaging is thus embedded within the social interaction as a way to refer to an object and also, in doing so, to perform social functions such as, in this case, blaming the more powerful interlocutor for not completing a task that would have potentially helped him with the reading task at the time. Thus, in a similar way to narratives (e.g. Georgakopoulou, 2006; Gordon, 2007), languaging episodes can be intertextually reproduced across time for multiple functions beyond simply language learning.

What-Questions as an Interactional Strategy

What-questions and the resulting languaging episodes also serve an interactional function in these conversations. For example, in the two excerpts given above (5.3 and 5.4), the children requested labels or definitions from their mother ('hot pads' and 'wreath'). In the first excerpt, Arkadiy selects his mother specifically (Kevin is in the room) and in the second Anna responds to her mother's talk with a definition request. In terms of setting up an interactional pattern in the family conversations, we can view these types of lexical talk elicitations by the children as a means for selecting their mother as interlocutor which excludes the other two members (father and other child) from the conversation and, if successful, focuses Meredith's attention on the child's problem (i.e. what to call something or what a word means). Recruiting Meredith's attention as interlocutor was important for Arkadiy and Anna because they spent less time with her than they did with Kevin, who was a stay-at-home dad. There are examples in the data of Arkadiy and Anna getting excited and interrupting other activities when their mother arrived home and also asking her about why she has to go to work on Monday. In some cases, Arkadiy and Anna can be seen to compete in vying for Meredith's attention through the use of alternating what-questions, as in Excerpt 5.7:

Excerpt 5.7 Corn
(2D, November 27, 2005; Arkadiy – six, Anna – four)

1	Arkadiy:	Mama, will /mom/ make anymore calendars ((pronounced calahndars)) because we have that one?
2	Meredith:	Yeh we'll just have to finish it.
3		Anna, use a fork.
4		Uhm, we'll take – . once it's [December]
→5	Anna:	[What is this]?
6	Kevin:	Corn.
7		Come on, eat.
8	Anna:	[What]?
9	Arkadiy:	[Mama]?

10	Kevin:	Just eat little girl.
11	Anna:	/???/
12	Arkadiy:	Mama?
→13		What kind number is December?
14	Meredith:	December is the last month of the year.
15	Kevin:	The month twelve.
16	Meredith:	And, the calendar there is to count down how many days [from the first day of Decem -
17	Anna:	[Remember we went
18	Meredith:	I – [I'm talking right now].
19	Kevin:	[/???/]
20	Meredith:	From the first day of December until the twenty-fifth of December
21		which is Christmas.
22		Christmas is the twenty-fifth of December.
23	Anna:	Mama Mama?
24	Meredith:	Yes.
25	Anna:	You know what?
26		This is corn.
27	Meredith:	Yes.
28		I know that.
29	Anna:	You know what Mama?
30		I like the red thing.
→31		What is that called?
32	Meredith:	Cranberry.
33		Do you want some more?

The what-questions in this excerpt provide a means for Arkadiy and Anna to enter into conversation with Meredith, and both children repeat this strategy when they lose their turn at talk with her (lines 5, 13, 31). In line 5 Anna interrupts Meredith with the question 'What is this?' after Meredith had corrected Anna about eating (line 3) and then resumed her own talk about decorating the house for Christmas. Kevin jumps in here perhaps to strengthen Meredith's earlier correction and to get Anna to 'focus' on eating. In lines 9 and 12, Arkadiy uses two attention-getters, 'Mama' to initiate conversation with his mother and draw attention away from Anna. Without success, in line 13 he asks a what-question, 'What kind number is December?'. This echoes Meredith's earlier talk about decorating the house in December (line 5) and successfully draws Meredith into languaging talk to discuss what month December is. The most successful strategy for engaging in conversation with Meredith so far has been to ask what-questions or very similar types of questions. Kevin's impatience with the disruption demonstrates his repeated concerns about Anna's inability to focus on the task at hand.

The interruptions from the children continue. In line 17 Anna attempts to interrupt Meredith's explanation again by initiating a narrative, 'Remember we went ...'. Meredith objects to this interruption, 'I'm talking right now', and continues. In line 23, Anna tries again, this time with a similar strategy used by Arkadiy, the attention-getter, 'Mama, mama, you know what?'. She then recycles the earlier word, 'corn', and displays her new knowledge, which is met with a lukewarm response, 'I know'. Finally, in line 31 Anna asks Meredith another what-question (What is that called?), which results in meaningful interaction (i.e. Meredith responds 'cranberry'). In this excerpt, Meredith responds to and ratifies contributions that take the form of what-questions and rejects other contributions such as a narrative initiation and Anna's display of new knowledge in the repetition of the word 'corn'. In this way, the patterns of what-questions and responses are collaboratively socialized in the family and recognized as a legitimate way for the children and parents to interact with one another.

Parents' Awareness of Questioning Strategies and Attention-Getters

In general, the pattern of questioning and response that developed in the Jackson-Wessels' interactions put Meredith and Kevin in a predominately reactive stance to the children, a phenomenon that the parents often commented on. In this interview, Kevin indicates that he had stopped responding to Anna's repeated use of 'You know what?', which developed as an attention-getter after the original what-questions were established as part of the family conversations.

Excerpt 5.8 You know what?
(March 23, 2006)

> K: Yeah, I'll say o.k. it should be this and like the thing lately they've been going 'What, what, what,' and you know that's their idea of a question.
> You know what, papa? You know, you know what?
> I said yeah, I know what, it's a four letter word w-h-a-t, it's a question word,
> And they're like, you know, now they're trying to get away from that because of the response.

Here Kevin talks about the strategy he uses to reduce the number of 'you know what' openers, suggesting that he is aware of the attention-getting strategy and wants to direct the children to making more meaningful contributions to the family talk.

Languaging, Cultural Models and Affect

Despite the annoyance or concern about the children's frequent questioning in the family, the languaging episodes in the Jackson-Wessels' talk, as in the other studies reviewed above, represented a kind of family pastime in which world views and identities were constructed, as well as a particular orientation toward language that emphasized accuracy or getting the 'right' word, as we will see below. The first two months of recording for the Jackson-Wessels family took place during November and December, during which the family celebrated both Thanksgiving and Christmas. The children had arrived the previous year in early December, but this was their first Thanksgiving in the United States. This holiday provided the topic of an extended discussion in transcript 2C.

Excerpt 5.9 Holiday
(2C, November 23, 2005; Arkadiy – six, Anna – four)

1	Anna:	Mama?
→2		What?
→3		Why tomorrow's holiday?
4		/???/.
5	Meredith:	Tomorrow's Thanksgiving.
→6	Anna:	What?
7		But Thanksgiving is holiday.
8	Meredith:	Yes.
9	Kevin:	Yeh.
10	Meredith:	A holiday is a special day like Christmas or,
→11	Anna:	Mom, what is [tomorrow day]?
12	Arkadiy:	[Mom look what] I found in my tomato.
13		/salad/.
14	Meredith:	Yeh.
15		That's a little of a sprout.
16	Arkadiy:	[Mom] what's a sprout?
17	Anna:	[m].
18	Meredith:	A sprout is when a seed starts to grow.
19		So your tomato [seeds] are starting to grow.
20	Anna:	[/???/]?

21 Meredith: Yes.
→22 Anna: Why /tomorrow's/ hol – what's tomorrow day called?
23   Kevin: /Now/ what would you say, Anna:?
24   What is tomorrow?
25   Anna: Holiday.
26   Meredith: What holiday?
27   Arkadiy: Thanksgiving.
28   M: [xx.
→29 Anna: [What is the name of the morning?
30   Meredith: Thursday.
31   Anna: Thursday.
32   Meredith: Thursday.
33   Anna: Thursday!
34   Kevin: Ah:
35   I got you.
36   Anna: Yeh!
37   hhh.
38   that's what I MEAN!
39   Meredith: Tomorrow is Thursday,
40   Anna: Thursday ((whispering)).
41   Meredith: but it's also Thanksgiving.
42   .. It's a holiday because it's a Thanksgiving not be
                    because it's –
43   not because it's Thursday.

Anna makes six attempts at what-questions in this excerpt, some more successful in eliciting the response she seemed to be after than others. In lines 2 and 6, in keeping with the interactional analysis above, 'What?' seems to function as a turn opener or attention-getter with a separate utterance following, 'Why tomorrow's holiday' and 'But Thanksgiving is holiday'. In addition, Anna uses the 'what' questions to interrupt Meredith's turn and to seemingly indicate that she wasn't getting the response she wanted. In line 10, Meredith begins to answer Anna's 'why' question, but Anna quickly interrupts here with another 'what' question in line 11 – 'Mom, what is [tomorrow day]?'. It's not clear what Anna is actually after, and in line 22 she begins again with the 'why' question but revises it to 'What's tomorrow day called'. At this point Kevin steps in and turns the tables and puts Anna in the reactive position by asking Anna the same question in line 24, 'What is tomorrow?', to which she responds, 'holiday' and 'Thanksgiving'. Anna then revises her question one more time, 'what is the name of the morning', at which point Meredith answers 'Thursday', and Anna expresses satisfaction with this reply.

In this excerpt, Anna is sorting out the meaning of an event (i.e. that tomorrow is a holiday and she will stay home from school) in relation to other things she is learning about (that tomorrow is also called Thursday). She is also playing with different question forms (why questions without inversion: 'Why tomorrow's holiday?') and 'what' questions with inversion ('What is tomorrow day called?'). It's not clear in the beginning of the excerpt that she is trying to elicit the word 'Thursday', and it may be that she does not determine that goal until later in the interaction. In fact, in the following excerpt Anna seems no longer concerned about the fact that tomorrow is Thursday, but rather wants to know more about Thanksgiving. In the next mealtime transcript (2D), which was recorded a few days after the one above, in fact, Anna asks at the opening of the recording 'But what is today?' and Meredith responds immediately with the day of the week, suggesting that she has been primed by this conversation to respond to such questions with the day of the week rather than other information.

The conversation about 'tomorrow' does not end with the naming of 'Thursday' in the above excerpt. In Excerpt 5.10, taken from the same mealtime conversation, Anna continues to talk about the event.

Excerpt 5.10 No fruit day
(2C, November 23, 2005; Arkadiy – six, Anna – four)

1	Anna:	Papa, Miss Karen said tomorrow's no fruit day.
2	Kevin:	Right.
3		Because no one's going to be there.
4	Meredith:	'Cause tomorrow's Thanksgiving.
5	Anna:	Yeh.
6		[And mama, we ever have] Thanksgiving?
7	Meredith:	[And Miss Karen and Miss Trish have to /have/ Thanksgiving].
8	Anna:	/No/.
9	Meredith:	/???/ your first Thanksgiving.

Anna introduces the topic of Thanksgiving to her father in line 1 by calling it 'no fruit day'. Here she seems to still be sorting out the significance of the day – why is there a holiday and what is Thanksgiving? In line 6 Anna asks a more information-oriented question about Thanksgiving, 'And mama, we ever have Thanksgiving?' (line 6). This time there is evidence that the name of the holiday, 'Thanksgiving', and the fact that Thanksgiving is not a regular or weekly event are understood. Now the focus is on Anna's desire to determine how this event fits into her past experiences. Through this line of questioning, 'Thanksgiving' becomes further narrowed to 'your first Thanksgiving' in line 9, signifying the holiday as a unique event in the children's lives. The topic of the first Thanksgiving evolves into a story about the prior Thanksgiving, as we see here in lines 1–12:

Excerpt 5.11 This is your first Thanksgiving
(2C, November 23, 2005; Arkadiy – six, Anna – four)

1	Meredith:	[This is your first].
2	Kevin:	[This is your first] Thanksgiving guys.
3	Meredith:	You haven't been here one year yet.
4		Last year . on Thanksgiving . you were in the detskiy dom ((orphanage)).
5	Anna:	You /used to/ Thanksgiving.
6	Meredith:	And we were thinking about you because we had already seen you one time.
7	Arkadiy:	And you were thinking how you were going to pick up us?
8	Meredith:	And we were thinking that next year, you would be here for Thanksgiving.
9		And now you are.
10	Anna:	Now we're here [all the time].
11	Kevin:	[/You're right/].
12	Anna:	But now we're your daughter and son!
13	Meredith:	mmhmm
14	Kevin:	Exactly.
15	Meredith:	Now you're here all the time and not just for Thanksgiving.
16	Anna:	Thanksgiving for /every/ gonna have Thanksgiving!
17	Arkadiy:	Uhm, not for /every/.
18	Meredith:	It's just one day.
19	Kevin:	But it'll come around next year.
20	Meredith:	Yep, next year we'll have Thanksgiving again.
21	Anna:	Whoo.
22		So I was right?

Anna's statement in this excerpt in line 12, 'But now we're your daughter and son!' constructs the significance of Thanksgiving as an event closely related to the children's membership in the new family. As we saw in the narratives of Ukraine produced by Sasha and Dima in Chapter 4, it is the child, Anna, who initiates this discussion and prompts her mother and father to connect the new event of Thanksgiving to her life story, although Meredith plays an active role in shaping this narrative. It is also Anna who concludes that being present in the family on Thanksgiving and 'all the time' relates to her new identity as a 'daughter' in the Jackson-Wessels family. Anna's questions about Thanksgiving, then, which began in Excerpt 5.9, evolved from a simple (if not a little confused) naming routine 'What is tomorrow day called?' that was common in this family's discourse to more complex questions about the significance of the event, and more importantly the significance of the event in their own personal histories. Reference to a concept of immediate relevance for Anna serves to connect her past experiences (from being in the orphanage) to projecting into the future (about celebrating Thanksgiving forever). Languaging allowed the family members a chance to build a model of what Thanksgiving meant to them as an individual family, a representation of a place and time when they were apart and thinking of one another to the projection of a long-lasting relationship that was characterized by the repetition of an annual event, Thanksgiving. Here we see how language learning, interaction and identity construction coincided in the discourse practices of this adoptive family. Furthermore, the child, Anna, guides and constructs this whole conversation through the use of questions that elicit the relevant information from her parents. In this way, Anna achieves agency through participation in the family routines and controlling the types of talk through such participation.

It was difficult to show longitudinal change in these patterns in this family because there were few recordings where the same family members were doing the same activities (e.g. mealtimes or book-reading sessions usually included different constellations of participants); however, it is clear that the children are playing an agentive role in shaping the interactional context in the family and therefore playing a role in language socialization in the family. The influence of the children is evident in the following excerpt where Kevin introduces a (metalinguistic) topic in conversation with his wife Meredith that he had discussed with Anna earlier in the day. Here Kevin takes on the role of questioner in place of the children to engage Meredith in a discussion of appropriate lexical items and word meanings. The conversation that develops between Meredith and Kevin leads to a focus on lexical accuracy (line 42) and, finally, a construction of identities of the two parents.

Excerpt 5.12 Cherries or berries?
1   Anna: That's all of the juice!
2   Kevin: All of the tomahtoes.

3	Anna:	TomAtoes.
4	Kevin:	Oh, I'm sorry.
5	Anna:	Tomah - but there's another word for tomah - tomatoes, /tomahdukes/.
6	Meredith:	Mhm <laughter>.
7	Anna:	Hhm, /???/.
8		And do you know what?
9		I saw some berries . on the way, home.
10	Kevin:	Yeh, we were debating that.
11	Anna:	Berries!
12	Kevin:	Ok, here's a question.
13	Anna:	Berries. Berry.
14		Blueberry!
15		/???/
16	Meredith:	Berries are a fruit.
17	Kevin:	Berries are a fruit, yes.
18		Are cherries a type of berry?
19	Meredith:	Mm-mm.
20	Kevin:	They're separate, right?
21	Meredith:	Mhm.
22	Kevin:	Now, are all berries in bushes?
23	Anna:	Yeh.
24	Meredith:	I think so.
25	Kevin:	Ok.
26	Anna:	[Yeh]!
27	Kevin:	[And so], [obvious]
28	Meredith:	[Or vines].
29	Kevin:	Ok, now.
30	Meredith:	Bushes.
31	Kevin:	Alina, then it was NOT a berry.
32		We were wrong.
33	Meredith:	Cherries [are a fruit].
34	Kevin:	[It was up in a tree].
35	Meredith:	They're in a tree.
36	Kevin:	Mkay, so fruits are trees, berries are bushes.
37	Meredith:	Yeh.
38	Kevin:	I mean eh, I mean [I -]
39	Meredith:	[I] wouldn't want to like stake my life on it, but I'm pretty sure.
40	Kevin:	Well, I wouldn't want to stake anyone's life on it.
41		So, hhhhhha.

42		I'm just tryin' to get more accurate.
43		So, we saw something that was red, and it looked,
44	Anna:	And prickle.
45	Kevin:	Cherry slash berryish.
46	Meredith:	Mmm!
47		[Nope]!
48	Kevin:	[In a] tree.
49	Meredith:	I'm wrong, I'm wrong, mulberries!
50	Anna:	[Why]?
51	Meredith:	[Mulberries] grow in trees.
52	Kevin:	Ah!
53		There we go, [mulberries].
54	Meredith:	[I don't know] if they're properly . berries, though.
55		Oh, I love mulberries.
56	Kevin:	/Those are bulberries/.
57	Meredith:	When I was a kid, we had a . mulberry tree.
58	Kevin:	You have a boysenberry tree?
59		I don't think so.
60	Meredith:	I think boysenberries are bushes, [I don't /really/ know].
61	Anna:	[Mommy]!
62		I broke it.
63	Kevin:	/???/
64		'Cause it looked very small, possibly cherryish,
65		but I don't know for sure.
66		Uh, what type of leaves do cherry trees have anyway?
67		Are they the kind of long and thin?
68		You come from a family of people who know plants I – I my family, . we're town folk.
69	Meredith:	Your mother's a master gardener.
70	Kevin:	Well she /learn -/ she picked it up /at/ – lo:ng after I left the house.

Here a discussion about how to pronounce the word 'tomatoes' (line 3) and subsequent language play with the word, 'there's another word for tomatoes . . . tomahdukes!', leads Anna to introduce the topic of the berries she and her father saw earlier that day. In this extended languaging episode that is initiated by Anna but which primarily involves Kevin and Meredith in conversation, accurate word definitions and names of objects are foregrounded. There is also reference to literate representations of language (cherry slash berryish), narratives of personal experience, 'Oh, I love mulberries', and representations of the parents' own families, 'your mother's a master garderner' that construct expertise in the interaction. The couple make fun of themselves for taking the naming and defining process so seriously, 'Well, I wouldn't want to stake anyone's life on it' (line 40) and become very engaged in thinking of the right name for the plant Kevin was describing. The role of the language-learning children in directing the parents' attention to new words, the names of new things and how to define or describe objects is evident here as Anna herself observed the 'berries' and introduced them into the family conversation (line 9). This episode shows how the children's questioning practices have shaped parents' focus on language and talk about talk even in conversation with each other. This discussion emerged out of Anna's curiosity and questions about a new object, as well as Kevin's focus on linguistic accuracy. This kind of talk about language becomes a type of language play or fun activity that allows the family members to construct their knowledge about the world around them as well as their own personal and family identities (e.g. 'We're town folk').

Conclusion

Asking questions is a primary way in which learners or novices can socialize experts and establish agency in interactions. Asking questions or making information requests typically fits into established norms for learner action and represents a complicit type of agency that is participatory and not, as in the previous chapter, resistant. Questions, however, can place the questioner in a position of power over other participants and therefore represent control in interactions. This tension over the children's control could be found in some of the parents' comments on the seemingly 'empty' questions the children asked. As Tannen (2007) notes, power maneuvers can also be interpreted as solidarity maneuvers. In this case, the direction of the family interactions by the children is related to two main processes: (a) the need to direct the level of conversation and obtain comprehensible input, and (b) the desire to engage the parent who worked outside of the home in conversation. That is, at the same time that Anna and Arkadiy exerted control over the types of talk in the family, they were also building solidarity with their parents by being interested participants in the conversations. The type of questions Anna and Arkadiy asked, primarily what-questions that queried the names of things or word meanings, connected with Meredith and Kevin's attention to language and interest in discussing metalinguistic topics for pleasure.

In these data, there is a relationship between longer episodes of languaging and actual storytelling or narrative events. This relationship has been noted in prior research (e.g. Beals & Snow, 1994). Explanations of word meanings or languaging episodes in these data could lead to narratives that help construct a world view, as described by Gee (2008). Thus the connection between metalinguistic talk or languaging and narrative allows the participants to move across time and place in defining words. These practices further connect with the children's literacy socialization and academic readiness and deserve further attention in second language-learning research.

The processes identified in the Jackson-Wessels family also have direct connections with what goes on inside the classroom. Boyd and Rubin (2002) found that student questions during class time provided a means to gain access to and potentially increase the comprehensibility of the L2 teacher talk. Student questions can also help teachers to understand their second language students' language use better in terms of predicting what words they know or don't know and how to negotiate meaning in effective ways. In a more complex discourse analysis of classroom interaction in mainstream US junior high and middle schools, Nystrand and colleagues (2003) found that student questions were important instigators of 'dialogic spells' that had been correlated in previous studies with student achievement. In this study, I have reported similar findings from the family context – learner questions lead to languaging episodes that open opportunities for learning and are also tied to social phenomena, such as establishing interactional roles and identities.

Kevin and Meredith engaged in these child-initiated languaging episodes as a form of rapport building (perhaps associated with their education level and professional interests, as lawyers are known to engage in 'lexical negotiation' as part of their professional practice [Cotterill, 2004]), and this further constructed these types of episodes as characteristic of the family discourse. The process is in some ways cyclical, with family members influencing each other over time. For the parents of transnational adoptees who enter the home with different linguistic and cultural backgrounds, part of the socialization process involves finding out what the children know and don't know, what they understand and how they learn. For the children, the process is slightly different – how to gain access to information, how to be ratified as a participant or member in the new family and how to understand new events, objects and even words in the new environment. These processes work together, and they result in local, personal family discourse practices that serve to construct meaning, relationships and understandings of the world. Finally, as the parents and children collaborated in arriving at a meaning of a word, they connected their past experiences across times and timescales to make sense of their new lives together. In this way, for this particular family, language-related episodes were a central part of how they learned about one another, how they interacted and how they made sense of their lives.

Notes

(1) Ely and Gleason (personal communication) noted that there was little to no multilingual activity in the Gleason corpus.
(2) Thanks to Michael Kieffer for this insight.

6 'We'll Help Them in Russian, and They'll Help Us in English': Negotiation, Medium Requests and Code-Switching

The previous chapters described adoptive families who, in different ways, had switched to English as the medium of communication in the family. Therefore, my analysis of language socialization in the previous two adoptive families focused on phenomena (narrative socialization and meta-linguistic talk) that were more relevant to monolingual contexts. Bi- and multilingual communication, however, entail a different level of analysis, in which code choice and alternation play a role in and are influenced by the social setting, linguistic competence and grammatical aspects of language (Gardner-Chloros, 2009). Both Russian and English were used in the daily communication of the third family, the Goellers, between the parents and their six adopted children and among the children themselves. In this chapter I examine how the family accommodated to the Russian language dominance of the newly arrived teenage members to the family (Lesya, 15 and Lena, 16), how a general progression to English was made over the course of data collection and how Lesya and Lena were able to maintain Russian in some interactions. In short, I focus on Lesya and Lena's agency in negotiating language choice in this family and, in doing so, demonstrate how learner agency as negotiation (through, for example, initiating their own and resisting others' medium requests) occurs in interaction.

In the Goeller family, all eight family members, including parents Melanie and Paul, as well as the six adopted siblings, used Russian in family interactions. In this chapter I look specifically at language negotiation sequences in which participants actively negotiate the language of interaction to show: (a) how an English-language context of interaction is negotiated between the parents and new arrivals over the eight months, and (b) how a Russian-language context of interaction is negotiated between the new arrivals and at least two of their siblings during the same time period. Although the family shifts from more Russian use to more English use at mealtime in the seven months after Lesya and Lena's arrival, in this chapter I show how the children are able to maintain Russian by narrowing its functions and using bridging strategies (such as translations to English) to include the whole family.

What is Code-Switching?

Code-switching is often defined as the 'use of more than one language in the course of a single communicative episode' (Heller, 1988: 1), and early approaches to the study of language alternation focused on the ways in which use of one or the other language indexed specific (ethnolinguistic) community identities and membership (e.g. Gumperz, 1982; Myers-Scotton, 1993). However, these approaches have been questioned in more recent perspectives on bilingual language use. There have been two main developments in the field in understanding when, why and how individuals code-switch. On the one hand, current research has noted that bilingual code-switching is not necessarily best defined as the alternation between two languages, but rather an alternative medium develops in bilingual language use that blurs the lines of static notions of 'language' (Gardner-Chloros, 2009; Torras & Gafaranga, 2002). Scholars in the emerging field of multilingualism have also pointed to the practice of 'languaging' (a different use of the term than that presented in Chapter 5) to describe this process of using linguistic resources from a number of codes to make meaning in conversation as well as writing (e.g. Jørgensen, 2008).

In the Goeller family, a clear distinction was often made in what language which family member was using. This separation of codes in this family's interactions was motivated both by an interest in talking about and encouraging the newly arrived teenagers' development of English and also the family members' demonstrated interests around language purism. The fact that the family members saw themselves as using two different codes independently of one another shaped the code-switching practices in this family and the comments and criticisms that were sometimes a part of conversations about code choice, as I will discuss further below.

A Sequential Approach

The second major development in the study of code-switching has been a move away from explaining language alternation through the use of we/they codes (Gumperz, 1982) to understanding how code-switching is sequential and locally occasioned. This approach has been particularly useful to understanding bilingual language use in unstable bilingual settings such as those associated with transnational and globalization processes (Auer, 1984). Auer (1984, 1998) proposed an approach to code-switching based on conversation analysis methodology in which code-switching is studied as a contextualization cue used in the sequential organization of talk. Auer (1984) views this 'interactional' approach to code-switching as falling between the 'grammatical', which is concerned with the forms of switches, and the 'sociolinguistic', which is concerned with macro issues of community language choice (where and why a language is used). Auer argues that simply looking toward societal patterns of language status will not explain why each language is used when in conversation because code-switching is locally produced and the choice of language in and of itself serves to contextualize the local interaction. That is, switching languages adds to the meaning of an utterance and its interpretation by an interlocutor by 'providing cues for the organization of the ongoing interaction (i.e., is it discourse related) or about attributes of the speaker (participant related)' (Auer, 1984: 12). Discourse-related code-switching, according to Auer, 'interrupts conversational continuity in order to set off something that has been said before against something that will be said now' (1984: 93). Participant-related code-switching, 'redefines the language of interaction' in order to make note of a speaker's unbalanced bilingual competence or a divergence in language preferences between two speakers (1984: 93). The interactional approach to code-switching also allows for the study of the processes of language negotiation and code selection, which can then be connected to larger macrosociolinguistic processes.

Gardner-Chloros supports this approach to code-switching (2009: 70):

> the notion that speakers make choices between codes and code-switch in accordance with indexical values external to the conversations and the speakers themselves has increasingly been regarded as insufficient.

Cashman (2005) further follows in this vein by expanding the notion of the ascription of 'individualistic preferences' to show how certain identity-related categories could also be ascribed through negotiations of language choice and how code-switching could serve to comment on other members' language competence and in-group status in interaction. Rather than taking a 'language reflects society view', Cashman finds that different identities are talked into being at the micro level (cf. Bucholtz & Hall, 2005). Such negotiations have also been tied to the construction of power relations amongst children (Cashman, 2008; Jørgensen, 1998), as well as individual ethnic membership within bilingual family interactions (Pasquandrea, 2008). In presumably less stable bilingual settings where community norms are not established or speakers from different ethnicities and backgrounds interact in two or more languages, code-switching practices are more likely tied to the construction of *local* meanings, such as the negotiation and ascription of participant identities (Cashman, 2005).

The Goellers were not recognized members of a minority language community where two languages were commonly spoken and were therefore not regularly exposed to the practice of code-switching. Communities of Russian bilinguals exist in nearly every major metropolitan area of the United States, and these communities have code-switching and language mixing practices that have been documented in research (Andrews, 1999; Angermeyer, 2005). However, transnational adoptive families, as I have reported in prior work (e.g. Fogle, in press), tend to have little contact with these communities. While adoptive parents might speak some Russian and attend Russian cultural events at local churches or embassies, they do not often use Russian outside of interactions with their children or socialize with Russian American families in the area. Models for Russian–English code-switching such as those associated with the New York Puerto Rican (Nuyorican) identity of El Barrio in New York city (Zentella, 1997), while potentially present in the larger Russian community in the United States, are not readily available to adoptive parents and adoptees. The use of both languages in the family sphere, however, can still play a role in identity construction for transnational adoptive families as family members find a way to maintain Russian against the external (and internal) pressures of English, as I will show in the data gathered from the Goellers.

In family units where community norms do not exist or are difficult to determine, such as transnational adoptive families with older children that do not fit neatly into mainstream English monolingual or immigrant bilingual communities, any number of ideological and interactional processes might be at play in code-switching practices. On the one hand, majority ideologies and concerns about English language competence suggest that adoptees would quickly 'replace' their first languages with English, and this has been the finding or conclusion of various studies on language attrition and theoretical perspectives on bilingualism for adoptees (Fogle, in press). However, language ideologies within the family and specifically the role of the children's native language in establishing family unity, as well as the fact that older children and particularly teenagers have been found to be harbingers of language change (e.g. Eckert, 1988; Hazen, 2002), can all play a role in maintaining Russian for the Goeller family.

In this chapter I will look specifically at how the negotiation of language competencies, individual language ideologies and family relationships intersect to establish certain patterns of code-switching in this family. While at times some of the Goellers mentioned in interviews not being aware of which language they were speaking, for the most part there was a clear separation of languages and consciousness of who was speaking English or Russian more frequently or less frequently and 'better' or 'worse' (usually in terms of pronunciation, lexical knowledge and sentence structures). The family members (usually Melanie, Lesya and Lena in interviews) often discussed each other's language competence, and Lesya and Lena in particular discussed a desire to maintain 'pure' Russian. This emphasis toward linguistic purity, and at times error correction, will serve as a backdrop for understanding the other dynamics, including relationships and power roles, that played a role in negotiating language choice in this family.

Participant-Related Code-Switching

The current analysis focuses primarily on participant-related code-switching, which Auer (1984) proposed as a contrasting phenomenon to discourse-related switching, both of which emerge in talk-in-interaction rather than reflect societal patterns. Participant-related code-switching, 'redefines the language of interaction' and in doing so signifies a speaker's unbalanced bilingual competence or a divergence in language preferences between two speakers (Auer, 1984: 93). The interactional approach to code-switching also allows for the study of the processes of language negotiation and code selection, which can then be connected to larger macrosociolinguistic processes. Shin and Milroy (2000) define participant-related switching as follows:

> Participant-related codeswitching . . . is motivated by a need to negotiate the proper language for the interaction – ideally, one that is both socially adequate and accommodates all parties' language competences and preferences. (Shin & Milroy, 2000: 370)

While the term 'proper' might be too normative in this context and implies linguistic prescriptivism (Lanza, personal communication), the notion of participant-related code-switching addresses the phenomenon in which individuals try to figure out which is the 'right' language to use with another speaker (e.g. which language feels comfortable, is comprehensible and shows the greatest respect to the interlocutor), and this process entails negotiation and 'trying out' different codes. This process does not always occur harmoniously, however. Interlocutors can diverge in language choice, and language negotiations can be related to negotiations over power, status and identity in the interactional context (Cashman, 2005; Hua, 2008; Jørgensen, 1998). Thus the choice of the 'right' code is in flux and such negotiations both construct and index larger social realities.

Another distinction in types of switching has been proposed by Torras and Gafaranga (2002), who distinguish between competence-related preference and ideology-related preference. In a study of the microinteractional processes of language shift in the family, Gafaranga (2010: 248) concluded that, 'in the case of the choice between Kinyarwanda and French by Rwandan children in Belgium, preference is strictly competence-related'. But little is known about the social side of competence-related switching. As noted in Chapter 2, emergent bilinguals who have uneven proficiency in their languages may refuse to communicate in their weaker language or resist learning altogether. Such resistance can be socially motivated or identity-related (Duff, 2012). Thus what is often deemed to be competence-related switching could also be motivated by a learner's resistance to the target language or their attempts to negotiate the language back to a preferred choice that fits with how the speaker sees him or herself or the role he or she is taking in the conversation, in addition to which language is dominant. As Gardner-Chloros (2009: 175) notes, there are difficulties in categorizing code-switching in second language-learning settings:

> Relatively little work has been done so far on C[ode] S[witching] by second language learners. It has been shown, however, that learners use words from their L1 to fill lexical gaps in their target language when this does not render them incomprehensible to their interlocutors. In practice it is not always easy to draw a line between such CS born of necessity and more discourse-oriented CS, which develops as soon as a greater level of fluency is achieved.

For the second and heritage language-learning adoptees in this study (as some of the children were primarily acquiring English while others were working on relearning their Russian), competence-related and ideology-related switching were intertwined. A powerful force in negotiating switching among the siblings toward Russian was the desire to learn, which was enmeshed in the desire to form relationships and establish Russian-speaking identities. In addition, Lesya and Lena's medium requests for Russian or Russian–English parallel conversations with their parents were tied to their weaker competence in English, but also to an implicit ideology toward pure speech and separation of codes that I will discuss below.

Children's Agency in Code Negotiation

In recent years studies of language maintenance and shift, and concomitantly code-switching in the family, have been interested in transnational or migrant families in which parents, caretakers or children are rooted in at least two national contexts with deep personal or practical connections to communities of practice and flows of information across national borders (Fogle & King, in press). Transnational families often involve members with uneven access to linguistic resources, and negotiations of language choice as well as language competence are prevalent (Canagarajah, 2008; Fogle & King, in press; Gafaranga, 2010; Kasanga, 2008). These studies have begun to point to the ways in which children in particular might influence code choice and family language policies in the home.

Gafaranga's (2010) work on Rwandan migrant families in particular has focused on understanding processes of language maintenance and shift in family interactions. Gafaranga argues that in order to understand how this happens, microinteractional studies need to be undertaken that explain the processes through which language shift occurs in parent–child interaction. Gafaranga describes a situation in Rwandan immigrant families in Brussels in which code-switching is unidirectional from Kinyarwandan to French and is shaped by children's strategies, specifically a 'medium request' that results in allowing the children the right to speak French. This study shows how 'the macro-sociological order can be seen as talked into being in the microconversational order' (Gafaranga, 2010: 233) and suggests how agency is afforded to the children in code negotiations with their parents through the macrolinguistic status of the majority language. The current study contributes to this line of research by foregrounding other aspects of the family communication, including establishing family membership, roles and bonds through language use that compete with the macrosociolinguistic norms and ideologies.

Other studies have also found that children play an agentive role in code selection in interaction with their parents. In these studies, younger generations are found to play an important role in negotiating code use in the home with parents and other siblings. In a study of Chinese diasporic families in the UK, for example, Hua (2008) found that code-switching strategies were used to negotiate, mediate and manage conflicts in values between parents and children (e.g. fulfilling family social obligations) and showed how cultural transformation occurred in talk in interaction in these families as children used heritage languages in strategic ways to influence their parents. Further, Kasanga (2008) focused on multilingual intragenerational interactions of extended families of Congolese origin that had migrated to different host nations. This study focused on micro interactions amongst family members, siblings (or cousins) from different families who had adopted French and English over the local family language, Kiswahili, and showed how they used coping strategies such as accommodation, crossing, code negotiation and negotiation for meaning to establish a mode of communication that met the interactional and social needs of the family members. Some of these strategies also occur in the data presented here; namely, negotiation for meaning occurs to maintain a monolingual mode of communication among family members (rather than a parallel conversation in two languages).

Slavic Identities and Linguistic Purism

In the analyses of the data in this book, I have rarely drawn on the children's backgrounds as Russian or Russian speakers to explain the interactional processes at home. I could not trace the questioning patterns of Arkadiy and Anna in the Jackson-Wessels family to a particularly Russian discourse style, nor could I find anything inherently Ukrainian about Dima's 'nothing' responses in the Sonderman family interactions (if anything this was a typical US preteen pattern). I have primarily focused on what I observed within the family setting and timeframe to explain the interaction patterns, although this certainly excludes an understanding of how these processes were shaped on longer timescales (Lemke, 2000). The two newly arrived teenagers in this chapter, Lesya and Lena, however, had a much longer socialization period in Russia than the other children and had been in school for eight or more years in Russia prior to arriving in the US (only one of the children, Dima, in the other two families had any schooling prior to the adoption). Ideologies that have been found to be related to language planning and teaching in the former Soviet Union surfaced in the children's discussions about language both in interviews and the interactional data. Specifically, Lesya and Lena talked about speaking 'correct' Russian and often compared themselves to other speakers of contact varieties of Russian in the data. This ideology of linguistic purism can serve as a backdrop for understanding some of the code negotiation processes in this family, as I will show below.[3]

According to Gorham (2000), purification of the Russian language from the modernist vernacular associated with the working class was a primary goal of Lenin in the early period after the Russian Revolution. This purism was a means of state building and a response to Russian émigrés' opposition to the new Russian or language of the peasants. Gorham (2000: 142) also suggests that constructing a standard Russian was a way to gain national power and unity after the turmoil: 'The fight for a clean, authoritative language was a matter of national legitimacy, identity, pride, and even survival.' Such ideologies have influenced teaching practices in schools as well as new struggles over revitalizing the national or native languages in the former USSR that were replaced by Russian during the Russification process.

In the 20th and 21st century, policies in Ukraine, for example, have sought Ukrainization within the nation primarily through the teaching of Ukrainian in schools. These efforts were documented in a language socialization study by Friedman (2010: 364) who found that ideologies of 'speaking correctly' and practices of intense error correction in the Ukrainian language classroom 'reflected and validated the valorization of pure language evoked through state-sponsored efforts to revitalize Ukrainian and establish it as a distinct language suitable for representing a distinct nation'. Thus language purism in Slavic contexts has been related to notions of a cohesive or unitary identity. These ideas will surface in Lesya and Lena's talk about their own and their family members' Russian use and potentially relate to a preference for not mixing languages in conversation, as will be shown below.

The Goeller Family

Lesya and Lena, ages 15 and 16 at time of arrival, were the oldest children to participate in the current study. One of the immediate concerns for Lena and her new mother Melanie was the fact that she would be required to enter a 'newcomer' program in the ninth grade. In Russia, Lena was in the 11th and final year of her vocational program (to be a professional chef), and completing four additional years of high school in the US seemed daunting. Melanie discussed potentially letting Lena start work and take General Educational Development (GED) tests that would lead to a High School Equivalency Diploma without actually finishing the coursework in school if the high school program did not work out. Lesya was younger, and the requirement to begin in the ninth grade in the US did not affect her educational program as greatly.

All three families who participated in this study were busy, but the Goellers probably had the busiest schedule. At the start of data collection with the Goellers, Melanie was at home with the children on family leave. She returned to work around the third month of the study. The family had also moved houses to a suburb further away from the city, and the children had changed schools because of that move. Melanie was looking for work closer to their new home, but for the duration of this study she commuted an hour and a half to work each day once her leave had ended. For this reason and because an au pair the family had hired did not work out, Lena, the eldest daughter, and also Lesya were sometimes responsible for babysitting the younger children after school.

The Goellers' Data

Data collection in the Goeller family began one week prior to the teenagers' arrival in June 2007, and extended eight months until the end of February 2008. The family was asked to self-record mealtimes once a week (in contrast to the once per month recording schedule established in the Sondermans and the Jackson-Wessels) in an effort to chart Lesya and Lena's early English language development. The family was very busy with after-school activities (gymnastics, tae kwon do, hockey, etc.) and other commitments, and although they did report regularly eating dinner together, they did not return as many recordings as the other two families in the study (only about four hours in total). Table 6.1 shows the total mealtime recordings conducted by the Goellers.

In addition, weekly interviews were conducted in Russian with Lesya and Lena in which the researcher asked them about their language learning, use of Russian and transition to school in the US. Table 6.2 shows the total amount of interview data collected including intermittent monthly interviews with Melanie and one interview with Melanie and Paul.

A total of four hours and 29 minutes of interview data, primarily in Russian with Lesya and Lena and English with Paul and Melanie, were collected in the Goeller family. The relatively small amount of actual recorded data for this family was augmented by more frequent visits to this family in their home.

Table 6.1 The Goellers' recordings

Date	Transcript	Type	Length
June 1, 2007	3A	Mealtime	22:49
July 18, 2007	3B	Mealtime	18:39
August 2, 2007	3C	Game	57:42
August 21, 2007	3D	Mealtime	15:22
October 25, 2007	3E	Mealtime	20:59
November 2007*	3F	Mealtime	15:21
November 2007*	3G	Mealtime	19:14
November 2007*	3H	Mealtime	10:29
November 12, 2007	3I	Mealtime	12:25
December 2007*	3J	Mealtime	16:25
February 23, 2008	3K	Mealtime	26:23

*Exact date unknown

Table 6.2 The Goellers' interview data in minutes:seconds

Date	Length	Participants
July 18, 2007	34:07	Melanie (M), Lesya (L), Lena (L)
July 27, 2007	22:47	L, L
August 2, 2007	16:02	L, L
August 22, 2007	29:17	M
August 22, 2007	18:51	L, L
August 31, 2007	15:10	L, L
September 28, 2007	31:16	L, L
October 27, 2007	25:45	L, L
November 10, 2007	41:22	L, L, M
January 6, 2008	34:30	L, L, M, Paul

Transcription

The data were transcribed and verified by two English–Russian bilinguals (the researcher and a native Russian speaker). After some discussion between transcribers, all utterances that could be determined to be in Russian were transcribed in the final transcripts using Cyrillic. Initially, the first transcriber (a native speaker of Russian) had transcribed phonologically 'native-sounding' Russian in Cyrillic and non-native sounding Russian in the Roman alphabet (representing a bivalency in script choice in the transcripts [Angermeyer, 2005]). Ultimately, the use of two scripts to represent Russian speech in the transcripts was problematic because it suggested that non-native productions of Russian were not 'real' Russian and obscured the current study's interest in switching between the two languages despite competence. In the excerpts presented here from the mealtimes, the Cyrillic transcript is presented followed by a Romanized version of the Russian and then an English language translation with the words originally uttered in Russian italics. In the text I use the Romanized version when referring to the transcripts.

Data Analysis

In taking an interpretivist stance to the data, in which I aimed 'to discover how people use language, what they believe about language, and why, as aspects of socially constructed reality' (Heller, 2008: 250), the phenomenon of negotiation of language choice and family language policies emerged as important aspects of the family conversations. A longitudinal perspective allowed for tracking developmental change in the participants' bilingualism (Hua & David, 2008). The changes I identify are primarily related to social relations and language practices in relation to the parents' changing language policies in the home. However, these changes also relate to the individual speakers' language competence and production. Thus while these areas have been addressed as different points of focus for code-switching, bilingual or second language-learning research, in this chapter I show how in some cases they can be understood as simultaneous processes (Gardner-Chloros, 2009; Moyer, 2008).

Coding

Utterances were initially coded for speaker and language. Utterances that were not coded for language (and therefore not considered to be switches) included: proper names, backchannels such as (oh, uh-huh, mhm), ok (which can be used in either language) and onomatopoeia. The analysis focuses on language negotiation sequences as described by Auer (1984). Language negotiation sequences were identified as episodes in which there was a noticeable divergence in language choice between speakers usually marked by one of the following cues:

(1) Switch away from a 'transepisodal' preference (Auer, 1984) or the language a speaker used more regularly in interaction.
(2) Disfluency or pause that precedes a switch (self-repair).
(3) Minimal response that maintains the language of interaction without extended contribution.
(4) Explicit comment about language choice or competence.

While Auer's negotiation sequence was meant to account for a range of situations and speakers, Gafaranga (2010) identified a specific type of language negotiation (i.e. other-initiated medium repair) in migrant family interaction that was typically child-initiated, unidirectional and could end in a parallel mode of communication (i.e. the parent speaks the minority language while the child speaks the majority language). This 'medium request', which Gafaranga found to be a primary mechanism for 'talking language shift into being', also plays a role in the Goeller family interactions as the teenage girls often shape the language of interaction in the family. However, these requests are not always unidirectional, a phenomenon related to uneven competencies in the two languages as well as ideologies of purism and mixing, as I discuss in the data analysis below.

Language Ideologies and Family Language Policy

As noted in Chapter 1, parents' and other family members' attitudes toward language choice and use can play a role in everyday family interactions; however, these relationships can also be bidirectional, and actual usage and interactional strategies can influence family members' attitudes. I start here with Lesya and Lena's discussion of learning English in the home when they first arrived. I also present Melanie and Paul's perspective on English language use in the family. I will then show how these attitudes actually played out and were constructed by the family interactions.

Lesya and Lena's perspectives

Lena and Lesya stated a preference for speaking English (or at least being spoken to in English in the family sphere) from very early on in the study. They saw the home environment as a good place to learn English:

Excerpt 6.1 It would be better
July 27, 2007 (Lesya – 15, Lena – 16)
> *Original:*
> Lena: Ну, лучше бы я сказала чего-то по-английски и они меня исправили слово там я не правильно там произнесла, лучше бы они меня исправили по-английски, как бы. . .
> Lesya: Потому что все еще ошибок очень много.
>
> *Translation:*
> Lena: Well, it would be better if I said something in English and they corrected the word, like I didn't pronounce it right like, it would be better if they corrected my English, like . . .
> Lesya: Because there is still a lot of mistakes.

Even after school started in September, Lesya and Lena suggested that they wanted to speak more English at home because they already understood everything at school. This was partly motivated by the fact that they felt they would do better at school if they had more English at home, and that they felt left out of some of the family interactions because they did not understand:

Excerpt 6.2 The first time we sat down as a whole family
August 2, 2007 (Lesya – 15, Lena – 16)
> *Original:*
> Lena: Ну, когда первый раз вообще, я помню, когда мы первый раз вообще сели всей семьей ужинать, как бы, мы вообще, неловко

чувствовали себя в этой ситуации, они чисто по-английски все говорят, чего-то даже про нас говорили, как бы, смеялись, нам обидно, мне обидно, как бы, чуть-чуть было, что мы не понимаем, то есть они смеются, а мы сидим с Лесей вот так на друг друга смотрим. То есть, а сейчас они даже вообще говорят, как бы, мы уже тоже понимаем уже.

Translation:
Lena: Well at first when, I remember, when we the first time in general sat down as a whole family to eat dinner, like, we in general, felt uncomfortable in this situation, they are speaking totally in English, they even said something about us, like laughed, it was offensive to us. It was offensive to me, like, a little bit it was, that we don't understand and that is they are laughing, and Lesya and I are sitting here so looking at each other. That is, but now even in general they are speaking, like, we already also understand already.

In addition to wanting to learn English (and to speak English with the family members), Lesya and Lena also stated a desire to maintain Russian and continue using Russian in daily life. They cited negative examples in interviews of other adopted children who lost Russian because their parents did not want them to maintain it and of Russian Americans whose Russian was, in their opinion, not 'pure'. The school environment provided less opportunity for Russian use and maintenance, and therefore Lesya and Lena had to find a way to reconcile their desire to use more English at home (for the sake of learning and fitting into the family) with maintaining their Russian. One of the main ways they accomplished this was narrowing their Russian in the family sphere to a specific domain of speaking with the other children (primarily with two more recently arrived and stronger Russian-speaking siblings) over time, and taking on the role of language teachers at home, as seen in this quotation.

Excerpt 6.3 They want to remember Russian
July 27, 2007 (Lesya – 15, Lena – 16)
Original:
Lena: Ну, они все хотят вспомнить русский, чтобы мы им помогли. То есть они нам помогут говорить на английском, а мы им по-русски.

Translation:
Lena: Well, they all want to remember Russian, they want us to help them. That is they'll help us speak English and we'll help them in Russian.

The teacher role extended to other spheres as well. Lesya in particular noted that she taught the Spanish-speaking boys at school some Russian, and even noted that sometimes they corrected their parents. The teacher role, then, allowed Lesya and Lena a reason to continue using Russian at the same time that they shifted to English more in interaction with their parents. Melanie and Paul, however, had slightly different views on Russian use in the family.

The Goellers also demonstrated a dual process of self-lowering and child raising, and language choice in this family was ultimately guided by parental ideologies along with the macrosociolinguistic context in which English was the majority language. In the first month after Lesya and Lena's arrival, Melanie and Paul accommodated to the teenagers by using Russian almost exclusively with them. As the family relationships evolved and changed, Melanie began to institute stricter English-only policies to encourage family unity and 'raising' the children linguistically to the communicative norms of the rest of the family. Both implicit and explicit beliefs about language influenced these trends. On the one hand, Melanie's immediate concern was promoting unity amongst the siblings who had different competencies in Russian, while, on the other, US norms made it easy to conceive of the adoptive family as an English-speaking family.

Melanie and Paul's perspectives

Although Melanie and Paul both spoke some Russian and used Russian in interaction with Lesya and Lena when they first arrived, they primarily viewed the family sphere as an English language environment. Melanie, in particular, felt that Lesya and Lena's growing English competence contributed to their 'fitting in' with the family more:

Excerpt 6.4 They are more a part of the family
November 10, 2007 (Lesya – 15, Lena – 17)
Melanie: They are speaking a lot more English.
Lyn: Both of them?
Melanie: Yes, Lesya not as much as Lena, but they are both speaking a lot more English. And I've noticed they are more part of the family, I think they are seeing us more as a family as opposed to them just kind of sitting around here whatever – you know, they are getting the idea of more, seem to be more relaxed...

This perspective coincides with Lena's statement above that they were uncomfortable at family dinners because they didn't understand what was being said. Although speaking English was seen to be key to becoming a member of the family, when asked what seemed to help Lesya and Lena learn English the most, both Melanie and Paul pointed to activities outside of the family environment. In an interview in January (six months after Lesya and Lena's arrival), both Melanie and Paul suggested that communicating with other English language-learning peers (mainly Spanish-speaking boys) outside of school had been a major factor in Lesya and Lena's acquisition of English. This also coincides with Lesya and Lena's early perceptions that the family environment was not as facilitative of English language development as they would have liked. The perception was that interactions that required the girls to use English for social and academic purposes (i.e. in peer groups and at school) played a greater role in their language development than interaction at home. This perception is most likely based on the sense that family members used a number of accommodating strategies to interact with each other that were initially aimed at facilitating family bonding. The family environment did contribute to Lesya and Lena's English language development, as well as their ability to maintain Russian over the eight months; however, these effects were perhaps hard to perceive for family members because of the other social factors involved.

By the third month of the study (September), divisions had begun to surface among the siblings as the more Russian-dominant girl (Valentina or 'Valya' for short) aligned with the teenagers, leaving the more English-dominant sister, Inna, out of the group. This grouping, along with some other power struggles and disruptive behaviors, prompted a family social worker to encourage the family to enforce English only as a way to assuage some of the conflict (and potentially give Melanie more access to the interactions that the children were having amongst themselves). Russian use had begun to be seen as something that divided the family because the first two arrivals, Inna and Tolya, did not have the same level of competence and therefore could not interact with Lesya and Lena as Valya and David did. In short, the parents' initial positive attitudes toward Russian and accommodation to Lesya and Lena by using Russian were drawn into conflict by concomitant processes of establishing interpersonal relationships in the family and constructing a cohesive family bond.

About five months into the study, I noticed that Paul, the father, used more Russian in conversations than Melanie. Melanie had also commented that Paul liked to use Russian, and in November I asked him about his Russian use. At this point Melanie reported using almost no Russian because she perceived that the girls' English was better than her Russian. Paul, on the other hand, had a slightly different view:

Excerpt 6.5 I should get something out of it
(January 6, 2008)

> Paul: I don't know, unfortunately part of it is, I'm really bad with languages and I feel like I put all this effort into it, and I should get something out of it, so maybe I use it more than I should. But usually it's – it's – I try to use it, if I'm trying to explain something that I can't explain in English, I guess, so I guess it's just another tool for getting things across. I'm trying to use it less, I am not sure if that bears out in the tapes or not.
>
> Melanie: I'm thinking over time we're gonna – it's gonna fade out.
>
> Paul: Yeah.
>
> Michelle: I mean the older girls might use it between themselves...

Here Paul cites two main reasons for continuing to use Russian with the teenagers: (a) he invested a good bit to learn the language himself, and (b) he sees it as a resource during communication breakdowns. This perspective contrasts with Melanie's emphasis on English as a family-building tool and the belief that communication breakdowns are better negotiated without the use of Russian. Although there is no real conflict between the two parents apparent in the data (Paul also agrees that English is important), there is some indication that Lesya, who preferred Russian, was more comfortable talking with her father, and Lena, who was the stronger English language learner, preferred conversation with Melanie (but this was also intertwined with Lena's attitudes toward men and the fact that Lena and Melanie travelled to the US together separately from Paul and Lesya).

She Speaks Too Much Russian

In addition to the attitudes expressed in the interview data, the importance of English was also established through explicit talk about English and Russian in family conversations. As mentioned above, proficiency in English symbolized belonging in the family for the Goellers, and this is evident in explicit talk about language competence. In the following excerpt, Melanie constructs Valentina's Russian competence as a detriment to her English development despite the fact that Valentina's ability to speak Russian often facilitated family communications with Lesya and Lena as she played the role of interpreter.

Excerpt 6.5 Valentina speaks too much Russian
(3E, October 25, 2007, Lesya – 15, Lena – 17)
(Cyrillic followed by Roman transliteration on second line and English translation on third line; words spoken in Russian are italicized)

1	Melanie:	Because Valentina,
2		*слишком много говорит по-русски,*
		slishkom mnogo govorit po-russkiy
		speaks too much Russian
3		*она по-английски [anh anh ph ph. <mock spitting>*
		ona po-angliski [anh anh ph ph <mock spitting>
		she speaks English [anh anh ph ph. <mock spitting>
4	Valya:	[/???/
5	?:	Hahhhh!
6	?:	Hhhh!
7	Melanie:	She speaks too much Russian and her English is getting bad.

Paul was out of town during this mealtime recording, and all of the children were present. Here Melanie switches to Russian to make her point about Valentina speaking too much Russian in lines 2–3, which makes the children laugh (presumably at the spitting noises that fill in for the more complex Russian construction, 'is getting bad'), and then summarizes what she has said in English in line 7. Melanie's use of both languages here makes the point clear to both the Russian-dominant and English-dominant children that Valentina is using Russian too much, and this, by extension, is because of Lesya and Lena's continued Russian use. Additionally, although the real problem with Valentina's Russian use has been the rift among the siblings that it created, here Melanie invokes a more macro-level ideology (i.e. that acquisition of one language leads to attrition or deterioration of another) to warn the children against using Russian even though the current conflicts are taking place at the micro, family internal, level. Thus micro- and macro-level phenomena are taken together here to construct parental language ideologies and power over the children's language choice.

Becoming an English-Speaking Family Member

Backtracking to the beginning of the data collection, in the first few months after Lesya and Lena's arrival in June, Melanie and Paul addressed the teenagers almost exclusively in Russian as seen in the following excerpt where Melanie switches to Russian to offer the girls food:

Excerpt 6.6 Cold beets
(3B, July 18, 2007, Lesya – 15; Lena – 16)

1	Melanie:	Anybody else want cold beets before I warm them up?
2	?:	Me please.
3		Right there.

4		Thank you.
5	Paul:	\<clears throat\>
6	Melanie:	Mkay.
7		Lena? Lesya?
8		*Ты хочешь?*
		Ti hochesh?
		Do you want some?
9	Lena?:	No.
10	Melanie:	*Холодно?*
		Holodno?
		Cold?
11		No?
12		*Хорошо.*
		Horosho.
		Ok.
13		((pause))

In line 1 Melanie offers 'cold beets' to the whole family in English (she is about to heat them up for one of the boys who has requested them hot). One child takes her up on the offer, and then in line 8 Melanie switches to Russian to offer the salad to Lesya and Lena, 'Lesya, Lena, ti hochesh?'. This type of participant-related switching represents an accommodation to the girls' Russian dominance, but it can also be alienating, as Auer (1984) indicates that at the same time that it implies accommodation, it also implies a face threat. Switching languages in this case sets Lena and Lesya apart from the rest of the family, who are addressed in English by their parents, and in interviews Lesya and Lena said that they would prefer family members spoke to them in English. Additionally, one of the girls responds here in English in line 9 ('no'), further suggesting a request to change the medium of communication. However, Lena and Lesya do not always request their parents to switch to English when addressed in Russian. The fact that one of them switches to English here might be related to the simplicity of the conversation (i.e. an offer of food). Potentially, a further implication might be that the girls are demonstrating a preference for their parents to use English while they continue to use Russian, as will be seen below.

Starting as early as the second month after Lesya and Lena's arrival, Melanie began to negotiate English language use from the girls and Lena in particular. Melanie suggested in interviews that these active efforts to encourage and support Lena's English productions were based on her judgments of Lena's language competence and readiness to speak English, as well as her concerns about some divisions that Russian use seemed to be causing between the siblings. Melanie initiates the following conversation, about some dental work Lena had done earlier that day, in Russian, but then slowly switches to English. Here Lena does not switch languages until prompted to do so by Melanie.

Excerpt 6.7 Teeth
(3D, August 21, 2007, Lesya – 15; Lena – 17)

1	Melanie:	*Хорошо?*
		Horosho?
		Ok?
2		It's ok?
3		*Не больно?*
		Ne bol'no?
		It doesn't hurt?
4	Lena:	Не привычно, что там ak ((creaky noise)) пломба.
		Ne privichno, shto tam ack ((creaky noise)) plomba.
		It's unusual, that there's ack ((creaky noise)) a filling.
5	Melanie:	Yes.
6	Lena:	*Дырка.*
		Dirka.
		A hole.
7	Melanie:	Yeh.
8	Lena:	*Сделали.*
		Sdelali.
		They made.
9	Melanie:	Yeh.
10	Lena:	*Не привычно.*
		Ne privichno.
		It's unusual.
11	Melanie:	Oh yeh, yeh.
12		Feels funny?
13	Lena:	*И зубы,*
		I zubi,
		And the teeth,
14		*Они были такие кч ((noise))*
		Oni bili takie kch ((noise))
		They were like kch ((noise))
15	Melanie:	Yeh.
16		((Paul talking in background))

17	Lena:	*Маленькие.*
		Malenkie.
		The small ones.
18		*Были большие,*
		Bili bol'shie,
		They were big,
19	Melanie:	Mhm.
20	Lena:	Mm.
21	Melanie:	Way back there?
22		Ah!
23	Lena:	/Yeh/.
24	Melanie:	Mhm.
25		So you still have three,
26		one over there?
27	Lena:	*Здесь* three uh huh huh. ((talking with mouth open))
		Zdes' three uh huh huh. ((talking with mouth open))
		Here three uh huh huh. ((talking with mouth open))
28	Melanie:	Three.
29	Lena:	*И,* three three.
		I, three three.
		And, three three.
30	Melanie:	Three and three?
31		Three, three, three, three?
32	Lena:	No!
33		Three *уже,*
		Three *uzhe,*
		Three *already,*
34	Melanie:	Yeh, already, yes.
35	Lena:	*Здесь.*
		Zdes'.
		Here.
36	Melanie:	Yes, those [three have to be done, yes
37	Lena:	[Three
38	Lena:	Uh,
39	Inna:	/Mommy/?
40	Lena:	Two.
41	Melanie:	Two over [there, yes.
42	Lena:	[*Моей*
		[*Moeyi.*
		[*Mine*
43	?:	/???/

44	Lena:	/???/
45	Melanie:	Yes, /plus those/.
46	Inna:	Mommy?
47	Melanie:	Yes.
48	Inna:	Uhm, daddy ah . said I have to take the uhm things out of the –
49		the napkins that people have thrown in the garbage.
50		I said, uh, I have to thro – th – reach my hand into the garbage.
51		I mean, I said I have to reach my hand into the toilet – I mean garbage.
52	Melanie:	Ok.
53	Inna:	And then I said at least it's better than the TOILET!
54	Melanie:	Thank you, Inna.
55	Lena:	Bl, bl, blblblbl ((imitating Inna's English)).

While Melanie initiates this episode in Russian, once she has Lena engaged, she begins to switch to English. Here Melanie has set up a Russian language context through her initial initiations of this conversation (she has spoken almost exclusively in Russian about the dentist office visit) and Lena follows by responding in Russian. Melanie begins to shift toward English as the conversation goes on – first just with backchannels 'yeh', 'oh yeh' (lines 11–12) and then with an approximate translation of Lena's repeated utterance, 'ne privichno', or 'feels funny'. Melanie continues to backchannel in English for several turns, 'yeh...mhm'. This allows Lena to maintain Russian use by showing understanding, but not requesting a medium change. Lena does simplify her Russian and uses sounds and one-word utterances in order to be understood (maintaining a Russian-language inter-action), using what Zentella (1997) calls an 'I speak mine, you speak yours' mode of communication and which Gafaranga (2010) notes as a parallel mode of conversation.

Finally, Melanie asks a direct question in English in line 21, 'Way back there?'. This question does function as a medium repair and causes Lena to shift to English in line 23, 'yeh', and then to mix English and Russian in her following responses. However, the only word that Lena utters in English during this exchange is the numeral 'three'. The other half of each utterance, 'zdes, uzhe and i' all of which are small words and easily translated to English, 'here', 'already' and 'and', she says in Russian. This is a type of discourse-related switching that can be explained in two main ways: (a) Lena is using Russian as a matrix language and slotting relevant English noun phrase into the Russian base, or (b) she is using repetition (both other-repetition of Melanie who first questions 'Three?') and then self repetition of the noun phrase 'three' to create cohesion and solidarity while maintaining Russian. Melanie attempts to repair again, correcting uzhe to 'already' in line 34, but Lena continues in a mixed code.

In an interview where Melanie listened to this clip, she commented that she knew Lena knew the word 'uzhe' and so repeated it in English to help her remember. Here we see the role that questions and other initiators (first pair parts) play in determining the language of interaction, as Melanie's questions trigger Lena to switch to English and reinforce the English language discourse context. Lena's English productions 'three' along with Russian adverbs and adjectives suggest that a type of discourse-related switching is also at play in that Lena repeats her mother, 'three', and maintains cohesion through choice of English for the numbers, while at the same time maintaining a Russian preference in choice of the function words.

At the end of this excerpt, Inna (one of the English-dominant adoptees in the family) recounts a story to her mother about putting her hand in the trash can (because people had thrown trash in the can when there was no bag). Melanie responds briefly in a slightly dismissive manner, 'Thank you, Inna', and Lena then imitates Inna's English with nonsense syllables 'bl, bl, bl'. Here the juxtaposition of Inna's story with Lena's effortful explanation of the dentistry work she had done, as well as Lena's metalinguistic comment, suggest rising tension between the English-dominant and Russian-dominant siblings.

In the previous four episodes that took place from July to August 2007, or the first two months after Lesya and Lena's arrival, Melanie shifts strategies to negotiate an English monolingual interactional context with Lesya and Lena. We also see at the end of Excerpt 6.7 that conflict, or at least resentment, had begun to arise between the siblings over language competence, and this was further confirmed by interview reports in which Melanie suggested that they would start English-only dinners to assuage some of the division. Melanie's increasingly explicit promotion of English as a family language, then, is primarily motivated by the immediate problem (which she did not anticipate) of Russian being a dividing force between the new siblings and also her desire to help Lena and Lesya speak more English. By November, Melanie reported in interviews using mostly English in her conversations with the children. In the following section I will examine how Melanie, Lesya and Lena negotiate communication breakdowns and language choice in the later transcripts (November to February) as Melanie's English-language policy becomes more explicit and Lesya and Lena's English competence increases.

Perhaps the most explicit example of divergence in language choice between Melanie and Lesya and Lena is found in data from a mealtime in October (three months after the girls' arrival). Here, Lena and Lesya maintain an 'I speak mine, you speak yours' in interaction with their mother. Melanie makes a medium request by responding in English each time, and further distances herself from the Russian-language conversation by recruiting other siblings to serve as interpreters.

Excerpt 6.8 *Eh, mama, eto bol'no*
(3E, October 25, 2007, Lesya – 15, Lena –17)

1	Lena:	*Э, мама, это больно.*
		Eh, mama, eto bol'no.
		Oh, mama, this hurts.
2	?:	*/???/ ничего не делала.*
		/???/ nichego ne delala.
		/???/ didn't do anything._
3	Lena:	*Мама.*
4		*Это /???/.*
		Eto /???/.
		This /???/.
5	Melanie:	Ok.
6		I'll get you something after dinner I'll give you some - some medicine.
7	Lena:	*/Я не люблю medicine/.*
		/Ya ne lublu medicine/.
		/I don't like ((also 'love')) medicine/.
8		*Я не люблю /???/.*
		Ya ne lublu /???/.
		I don't like ((love)) /???/.
9	Valentina?:	/???/
10	Lesya:	*Почему ((to Valentina))?*
		Pochemy ((to Valentina))?
		Why ((to Valentina))?
11	Melanie:	She doesn't love what?
12	?	/???/
13	Valentina?:	/???/
14	Lesya:	*У нее горло [болит сегодня.*
		U nee gorlo [bolit segodnia.
		Her throat [hurts today.
15	Melanie:	[When /your/ head hurts?
16	?:	Uh, uh, uh!

17	Melanie:	Yeh, nobody does.
18		Yeh, nobody likes it.
19	?:	I like it.
20	Melanie:	No, you do not.

Here, Melanie used several strategies to negotiate the conversation away from Russian. Lena complains in Russian directly to her mother in line 1 that something hurts. Melanie responds directly in English in lines 5–6 ('Ok. I'll get you something . . . I'll give you some . . . medicine'). Lena does not initially acknowledge the medium request and continues in her preferred choice of Russian, but then uses the English word 'medicine' in line 7. Melanie then further diverges and dismisses Lena's Russian by recruiting another sibling to translate, 'What doesn't she love?', even though the object in question (i.e. medicine) was stated in English. The selection of another speaker as interpreter here further distances Melanie from the Russian-language conversation and signals a refusal to participate. Melanie then directs her next turns toward her again, 'When your head hurts? . . . Yeah, nobody does'. In this sequence, both Lena and Melanie make their code preferences clear through medium requests/repairs and refusals to switch to each other's chosen language. This pattern might suggest a preference for a parallel conversation in which Melanie used English and Lena used Russian, but Melanie's strategies of distancing Lena by recruiting a third interlocutor as translator suggest a frustration with and dismissal of Lena's continued use of Russian. Thus while Lena has established agency in negotiating her code preference, it has been at the expense of her mother's patience and accommodation in this episode.

The previous excerpts have demonstrated how code negotiations between Lesya and Lena and their parents were related to parental accommodation and divergence, as well as assumptions about linguistic competence (e.g. Melanie felt that Lena should be able to use the English words when talking about her teeth in Excerpt 6.7). As Russian came to be viewed as a disruption in the family unit, Melanie used more explicit strategies to negotiate away from its use. The active negotiation away from Russian coincides with the perception of Lena as a good English-language learner and potentially better and faster than the other siblings at learning language. Framed in this way, Melanie's efforts to negotiate toward English in conversation with Lena are part of a solidarity-building process as she encourages Lena to speak more English and to learn (as in Excerpt 6.8). However, a parallel process occurred in which Lesya and Lena demonstrated preference for a parallel mode of communication in which their parents used their dominant language, English, while the teenagers used their dominant language, Russian. This preference was potentially related to Lesya and Lena's focus on the purity of Russian. For example, Lena in particular noted the mistakes that Melanie made when speaking Russian:

Excerpt 6.9 Russian is the hardest language
(Interview C; August 2, 2007)
  Original
  Lena: Мама говорит: Я возьму..., а Тебе сколько надо: два банка? Я такая: Мама, 'банка' – она моя, ну, женского рода, как бы, то есть это будет получается 'две банки', а 'стакан' – 'два стакана' там, 'десять стаканов', а она говорит: 'Почему?'. Она вот не понмает этого, то есть я ей объясняла, объясняла, она говорит: 'Ай, я не понимаю!' То есть в английском такого нету, как бы... Ну, русский вообще самый сложный язык, вообще как бы.

  English translation
  Lena: Mama says, I will take or how many do you need? Two jars? I say, Mama, banka – it is 'mine' [feminine singular] – well, feminine gender, like it will be 'dve banki' [feminine plural], and 'stakan' will be 'dva stakana' [masculine plural] and 'desyat' stakanov' [masculine plural], and she says, Why? She doesn't understand this, that is I explained it to her, explained it, and she says, 'Ay! I don't understand!' That is English doesn't have this, like, ... well, Russian in general is the hardest language, like in general.

In addition, Lena at times displayed frustration with mixing her languages and not being aware of which language she was speaking. Lesya, on the other hand, while also commenting on heritage Russian speakers' 'incorrect' varieties of Russian and a desire to maintain her 'better' Russian, did not correct her parents in interaction.

They Will Help Us in English, and We Will Help Them in Russian

While the two teenagers, Lesya and Lena, began to use more English with their parents over the eight months of the study, they also found ways to maintain Russian language use with the other siblings, primarily Valentina and David who had arrived more recently than Tolya and Inna, and initially were better able to communicate with Lesya and Lena in Russian. As mentioned above, family members noted that Valentina in particular began to speak more and better Russian after the teenagers arrived. This caused a rift in the family as Inna was left out of the Russian-speaking girls' interactions. At first, gender seemed to play a role in who spoke what language in family interactions, but over time David, Valentina's biological brother, also began to speak more Russian and be included in the three girls' Russian conversations. David's own medium requests (for Russian) ultimately played a role in the teenagers' use of Russian with him in interaction.

In Excerpt 6.10 from July, one month after Lesya and Lena's arrival, David seems unwilling to switch to Russian to interact with Lena.

Excerpt 6.10 *On strashniy?*
(3B, July 18, 2007, Lena – 16, David – nine)

1	Lena:	*Ну и как Давид, он страшный?*
		Nu i kak David, on strashnyi?
		Well and what's he like, David, is he weird?
2	David:	/I don't know what you're asking me/
3	Lena:	*Страшный?*
		Strashnyi?
		Weird?
4	David:	What?
5	Lena:	*Откуда – .. откуда они его знают?*
		Otkuda – .. otkuda oni ego znayut?
		How – how do they know him?
6	?:	*Они - [они.*
		Oni – [oni
		They – [they.
7	David:	[*Он /ходил/* tae kwon do.
		[*On /hodil/* tae kwon do.
		[*He /went/* tae kwon do.
8	Valentina?:	*Он хоДИЛ там.*
		On hoDIL tam.
		He WENT there.
9	Melanie:	((*from other room*)) Lesya!
10	Paul:	Do you have tae kwon do today? Valya ((Valentina))?

Lena initiates the conversation with a question in Russian in line 1. David responds that he doesn't understand, 'I don't know what you're asking me', in line 2. This is an explicit comment that addresses both David's language competence and potentially Lena's code choice. However, Lena does not switch to English at this point nor does she recruit Valya to help out. Instead she chooses to negotiate for meaning in Russian and simplifies the question by repeating the word 'strashniy' or 'weird'. Lena's continuation in Russian is most likely related to her language competence – this is only the first month after their arrival, and the teenagers are not using much English in family conversations at this point. However, David's response changes as the two negotiate over code choice and meaning.

In line 4 David replies to the simplified Russian again in English with a clarification request, 'What?'. At this point Lena directs a completely different question to Valya who often played the role of language broker in the family, 'Otkuda oni ego znayut', (How do they know him?). Now David understands the question and responds in Russian, 'On hodil tam' (line 7), which Valya repeats. David's Russian response even after Lena had dropped him as a conversational partner (turning to Valya and referring to David and his brother Tolya as 'they'), suggests that David is willing to and even wants to take part in the Russian conversation with Lena as long as it is at a level that he comprehends and in which he can participate. This example suggests, in keeping with Kasanga (2008), that negotiation over language choice also involves negotiation for meaning. That is, in order for Lena to maintain the Russian language context with her siblings, she is required to simplify and revise her questions so that she is understood.

In this way, the process of language learning shapes the interactional context and the actual meanings that are conveyed in the interaction. Negotiation for meaning serves a social goal of accommodating to speakers' language competencies in much the same way that code-switching can. Once Lena makes accommodations to her interlocutors' language competence, David converges in turn by responding in Russian. The negotiation of language choice therefore involves not only pragmatic functions of deciding on the language between interlocutors, but also negotiations of language competence. Successful negotiations lead to increased use of Russian by the bilingual children and finally the building of relationships because of the ability to speak Russian.

In the following excerpt, taken seven months later, at the end of the study, David demonstrates an active preference to speak Russian with Lesya, the other sister. Here Lesya initiates a conversation about food with David in Russian.

Excerpt 6.11 *Ne takuyu.*
(3K, February 23, 2008, Lesya – 15, Lena – 17)

1	Lesya:	/???/ *дай* /???/ *пожайлуйста* /???/.
		/???/ *give me* /???/ *please.*
2	Melanie:	She has some potato on her plate, I [see that.
3	David:	[Mm?

4	Lesya:	/???/
5	David:	Mm?
6	Lesya:	That.
7	?:	And corn.
8	David:	*Какую?*
		Kakuyu?
		Which one?
9	Lesya:	*[Любую.*
		[Lubuyu
		[Any one.
10	?:	[We -
11		/the/ juice.
12	David:	/???/
13	Lesya:	*Не большую, маленкую.*
		Ne bol'shuyu, malenkuyu.
		Not a big one, a small one.
14	Paul:	/???/ then you can have five of em?
	Lesya:	<burps> *[Нет не такую!*
		[Nyet ne takuyu!
15		*[No, not that one!*
16	Paul:	[/???/
17	?:	Hmm.
18	Paul:	Is that one too small?
19	Lesya:	*Не, не такую!*
		Ne, ne takuyu!
		No, not that one!
20		<laughter>
21	Lesya:	*[Нет, не такую.*
		[Nyet, ne takuyu.
		[No, not that one.
22	?:	[/???/
23	Lesya:	*Да, такую Давид.*
		Da, takuyu David.
		Yes, that one David.
24	?:	[Ye::h!
25	Inna?:	[This one!
26	David:	She picked for this one!
27	Tolya?:	Ho ho!
28	Paul:	I thought she said small, not big?
29	David:	[She said medium
30	Tolya?:	[Ho hoho!

31	Paul:	That's - that's not medium.
32	Tolya?:	[That's large!
33	David:	[That's the biggest one!
34	Melanie:	That's the biggest one in the pot.
35	Paul:	Hahhhh
36	?:	/???/
37	Melanie:	Mhm!

David responds to Lesya's requests for a potato with a minimal grasp in lines 3 and 5, 'Mm?'. Lesya interprets these responses as a need to switch languages (either because David does not understand her or because he doesn't want to be addressed in Russian). This is a similar strategy reported by Lanza (1997/2004), but in those data the mother used this technique as a response to her child's utterances that negotiated the conversation toward the other language. This demonstrated that even very young children were attuned to the interactional demands of the situation. Here, Lesya seems attuned to David's competence and the wider context of the English-speaking family. When David doesn't understand, she switches to his dominant language, English, 'that'; however, David leads the switch back to Russian in line 8 by asking 'Kakuyu?' or 'Which potato?'. This interaction suggests a desire on David's part to maintain the Russian-speaking context with Lesya, whether this be in relation to her older age and potentially higher status in the family or his own personal goals of remembering Russian as represented in Lesya and Lena's interview quote above.

Once Russian is established as the language of interaction, the question–answer sequence turns into a sort of a game as Lesya repeatedly corrects David's choice of potatoes from the pot. The whole family laughs at the 'This one? No, not that one' routine until Lesya finally selects a potato. David then comments on the interaction in English to the rest of the family members in line 26, 'She picked for this one', following Inna's switch to English. David's switch to English is participant-related as it shifts the conversation from a dyadic (i.e. David and Lesya) to multiparty interaction (i.e. the whole family). In line 28 Paul appears to be an eavesdropper on the children's conversation, 'I thought she said small, not big?', David's strategies here seem to build solidarity by including the English-dominant family members in the Russian language interaction. At the same time, this switch serves to construct the domains for the two languages in the whole family interaction where Russian can be used between Lesya and him, but English is for whole family use. Or more generally, Russian is used amongst the bilingual or Russian-dominant siblings (i.e. Lesya, Lena, Valya and David), and English is used when the English-dominant family members are involved. At the same time that these processes build solidarity, however, they also imply face threats by leaving some family members out of the interactions. Lesya and David, for example, exclude the rest of the family in their Russian talk, but when David switches to English to tell the rest of the family about the interaction, Lesya is then excluded. Thus code negotiation in this family was tied to constructing family relationships and solidarity building. The transnational adoptive family as a bilingual family, at least for the Goellers, is in a state of flux and conflict with code use intimately tied to power, status and language competence in the family sphere.

Conclusion

The assumption is often made that when second language learners switch languages it is usually because of a lack of knowledge in the second language. In the examples above, participant-related switching, and in some cases discourse-related switching, were both shaped by and shaped the social processes of establishing family relationships and family bonding in the Goeller family. Language learners can and do switch languages for social purposes, and speakers with very limited competencies in their second or other languages can make a choice to accommodate to their interlocutors by initiating negotiation for meaning in the weaker language. The choice of which language will be negotiated is related to both the social goals of interlocutors and the knowledge of the languages. Further, language competence played an important role in the family dynamics of this adoptive family specifically around power relations between the mother and two teenage girls, as well as establishing sibling relationships. The data here suggest that code-switching in intergenerational communication can not only point to negotiation of cultural norms and values between older and younger generations, but also to what it means to be a family. Language competence, proficiency and preference all play a role in how family members regard one another and establish relationships. More specifically, in this family the choice to actively negotiate an English-only context by the mother was tied not only to the status of English and language ideologies, but also to the divisions that the use of two languages by the siblings was perceived to create in the family sphere (i.e. by excluding the weaker Russian speakers).

The findings in this chapter contribute to recent work on language maintenance and shift, which has begun to focus on micro interactions to better understand how these processes are 'talked into being' (Gafaranga, 2010). Such studies have further pointed to the role of macrosociolingusitic realities in shaping family internal language use patterns (Canagarajah,

2008; Gafaranga, 2010). Macrolinguistic factors contribute to children's agency by providing the impetus for a shift in the first place and reinforcing the use of the majority language in the family sphere by shaping parental language ideologies. This chapter has examined these processes in a different type of transnational family (i.e. the adoptive family where the children are expected to learn and use the majority language as the language of the family). In these data, the children's agency, as instantiated in code negotiation and the continued use of Russian, is achieved in two main ways: (a) the parents' accommodation and learning of Russian, and (b) the sibling culture that emerges outside of parent–child interaction.

In this family, macrosociolinguistic phenomena such as English as the community language and the need to learn English to succeed in school shaped, but did not solely determine, the language use patterns in the Goeller family. In fact, Melanie only began to invoke these ideologies once disturbances arose in the family among the children and language competence seemed to deepen these rifts (i.e. Lesya, Lena and Valya were leaving the fourth daughter Inna out of their Russian language interactions). More often, micro-level interactions and politics of status and power in the family relations played a role in who spoke what language to whom. The ability and willingness to speak Russian also played a role in the relationships the four previously adopted children made with the new arrivals Lesya and Lena. As the parents and children sorted out these new realities, the four more dominant Russian-speaking children were able to carve out a space in the family interactions for Russian language use and manage interactions in such a way that Russian and English could be used in the family sphere. These findings suggest the ways that children might actively negotiate language shift toward a dominant language in minority language families, as well as how children's preferences and competencies influence their interlocutors' code choice. Further, these findings suggest that these phenomena are mediated by ideologies of language as well as the need to form bonding relationships.

As discussed at the outset, linguistic purism is an aspect of Russian language ideologies. Lesya and Lena often cited a need to separate languages or speak pure Russian. In several cases they exhibited low tolerance for learner Russian or contact varieties of Russian. This ideology potentially provided a backdrop for the language negotiations that went on in the family. In some cases, power dynamics shifted as Lena in particular corrected her mother's Russian. Further, the desire to not mix languages potentially competed with Melanie's efforts to encourage the girls to speak English. The girls tended to prefer a 'you speak yours; I'll speak mine' or parallel mode of communication with their parents. Purism also determined with whom the girls tried to speak Russian as they continued to use Russian with the two middle adoptees throughout the data collection. Thus the Goeller family represented a complex intersection of language ideologies, bonding processes and language learning that shaped and were shaped by code negotiation in family conversations.

Notes

(1) I am grateful to the anonymous reviewer of the manuscript for this perspective.

7 Conclusions and Implications

Building on prior language socialization research in first language and bilingual contexts, in this book I have discussed how language socialization processes (e.g. telling stories about the day, talking about language and code-switching) play out in the second language-learning context of the adoptive family. I have examined how older transnational adoptees as second language learners play an active role in second language socialization processes in their new families. By taking a language socialization approach, I have shown that language learning is shaped by and shapes the discourse context of the family as well as ideological perspectives and identities in family interactions. To conclude this book, I will return to the discussion of learner agency in second language studies that I began in Chapter 2, and will consider how second language research could better employ the construct in light of the findings of this study. I will also talk about identities and speaker roles, focusing on how more in-depth research into the micro identities constructed in interaction can inform second language-learning research. Finally, I turn to the implications of the findings from this study for providing support for older transnational adoptees as they learn a new language in their new home contexts.

Agency in Language Socialization

As I pointed out in Chapter 2, the role that children themselves play in language socialization processes might best be explained with reference to the construct of agency or 'the socioculturally mediated capacity to act' (Ahearn, 2001) that is achieved in interaction (Al Zidjaly, 2009). Child agency is a significant force in language socialization that can determine family language policies, parental interactional strategies and children's outcomes (Fogle & King, in press). From a macrosociolinguistic perspective, children's agency also determines societal processes of language maintenance and shift, as well as cultural transformation and change (Gafaranga, 2010). Further, as shown in this study, transnational adoptees' achievement of interactional agency is one means through which adoptive families are transformed into a new kind of US family. It is also a key to how and what adoptees learn.

Most studies of second language learning focus on one type of agency (i.e. of participation or control) that connects with and facilitates learning outcomes. However, facilitative agency is not the only type of agency children achieve in learning contexts. In fact, more often, resistance in learning processes leads to negative representations and failure to learn. In this book I have demonstrated that different types of agency emerge in different contexts and that types of agency that might not be facilitative in one context (e.g. resistance) could potentially have a completely different effect in another context. The three types of agency I have identified in this book, resistance, participation and negotiation, all led to changes in the interactional environment and increased opportunities for language learning and identity construction for the children.

In the Sonderman family, Dima's resistance to a socializing routine was instantiated in a 'nothing' response to his father's narrative prompts. While this type of linguistic resistance would most likely not fare well in the classroom, in this family it opened up interactional space for new types of discourse. In the Jackson-Wessels, the high-level of conversation that was ongoing between the parents was negotiated by the children's frequent use of what-questions that afforded the children agency in selecting themselves as speakers and placing the parents in a responsive role. The use of what-questions opened up opportunities for learning through the initiation of languaging episodes or metalinguistic discourse by the parents. In the third family, the Goellers, the children exercised agency in choosing and/or shaping the language of interaction in different situations in the family. While much of the family's conversations were negotiated toward English, over the course of the study the newly arrived teenagers were able to carve out a domain for Russian language use among the Russian-competent siblings. In addition, the processes through which the adoptees in this study developed agency in their interactions with parents socialized the children into practices that could help them assert such agency, through asking for assistance or rejecting representations that did not fit with their own sense of self.

The Conflicted, Complex Nature of Agency

Studies in second language learning have begun to take an 'agency' turn. Agency is cited as an explanatory factor for learners' successful participation in interactional tasks and classroom-based learning. Agency and identity are related constructs in language learning, and the relationship between the good learner identity and actual learning is potentially mediated by agency, as discussed in Chapter 2. Learners who both conform to expectations and norms in the classroom and find ways to act to obtain necessary input, interaction and scaffolding that meet their individual needs most likely have a better chance at learning by mainstream standards than those who passively take on the good student role (e.g. Rymes & Pash, 2001) or who actively resist the structures of the classroom (McKay & Wong, 1996). Recent approaches to language teaching have further outlined approaches to teaching designed to facilitate learner agency (e.g. van Lier, 2007). These approaches seem fruitful in directing teachers' and researchers' attention to the structures in the learning environment that constrain learner agency.

However, agency is multiple and varied and greater attention to the interactional processes through which agency is achieved in second language learning is necessary to continue our work in this area. Al Zidjaly (2009) concluded that the participants in her study achieved agency through multiple strategies, including asking questions, speaking for another and asserting expertise among others. Gafaranga found that a strategy of 'medium request', or not following parents' language choice, led to agency in code choice by children. Further, Kasanga's (2008) findings that teenage peers in interaction with one another found ways to negotiate for meaning in order to accommodate to others' code preferences also point to ways in which accommodation affords agency in interaction. In the current study, resistant strategies in the form of 'nothing' responses were an additional example of the assertion of agency in interaction. All of these strategies represent or can lead to more than one type of agency. Dima's resistance, for example, led to greater participation in other types of discourse. Anna and Arkadiy's questioning strategies as participation often crossed a fine line toward control and sometimes resulted in negative evaluation from the parents. Lesya and Lena's negotiation strategies represented active participation at the same time as they divided the family and created new relationships and domains. Further studies in this area will surely lead to understanding other ways of interactionally achieving agency and the implications not only for learning processes, but also for social change and cultural transformation. One future goal of this research should be toward a greater understanding of the complex nature of agency in learning and how agencies interact and influence learning processes.

In conclusion, it is not the children's actions in and of themselves that I have found theoretically interesting in these analyses. Rather, actions imply a result, and the effect that learner agency has on experts or other members of a community of practice (e.g. family or classroom) seems key to understanding the role of agency in language learning and socialization. While the parents in the three families examined here expected their children to fit into certain norms and practices, they were willing to adjust to children's resistance and control. This accommodation might have contradicted parents' stated beliefs, but it did not seem to conflict with their notions of what it meant to be a 'good child' or a 'good parent' (e.g. none of the parents in this study expressed any kind of sentiment like they could not parent their adopted child or that their children did not belong in their home). The accommodations that experts make to novices (or interlocutors in general) in interaction over time imply transformation and change on both the micro and macro level. From a macro perspective, children's practices (and parents' responses to them) can account for language change and shift. Although studies of language shift have focused on parent ideologies and have made a strong case that preexisting beliefs about children and the status of local languages have affected change (King, 2000; Kulick, 1993), it seems there is also reason to examine how children's practices affect parents' ideologies (Fogle & King, in press).

Adoptive families are changing the social fabric of US family life in terms of how we view kinship and multiculturalism – some white mothers of Chinese children have come to consider themselves Asian American (Jacobson, 2008) and English-speaking parents, like the ones in this study, learn Russian and develop transnational ties with people on a different continent who were involved in their adopted children's early life. These phenomena are related to culture-specific notions about accommodating to children, and it seems that parents who are able to negotiate their own beliefs about family and allow adopted children agency in the process of forming family are better equipped and have more successful outcomes (Stryker, 2010). Further, in situations where parents are not sure what learning a second language is like or do not initially understand their children's linguistic needs, the bidirectional socialization process is crucial to creating a beneficial learning environment for the children and promoting family bonding. In this way, second language learning in families with older adoptees is a process of learning to be a family.

Second language teachers and researchers can take from these findings a sense of the unique way that establishing bonding relationships and affect facilitated second language-learning processes. One of the major differences between the adoptive family environment and the classroom is the relationship that forms between adults/experts and children/novices. In prior work with these transnational adoptive families, I have argued that examining the family discourse can provide a better understanding of what learners can do in one-on-one interaction with caring adults (Fogle, 2008b). Several classroom-based studies have also reported on the benefits of close interaction with a more competent adult outside of teacher-fronted instruction. In an often-cited study of variation in SLA, Tarone and Liu (1996), for example, found that one boy's acquisition of higher stage question forms occurred in interaction with an adult tutor (and not in other contexts such as the classroom and peer interaction). Further Kotler *et al.* (2001) found that children who participated in a conversation partners program with working adults from the community made rapid gains. Together, these studies argue that children are able to take more risks in comfortable situations such as tutor sessions, and that the one-on-one time with an adult leads to more scaffolded interaction that guides the learners.

In addition, such contexts and the relationships that are formed with adult interlocutors (i.e. the boy in the Tarone and Liu study was *friends* with his tutor) provide possibilities for learners to imagine themselves in English-speaking roles and identities outside of the classroom. Thus, constructing some kind of second language identity in parallel to the 'English learner' or 'good student' identity can facilitate language learning not only by encouraging risk taking, but also by providing an additional purpose and more authentic social goal for interacting in English. These findings connect with the recent work of Lapkin *et al.* (2010) on languaging with elderly dementia patients. Their study found that establishing affect and a personal bond were related to the assertion of agency in the learning process. These processes helped to construct new zones of proximal development between the patient and more competent interlocutors that led to learning. Understanding when, where and with whom learners use their second languages outside of the classroom seems crucial to understanding the complex social processes involved in language learning within the classroom.

The complex nature of agency, and specifically the extent to which it is mediated by external, contextual factors, has prompted some to question whether the concept has any theoretical validity at this point (Norris, 2005). Other approaches are beginning to emerge in second language learning and bilingual research (e.g. nexus analysis [Hult, 2010] and complexity theory [Larsen Freeman & Cameron, 2008]) that emphasize the importance of external and historical processes. However, as the analyses in this book show, the affordance of individual agency makes a difference in learning processes for children. Further research in these areas will help us to contextualize the individual further and understand how culturally sensitive our own research paradigms are.

Learner Identities: Summing Up

Related to the construct of agency, the concept of identity and positive identity formation has also played an important role in education research. Bilingual children have been found to perform better in valorized environments such as two-way immersion programs (Cummins, 2001). Discontinuities between home and school identities have been found to lead to school dropouts and other perceived social problems (Lin, 2007). Further, establishing affiliative identities with schooling has been found to facilitate second language acquisition and school performance (Hawkins, 2005; Willett, 1995). In addition, identity and specifically constructing an adoption narrative, has been viewed as important to the mental health and school success of child adoptees (Grovetant, 1997). In this study I have shown how second language-learning children construct discursive identities on three main levels in the supportive environment of the family: through taking on different speaker roles, through the repetitions of these roles and stances in everyday interactions and through reference to distant times and places. Prior studies of language socialization have focused on speaker roles and participation structures to show how children and other novices acquire communicative competence through routines. These studies show the importance of examining speaker roles in family interactions and the repetitions of these roles over time. They do not, however, touch on what other types of identities can be established in families when family members break away from these routines.

Speaker roles, identified through patterns of initiation and response, were found to be important in the current study in constructing everyday power relations in the family conversations and negotiating the types of discourse activities that took place in those interactions. The repetition of these roles and the evaluative stances that went along with them (e.g. persistently resisting another speaker's elicitations) led to constructions of family identities such as Dima, a preteen boy, being 'unwilling' to talk about himself. Such repetitions of the everyday are considered to be elemental, in terms of the individual, to making up a coherent 'self' (Lemke, 2000), and in terms of the family are characterized by Garrett and Baquedano-Lopéz (2002: 343) as the 'warp and woof of human sociality'.

While the mundane and the routine serve to explain continuity across generations in a culture or a self across contexts, focus on the everyday has in some ways precluded consideration of the momentary, ephemeral events that might also have importance in socialization processes. Surprising, out-of-the-ordinary or innovative events (including conversations) can have lasting effects on people's beliefs and practices, although they might not hold the same type of analytical power as uncovering patterns in repetition. Experiencing war, the loss of loved ones or another type of trauma are extreme examples of out-of-the-ordinary events that can influence a person's developmental trajectory. In the same way, unexpected conversations or memorable utterances such as confessions of love, jokes, denigrations or criticisms and other speech acts can stay with an individual over time and influence future behaviors.

In these data I have singled out talk about pre-adoption time in Ukraine and Russia to show how family members in two of the families broke from regular routines to construct a shared history or at least part of a shared adoption narrative. These out-of-the-ordinary instances, I argue, allow for connection of the momentary discussion (in these cases about the meanings of words) to longer timescales through reference to the distant past. These narrative activities, which were not everyday events, allowed the family members to conceptualize themselves in relation to the current time and place (i.e. urban, middle-class English-speaking families in the United States). Because the process of becoming a family across times and places is of immediate importance in these transnationally adoptive families, the need to step out of everyday routines to do this kind of discursive identity work on longer timescales is apparent.

In much the same way that constructing an adoption narrative or telling stories about Ukraine and Russia gave the children in the Sonderman and Jackson-Wessels families a way to connect their pasts to their present lives, Lesya and Lena in the Goeller family used Russian in communication with the other adoptees to symbolically maintain a connection with the past time and place. As a heritage language within this family, the use of Russian served to remind family members of where the children came from and what they knew and did before their arrival in the United States. These examples of the children taking an agentive role in finding opportunities for long-term identity construction connect with what Grovetant *et al.* (2007) describe as an 'integrated' or unified adoptee self identity that can have benefits in schooling and post-school careers (although, of course, this narrative is only one display of self and identities are multiple and con-textual). The findings from this study contribute to this line of research by showing how such narratives are initiated and constructed in the family interactions, as well as the fact that other types of language use such as maintaining a heritage language can contribute to developing a sense of self.

While these findings have important implications for adoption research, they can also be applied to research on other child second language learners. Recent studies in Native American heritage language communities have found that children often have positive attitudes toward their native languages and even criticize members of older generations who no longer speak the languages in day-to-day interactions (McCarty, 2009). These attitudes and the efforts younger generations have been found to make in revitalizing heritage languages have led researchers such as McCarty to refer to children in these communities as 'the youngest policymakers'. Connecting the past with the present, then, has implications for all language learners, and particularly those in transnational settings, who have an interest in revitalizing or maintaining their languages or even creating a sense of self across discontinuities such as language shift, migration or other sociopolitical/sociohistorical disruptions. In these data I have shown that the children are able to begin to do this through self-initiated narrative activities and language negotiations that maintain the use of their native languages. In other words, as argued in this book, learner agency is essential to these processes.

Implications for Supporting Transnational Adoptees

When school-age adoptees arrive in new homes in the US they have the potential to be bilingual and, in the early months of their lives in the home, are best seen as emergent bilinguals. Aside from the typical reasons cited by US parents for wanting to raise their children bilingually – e.g. it will help with future career development, it will maintain cultural ties and heritage and it will potentially provide some cognitive benefits (Bialystok, 2009; King & Fogle, 2006) – there are three main reasons why parents might wish to actively support adoptees' first language maintenance after arrival: (a) speaking Russian or the child(ren)'s first language at home smoothes the transition to the new family and makes the family environment less threatening; (b) maintaining the child's first language facilitates academic development; and (c) maintaining the first language provides long-term possibilities for belonging in two cultures and retaining the child's heritage, which will be important in later years. I discuss each of these points in detail below.

Much of the advice provided to adoptive parents about language has been based on clinicians' observations rather than empirical data, and linguistic theories have been misinterpreted in some of this literature, as discussed in Chapter 3. That work has narrowly focused on the prior lives of adoptees and the potential for risk associated with their backgrounds. However, the immigrant experience itself can be disruptive, and the transition to a US English-speaking home in and of itself possesses inherent disruptions and incongruencies for children. Thus, as Stryker (2011) argues, interventions and treatments for adoptees should consider the context of development within the new family. For language, this should take into account best practices for bilingual children that center on ways to maintain and develop competence in both languages.

As noted above, there are three main reasons for supporting older adoptees in the maintenance of their first languages. First, as adoptive parents suggested in interview data (Fogle, in press) and was seen in both the Sonderman and Goeller families in this study, Russian can be a useful resource in smoothing the transition to the new home and parents' use of Russian in particular can facilitate emotional bonding between parents and children. In this sense, the home becomes a safe place where Russian can be spoken and the outside world is the domain of English. Adoptive parents and the therapists and other professionals who work with them should be aware that learning English can be a challenging and frustrating process for young children that takes time. We tend to think of children as 'sponges' who soak up knowledge and language easily, and children often do appear to pick up conversational competence in another language easily. However, countless studies, including this one, have shown the laborious cognitive, social and emotional processes involved in childhood language learning (Cruz-Ferreira, 2006; Toohey, 2000; Willett, 1995). Levine (1995), for example, has written an award-winning children's book about school-age English language learners' experiences entitled *I Hate English!* that sympathizes with and represents the child's point of view. One of the easiest ways to smooth these transitions is to maintain a mode of communication (i.e. the children's first language) between parents and children in which children can express their confusion, frustration or even sadness in leaving their friends and extended family in their prior homes.

Despite parents' and sometimes therapists' fears about use of the first language, use of the children's first language by parents, family members or caregivers validates adoptees' prior experiences and knowledge and provides a way to deal with emotional difficulties and talk about problems as they arise. Otherwise, children are required to make sense of the new environment on their own without explanation or the ability to ask questions. When I worked as a tutor for two adoptees, for example, they asked me questions in Russian like 'Why can't we drink tea at breakfast?' (which was considered healthful for children in Russia) and 'Why do we need to wear button-down shirts or fancy clothes' (and not t-shirts) around the house. Very basic aspects of US parenting and culture (i.e. that children shouldn't have caffeine or that people wear their 'nice' clothes in the house and do not change into more comfortable clothing immediately when they come home) were not apparent to the children and needed explanation. These may seem to be simple things to explain, but they point to deeply ingrained cultural differences and changes in their everyday lives that adopted children are trying to sort out and understand as they become members of the new family. It is not hard to imagine the kinds of explanations children *might* come up with on their own in explaining these difference (e.g. 'our parents don't like us, that's why they won't give us tea' or 'our parents didn't like the clothes we brought with us', etc.), which are far from the original intentions of the parents. Giving adoptees a voice in the early months as they transition to a new home, either through the parents' use of the first language or regular visits from an interpreter (e.g. a bilingual social worker) who can spend time talking with the children, is crucial.

Second, providing academic support in Russian from the start with Russian-speaking tutors or, if available, Russian-medium education, can assist adoptees in catching up to school expectations and norms. Extensive research demonstrates the benefits of first language maintenance and the development of literacy in a first language to young bilinguals' educational development and academic success (see for example discussions in Baker, 2000; Hornberger, 2003; King & Mackey, 2007). Russian children who have moved to Hebrew-medium schools in Israel at school age, for example, were found to take between seven and eight years to catch up to grade-level norms in math (Levin et al., 2002 reported in Shohamy, 2006). Maintaining an adoptee's first language during the transition to the US school system, and if possible beyond, could be the most valuable thing that parents do for their children academically.

In this study, this process was evident with John Sonderman's use of Russian at home (Chapter 4). Although, the data collection began after the children had switched to English, the ease with which Dima and Sasha transitioned to the US school and their literacy outcomes can, in comparison with prior research, be attributed to John's choice to use Russian, hire Russian tutors and help the boys with their homework and school routines in Russian. From a linguistic perspective these strategies gave the boys a boost academically that was clear when comparing Dima and Sasha to their peers in this study. In addition, Dima's one year of schooling in Ukraine most likely helped him in the transition to the US school as he was already reading above grade level by the end of the second year in the States. For Lesya and Lena in the Goeller family (Chapter 6), prior schooling helped, but their ages made the prospect of staying in school for an additional four years in the US daunting.

Third, maintaining Russian can help adoptees find a sense of belonging both in the new family and their culture and place of origin for the long term. Understanding the role of first language maintenance and heritage language learning for transnational adoptees should be a future goal for research in language and transnational adoption (see Higgins & Stoker, 2011). As this most recent wave of transnational adoptees from Eastern Europe and Asia grow into adolescence and adulthood, new studies are beginning to understand how they see themselves and how they belong in the transnational spaces they have occupied (Higgins & Stoker, 2011; Lo & Kim, 2011). Desires to return to birth cultures surface in some cases as an important part of being an adult adoptee, and one aspect of this is a desire to relearn first languages. What didn't seem possible to adoptive parents early on then becomes an aspect of family life through high school foreign language and other language programs (Fogle, in press). In addition, making heritage language maintenance an important part of family life, and not just the responsibility of the individual child, can also validate the children's experiences and help to construct a new, transnational adoptive family identity. In this study, two families (the Sondermans and the Goellers) made the children's first language a part of their everyday life, at least in the early period. Ironically, the US parents knew more Russian than some of the children after they had been in the States for an extended time. Bringing the children's first language into the adoptive home validates their past knowledge, competence and experiences. First language use in the adoptive family situates belonging to two cultures within the adoptive family and creates a safe space for adoptees to be who they are and imagine who they will become and involves the whole family in that process.

In conclusion, this book has followed trends in second language-learning research to take a more contextually sensitive approach to learning processes that views learning as tied to interactional processes of identity construction. In examining second language socialization in transnational adoptive families, I have shown how parents' ideologies and accommodation to their children intersect with children's needs to negotiate the interactional context for language learning and identity construction purposes. In each of these families, children are both allowed and achieve agency to affect long-term socialization processes through specific interactional roles. In this book I have argued that the ability of children or learners to change or transform experts' beliefs and practices is at the heart of findings on the outcomes of learner agency in second language learning. That is, as a construct, learner agency in second language learning has the most explanatory power when it affects change in the interactional context (e.g. classroom or family interactions).

Learners' desires, language competencies and expert ideologies drive negotiations in transnational language socialization processes where collaboration and accommodation are essential to establishing relationships. The children in the three families described in this book had varying alignments to their birth cultures and first languages, but all of them found ways to meet their needs in terms of language learning and identity construction in interaction with their parents. These findings suggest that transnational adoptees potentially enter the classroom with a sense of agency socialized in middle-class families in the US. It also points to a need to examine these processes in the classroom more carefully with more attention paid to connections between home and school contexts. In addition, as children move across educational systems, cultures and languages in transnational flows, understanding what values and desires these children have and how they negotiate their new identities and competencies is crucial to providing meaningful support for them.

8 Epilogue

At the time of finishing this book, the transnational adoptees who took part in this study (four to eight years ago) have entered middle and high schools and followed other paths into adulthood. I recently reconnected with all of the parents who had participated in the original data collection through videoconference interviews to ask them what they thought about language socialization processes in their families. (They had previously read versions of the chapters of this book in which I wrote about them.) Additionally, I asked them what advice they would give to parents planning on adopting older children from abroad. Here is what they had to say.

John Sonderman

Both Dima and Sasha are now teenagers in high and middle school respectively. Dima attends a small public school with a college preparatory curriculum that focuses on self-directed learning and uses alternative assessments. The school has a competitive admissions process, and it was an accomplishment for Dima to be admitted. Sasha had started a school for children with learning disabilities and had some more behavioral issues. John indicated that both children had been diagnosed with learning and language disabilities. Dima showed a high-level of academic aptitude and had high scores on his Preliminary Scholastic Aptitude Test (PSAT) (a common standardized aptitude test used for university admissions in the US) despite being diagnosed with ADHD. John felt that both boys showed low motivation in the classroom, but had the potential to finish school.

Despite the challenges, John was optimistic that both boys would go to college and find success in their adult lives. Sasha in particular liked to work with his hands and frequently used the shop area at the condo community where they lived. Dima showed an interest in learning other languages and enjoyed studying Spanish in school – he even spoke Spanish with the bilingual toddler who lived next door, although the boys did not use Russian anymore and did not show interest in it. As John stated, he knows more Russian than his sons at this point. He also suggested that the patterns of resistance that I identified in Dima's interactional style continued into his teenage years, and he felt that this was a pervasive strategy of Dima's that carried over into other activities, 'If Dima could find a way to put "no" into his answer, or the meaning of "no" in his answer, he will'. In reflecting on what had been successful for him in parenting older adoptees, John suggested that living in a multicultural community where neighbors knew one another had been useful to him. He also noted that his next-door neighbor had adopted an older child and had been a good support and model for him as an adoptive parent. He said he had learned to revise his expectations for the boys and specifically his own notions of what it means to be a good student. John also continues to believe that learning and speaking Russian with the children from the outset had been one of the best ways to establish early bonding with Dima and Sasha. Finally, he felt that the regular literacy events the family had participated in from the start, such as listening to and talking about audiobooks during car rides, had become practices that helped them 'do' being a family together.

Kevin and Meredith Jackson-Wessels

At the close of the data collection in the Jackson-Wessels, both children had been enrolled in public schools for the following year. Anna and Arkadiy Jackson-Wessels are now in middle school after both had changed schools at least once. Changing schools for Arkadiy, according to his father Kevin, had given him a chance to start over and transform some of the negative interactional routines that had started at his old school after the data collection for this study. Anna had also begun the same school after spending a year being homeschooled by Kevin. As in the early interviews, Kevin and Meredith still saw defiant behaviors that continued for Arkadiy and were also manifested by Anna at some times. These behaviors seemed to have affected the children's performance in school as well as their activities at home. For example, Anna had been enrolled in a French language immersion program for her first year of school, but had not received enough support in relation to her special needs there. She had been good at French, her mother said, and after leaving the immersion program had expressed a desire to relearn Russian. So Anna and Arkadiy had gone back to the Russian supplementary school. After a few sessions, however, the Russian teacher noted that they were disruptive in the class, and Anna and Arkadiy eventually stopped attending because of their behavior problems.

Kevin and Meredith said that teachers often told them that the children had strong 'background knowledge', referring to the highly literate environment they were being socialized in at home which was documented in this study. Both children also showed an enjoyment in reading, which also connected with Kevin and Meredith's love of books. However, Kevin and Meredith suggested that they had needed to revise their expectations for being a family over time. For example, Kevin said that he loved to play games and had always imagined having family game night. Anna and Arkadiy, however, would dispute the rules of the games when the family tried to play together, which resulted in making the game a contentious, rather than harmonizing, activity. The family had found other ways to enjoy their free time and were able to find quiet moments when they could be a family. When asked what advice they would give other families, Kevin and Meredith said that rethinking expectations was a big part of being a parent of older adoptees – that adoptive parents' vision of a successful family (i.e. as a family who reads together or has family game night) might not reach fruition. They also suggested that, after trying homeschooling twice, it had not been the best option for them because of the intense demands it placed on the homeschooling parent.

Melanie and Paul Goeller

Melanie and Paul reported that, in the summer of 2008, soon after the data collection had ended, Lena, Lesya and Melanie took a trip back to Russia to visit some family members and friends. At that time Lena decided to leave the family and remain with her birth mother in Russia. She now has one child and is expecting a second as I write this final chapter. She and Lesya keep in touch over the telephone, and Melanie and Paul continue to also have contact with Lena. They felt that Lena's decision to return to Russia had to do with being uncomfortable with being a member of a loving family.

The younger teenage adoptee, Lesya, also did not complete the high school program she had entered when she arrived in the US. However, Lesya decided to stay in the US and remain at home with the Goeller family. She was working in a nursing home for elderly people at the time of the interview and her parents said she was getting ready to enter a community college program to obtain her General Education Diploma (GED) in lieu of completing high school. Melanie reported that Lesya had expressed the desire to own a funeral home. When I asked why Lesya had chosen funeral home directorship as a future career option, Melanie told me that the director of the orphanage in which Lesya had lived had a hobby of searching for the remains of soldiers from World War II in the forests in the region. She and the children would collect remains, identify their nationality based on their uniforms and give them proper burials. Lesya's imagination had been captured by these activities, and this is an interesting example of how a child's socialization in the Russian orphanage can create a constructive opportunity and area of expertise that has helped her to imagine a concrete future in the US.

Melanie and Paul remarked on the apparent paradox that Lena had proved to be the faster English language learner and better student of the two children, but had not succeeded in her new life as a member of the US family. Lesya's more laid-back approach seemed to have facilitated integration into the new family and a longer-term identity as an American. Both parents said they were glad that they had learned and used Russian with their children. Paul remarked that it validated the children's prior knowledge and competence. While Russian is no longer used regularly in the Goeller household, Lesya still talks on the phone with Lena in Russian, and Valya wants to establish a Russian language class at her new school. (If all the siblings from her family join, they will have enough students to request it from the administration according to school policy.) Even though Melanie and Paul both also said that adoptive parenting required revising expectations, they said it was worth it to have a family.

Three Themes

In sum, three major themes arose in these final interviews. First, learning and using older adoptees' first language was beneficial to the families who participated in this study. Second, English language learning happens fast for adoptees, and parents should not worry about this process at the outset. Third, adoptive parenting requires revisions of what it means to be parents and children in a middle-class US home, but it is worth it in the end. For these parents, this is what it means to be a 'new' US family. As researchers, therapists and teachers it is our job to understand our transforming society and support these parents and children in culturally responsive ways.

References

Adler, P.A. and Adler, P. (1984) The carpool: A socializing adjunct to the educational experience. *Sociology of Education* 57 (4), 200–210.

Ahearn, L.M. (2001) Language and agency. *Annual Review of Anthropology* 30, 109–137.

Al Zidjaly, N. (2009) Agency as an interactive achievement. *Language in Society* 38 (2), 177–200.

American Speech-Language-Hearing Association (ASHA). Online document: http://www.asha.org/default.htm

Andrews, D. (1999) *Sociocultural Perspectives on Language Change in Diaspora: Soviet Immigrants in the United States*. Amsterdam: John Benjamins Publishing Company.

Angermeyer, P.S. (2005) Spelling bilingualism: Script choice in Russian American classified ads and signage. *Language in Society* 34 (4), 493–531.

Atkinson, D. (2002) Toward a sociocognitive approach to second language acquisition. *The Modern Language Journal* 86 (4), 525–545.

Atkinson, D. (2011) *Alternative Approaches to Second Language Acquisition*. London: Routledge.

Auer, P. (1984) *Bilingual Conversation*. Amsterdam: John Benjamins Publishing Company.

Auer, P. (1998) Introduction: *Bilingual Conversation* revisited. In P. Auer (ed.) *Code-switching in Conversation: Language, Interaction and Identity*. London: Routledge.

Baker, C. (2000) *Care and Education of Young Bilinguals*. Clevedon: Multilingual Matters.

Barnes, J.D. (2006) *Early Trilingualism: A Focus on Questions*. Clevedon: Multilingual Matters.

Bauman, R. (1977) Linguistics, anthropology, and verbal art: Toward a unified perspective, with a special discussion of children's folklore. *Georgetown University Round Table on Languages and Linguistics* (pp. 13–36). Washington, DC: Georgetown University Press.

Bayley, R. and Schecter, S. (2003) *Language Socialization in Bilingual and Multilingual Societies*. Clevedon: Multilingual Matters.

Beals, D.E. and Snow, C. (1994) 'Thunder is when the angels are upstairs bowling': Narratives and explanations at the dinner table. *Journal of Narrative and Life History* 4 (4), 331–352.

Bialystok, E. (2009) Bilingualism: The good, the bad, and the indifferent. *Bilingualism: Language and Cognition* 12 (1), 3–11.

Block, D. (2007) *Second Language Identities*. London: Continuum.

Blum-Kulka, S. (1997) *Dinner Talk: Cultural Patterns of Sociability and Socialization in Family Discourse*. Mahwah, NJ: Lawrence Erlbaum.

Boehm, D. (2008) 'Now I am a man and a woman': Gendered moves and migrations in a transnational Mexican community. *Latin American Perspectives* 35 (16), 16–30.

Bongartz, C. and Schneider, M.L. (2003) Linguistic development in social contexts: A study of two brothers learning German. *The Modern Language Journal* 87 (1), 13–37.

Bourdieu, P. and Passeron, J.C. (1977) *Reproduction in Education, Society, and Culture*. London: Sage.

Boyd, M.P. and Rubin, D.L. (2002) Elaborated student talk in an elementary ESOL classroom. *Research in the Teaching of Reading* 36 (4), 495–530.

Brodzinsky, D.M. (1993) Long-term outcomes in adoption. *The Future of Children* 3 (1), 153–166.

Brodzinsky, D.M. and Palacios, J. (eds) (2005) *Psychological Issues in Adoption: Research and Practice*. New York: Greenwood.

Bucholtz, M. and Hall, K. (2005). Identity and interaction: A sociocultural linguistic approach. *Discourse Studies* 7 (4–5), 585–614.

Byram, M. (2008) *From Foreign Language Education to Education for Intercultural Citizenship: Essays and Reflections*. Clevedon: Multilingual Matters.

Canagarajah, A.S. (2008) Language shift and the family: Questions from the Sri Lankan Tamil diaspora. *Journal of Sociolinguistics* 12 (2), 143–176.

Cashman, H. (2005) Identities at play: Language preference and group membership in bilingual talk in interaction. *Journal of Pragmatics* 37 (3), 301–315.

Cashman, H. (2008) You're screwed either way: An exploration of code-switching, impoliteness, and power. In D. Bousfield and M. Locher (eds) *Impoliteness in Language* (pp. 255–279). Berlin: Walter de Gruyter.

Choi, S. and Gopnik, A. (1995) Early acquisition of verbs in Korean: A cross-linguistic study. *Journal of Child Language* 22 (3), 497–529.

Corsaro, D.W.A. (2004) *The Sociology of Childhood* (2nd edn). Thousand Oaks, CA: Pine Forge Press.

Cotterill, J. (2004) Collocation, connotation, and courtroom semantics: Lawyers' control of witness testimony through lexical negotiation. *Applied Linguistics* 25 (4), 513–537.

Cruz-Ferreira, M. (2006) *Three is a Crowd?: Acquiring Portuguese in a Trilingual Environment* (illustrated edn). Clevedon: Multilingual Matters.

Crystal, D. (1986) Grin and swear it. *English Today* 7, 34–35.

Cummins, J. (2001) *Negotiating Identities: Education for Empowerment in a Diverse Society* (2nd edn). Los Angeles: California Association for Bilingual Education.

Cummins, J., Baker, C. and Hornberger, N.H. (2001) *An Introductory Reader to the Writings of Jim Cummins*. Clevedon: Multilingual Matters.

Dauenhauer, N.M. and Dauenhauer, R. (1998) Technical, emotional, and ideological issues in reversing language shift: Examples from Southeast Alaska. In L.A. Grenoble and L.J. Whaley (eds) *Endangered Languages: Current Issues and Future Prospects* (pp. 57–116). Cambridge: Cambridge University Press.

De Fina, A. (2003a) Crossing borders: Time, space, and disorientation in narrative. *Narrative Inquiry* 13 (2), 367–391.

De Fina, A. (2003b) *Identity in Narrative: A Study of Immigrant Discourse*. Amsterdam: John Benjamins Publishing Company.

De Fina, A., Schiffrin, D. and Bamberg, M. (eds) (2006) *Discourse and Identity*. Cambridge: Cambridge University Press.

De Geer, B., Tulviste, T., Mizera, L. and Tryggvason, M-T. (2002) Socialization in communication: Pragmatic socialization during dinnertime in Estonian, Finnish and Swedish families. *Journal of Pragmatics* 34, 1757–1786.

De Houwer, A. (1999) Environmental factors in early bilingual development: The role of parental beliefs and attitudes. In G. Extra and L. Verhoeven (eds) *Bilingualism and Migration* (pp. 75–96). New York: Mouton de Gruyter.

Department of Homeland Security (2009) *Yearbook of Immigration Statistics*. Online document: http://www.dhs.gov/files/statistics/publications/yearbook.shtm

Donato, R. (2001) Sociocultural contributions to understanding the foreign and second language classroom. In J.P. Lantolf (ed.) *Sociocultural Theory and Second Language Learning* (pp. 27–50). Oxford: Oxford University Press.

Duff, P.A. (1995) An ethnography of communication in immersion classrooms in Hungary. *TESOL Quarterly* 29 (3), 505–537.

Duff, P.A. (2002) The discursive co-construction of knowledge, identity, and difference: An ethnography of communication in the high school mainstream. *Applied Linguistics* 23 (3), 289–322.

Duff, P.A. (2008a) *Case Study Research in Applied Linguistics*. New York: Lawrence Erlbaum Associates.

Duff, P.A. (2008b) Language socialization, participation and identity: Ethnographic approaches. In P. Duff and N. Hornberger (eds) *Language Socialization: Encyclopedia of Language and Education* (Vol. 8) (pp. 107–119). New York: Springer.

Duff, P.A. (2011) Second language socialization. In A. Duranti, E. Ochs and B. Schieffelin (eds) *Handbook of Language Socialization*. New York: Blackwell.

Duff, P.A. (2012) Identity, agency, and second language acquisition. In S.M. Gass and A. Mackey (eds) *The Routledge Handbook of Second Language Acquisition*. London: Routledge.

Eckert, P. (1988) Adolescent social structure and the spread of linguistic change. *Language in Society* 17 (2), 183–207.

Ely, R., Berko Gleason, J., MacGibbon, A. and Zaretsky, E. (2001) Attention to language: Lessons learned at the dinner table. *Social Development* 10 (3), 355–373.

Ervin-Tripp, S., O'Connor, M.C. and Rosenberg, J. (1984) Language and power in the family. In C. Kramarae, M. Schulz and W.M. O'Barr (eds) *Language and Power* (pp. 116–135). Beverly Hills: Sage.

Esposito, D. and Biafora, F.A. (2007) Toward a sociology of adoption: Historical deconstruction. In R.A. Javier, A.L. Baden, F.A. Biafora and A. Camacho-Gingerich (eds) *Handbook of Adoption: Implications for Researchers, Practitioners and Families* (pp. 17–31). London: Sage.

Feiler, B. (2004) A game that gets parents and kids talking [Electronic Version]. *Parade Magazine*. Online document: http://www.parade.com/articles/editions/2004/edition_08-15-2004

Felling, S. (2007) Fading Farsi: Language policy, ideology, and shift in the Iranian American family. Unpublished PhD dissertation: Georgetown University.

Fogle, L.W. (2008a) Questions, beliefs, and interaction in the internationally adoptive family. Paper presentation, American Association of Applied Linguistics (AAAL). Washington, DC.

Fogle, L.W. (2008b) Home-school connections for international adoptees: Repetition in parent-child interactions. In J. Philp, R. Oliver and A. Mackey (eds) *Child's Play? Second Language Acquisition and the Younger Learner*. Amsterdam: John Benjamins.

Fogle, L.W. (2009) Language socialization in the internationally adoptive family: Identities, second languages, and learning. Unpublished PhD thesis: Georgetown University.

Fogle, L.W. (in press) Parental ethnotheories and family language policy in transnational adoptive families. *Language Policy*.

Fogle, L.W. and King, K.A. (in press) Child agency and language policy in transnational families. *Issues in Applied Linguistics*.

Fortune, A. (2005) Learners' use of metalanguage in collaborative form-focused L2 output tasks. *Language Awareness* 14 (1), 21–38.

Fortune, A. and Thorp, D. (2001) Knotted and entangled: New light on the identification, classification, and value of language related episodes in collaborative output tasks. *Language Awareness* 10 (2&3), 143–160.

Friedman, D.A. (2010) Speaking correctly: Error correction as a language socialization practice in a Ukrainian classroom. *Applied Linguistics* 31 (3), 346–367.

Gafaranga, J. (2010) Medium request: Talking language shift into being. *Language in Society,* 39 (2), 241–270.

Gallagher, S. (2007) Agency, resources, and identity. *Gender & Society* 21 (2), 227–249.

Gardner-Chloros, P. (2009) *Code-switching.* Cambridge: Cambridge University Press.

Garrett, P.B. (2004) Review of *Language Socialization in Bilingual and Multilingual Societies. Language in Society* 33 (5), 776–779.

Garrett, P.B. and Baquedano-Lopéz, P. (2002) Language socialization: Reproduction and continuity, transformation and change. *Annual Review of Anthropology* 31, 339–361.

Gass, S.M. and Mackey, A. (2000) *Stimulated Recall Methodology in Second Language Research.* Mahwah, NJ: Lawrence Erlbaum.

Gee, J.P. (2008) *Social Linguistics and Literacies: Ideologies in Discourses* (3rd edn). London: Routledge.

Genesee, F. (2004) What do we know about bilingual education for majority students? In T.K. Bhatia and W.C. Ritchie (eds) *The Handbook of Bilingualism* (pp. 547–567). Oxford: Blackwell.

Georgakopoulou, A. (2006) Small and large identities in narrative (inter)action. In A. De Fina, D. Schiffrin and M. Bamberg (eds) *Discourse and Identity* (pp. 83–102). Cambridge: Cambridge University Press.

Georgakopuolou, A. (2007) *Small Stories, Interaction, and Identities.* Amsterdam: John Benjamins Publishing Company.

Gindis, B. (2000) Detecting and remediating the cumulative cognitive deficit in school age internationally adopted post-institutionalized children. *The Post (The parent network for the post-institutionalized child)* 27, 1–6. Online document: http://www.bgcenter.com/CCDPost.htm

Gindis, B. (2005) Cognitive, language, and educational issues of children adopted from overseas orphanages. *Journal of Cognitive Education and Psychology [online]* 4 (3), 290–335.

Glennen S. (n.d.) *Language and the older adopted child.* Towson University, Language Development in Internationally Adopted Children – Online document: http://pages.towson.edu/sglennen/Olderchildrenandlanguage.htm

Glennen, S. (2002) Language development and delay in internationally adopted infants and toddlers: A review. *American Journal of Speech-Language Pathology* 11, 333–339.

Glennen, S. and Bright, B. (2005) Five years later: Language in school-age internationally adopted children. *Seminars in Speech and Language* 26 (1), 86–101.

Glennen, S. and Masters, M.G. (2002) Typical and atypical language development in infants and toddlers adopted from Eastern Europe. *American Journal of Speech-Language Pathology* 11, 417–433.

Goodwin, M.H. (1997) Children's linguistic and social worlds. *Anthropology Newsletter,* 38 (4).

Gordon, C. (2007) 'Al Gore's our guy': Linguistically constructing a family identity. In D. Tannen, S. Kendall and C. Gordon (eds) *Family Talk: Discourse and Identity in Four American Families.* Oxford: Oxford University Press.

Gorham, M.S. (2000) Mastering the perverse: State building and language 'purification' in early Soviet Russia. *Slavic Review* 59 (1), 133–153.

Gregg, K. (2006) Taking a social turn for the worse: The language socialization paradigm for second language acquisition. *Second Language Research* 22, 413–442.

Greko-Akerman, J. (2006) Homeschooling the older, adopted child. Online document: http://homeschooling.gomilpitas.com/articles/051806.htm

Grovetant, H.D. (1997) Coming to terms with adoption: The construction of identity from adolescence into adulthood. *Adoption Quarterly* 1 (1), 3–27.

Grovetant, H.D., Dunbar, N., Kohler, J.K. and Esau, A.M.L. (2007) Adoptive identity: How contexts within and beyond the family shape developmental pathways. In R.A. Javier, A.L. Baden, F.A. Biafora and A. Camacho-Gingerich (eds) *Handbook of Adoption: Implications for Researchers, Practitioners, and Families*. Thousand Oaks, CA: Sage.

Gumperz, J.J. (1982) *Discourse Strategies*. Cambridge: Cambridge University Press.

Hahn, D., Allers, R. and Minkoff, R. (1994) *The Lion King*. United States: Walt Disney Pictures.

Hamilton, L., Cheng, S. and Powell, B. (2007) Adoptive parents, adaptive parents: Evaluating the importance of biological ties for parental investment. *American Sociological Review* 72, 95–116.

Harklau, L. (2000) From the 'Good Kids' to the 'Worst': Representations of English language learners across educational settings. *TESOL Quarterly* 34 (1), 35–67.

Hart, B. and Risley, T.R. (1999) *The Social World of Children Learning to Talk*. Baltimore, MD: Paul H. Brookes Publishing Company.

Hatch, E., Peck, S. and Wagner-Gough, J. (1979) A look at process in child second-language acquisition. In E. Ochs and B.S. Schieffelin (eds) *Developmental Pragmatics*. New York: Academic Press.

Hawkins, M. (2005) Becoming a student: Identity work and academic literacies in early schooling. *TESOL Quarterly* 39 (1), 59–82.

Hazen, K. (2002) The family. In J. Chambers, P. Trudgill and N. Schilling-Estes (eds) *The Handbook of Language Variation and Change* (pp. 500–525). Malden, MA: Blackwell.

Heath, S.B. (1982) What no bedtime story means: Narrative skills at home and school. *Language in Society* 11, 49–76.

Heath, S.B. (1983) *Ways with Words: Language Life and Work in Communities and Classrooms*. Cambridge: Cambridge University Press.

Heath, S.B. (2006) Commentary 2: Building the micros toward seeing the macro. *Text & Talk* 26 (4–5), 627–634.

Heller, M. (1988) *Codeswitching: Anthropological and Sociolinguistic Perspectives*. Berlin: Mouton De Gruyter.

Heller, M. (2008) Doing ethnography. In L. Wei and M.G. Moyer (eds) *The Blackwell Guide To Research Methods In Bilingualism And Multilingualism* (pp. 249–262). Oxford: Blackwell.

Heller, M. and Martin-Jones, M. (2001) *Voices of Authority: Education and Linguistic Difference*. Westport, CT: Ablex Publishing.

Higgins, C. and Stoker, K. (2011) Language learning as a site for belonging: A narrative analysis of Korean adoptee-returnees. *International Journal of Bilingual Education & Bilingualism* 14 (4), 399–412.

Hornberger, N.H. (2003) *Continua in Biliteracy: An Ecological Framework for Educational Policy, Research, and Practice in Multilingual Settings*. Clevedon: Multilingual Matters.

Hough, S. (2005) Language outcomes in school-aged children adopted from Eastern European orphanages. Unpublished PhD Thesis: University of Pittsburg.

Howell, S. (2007) *The Kinning of Foreigners: Transnational Adoption in a Global Perspective*. New York: Berghahn Books.

Hua, Z. (2008) Duelling languages, duelling values: Codeswitching in bilingual intergenerational conflict talk in diasporic families. *Journal of Pragmatics* 40, 1799–1816.

Hua, Z. and David, A. (2008) Study design: Cross-sectional, longitudinal, case, and group. In L. Wei and M.G. Moyer (eds) *The Blackwell Guide to Research Methods in Bilingualism and Multilingualism* (pp. 88–107). Oxford: Blackwell.

Hult, F.M. (2010). Analysis of language policy discourses across the scales of space and time. *International Journal of the Sociology of Language* 202, 7–24.

Isurin, L. (2000) Deserted island or a child's first language forgetting. *Bilingualism: Language and Cognition* 3 (2), 151–166.

Jacobson, H. (2008) *Culture Keeping: White Mothers, International Adoption, and the Negotiation of Family Difference*. Nashville: Vanderbilt University Press.

Jacoby, S. and Gonzales, P. (1991) The constitution of expert-novice in scientific discourse. *Issues in Applied Linguistics* 2 (2), 149–181.

Javier, R.A., Baden, A.L., Biafora, F.A. and Camacho-Gingerich, A. (eds) (2006) *Handbook of Adoption: Implications for Researchers, Practitioners, and Families*. Thousand Oaks, CA: Sage.

Johnstone, B. (2001) Discourse analysis and narrative. In D. Schiffrin, D. Tannen and H. Hamilton (eds) *The Handbook of Discourse Analysis* (pp. 635–649). Malden, MA: Blackwell.

Jones, R. (2005) 'You show me yours, I'll show you mine.': The negotiated shifts from textual to visual modes in computer-mediated interaction among gay men. *Visual Communication* 4 (1), 69–92.

Jones, R.H. and Norris, S. (2005) *Discourse in Action: Introducing Mediated Discourse Analysis*. London: Routledge.

Jørgensen, J.N. (1998) Children's acquisition of codeswitching for power wielding. In P. Auer (ed.) *Codeswitching in Conversation* (pp. 237–262). London: Routledge.

Jørgensen, J.N. (2008) Urban wall languaging. *International Journal of Multilingualism* 5 (3), 237–252.

Kasanga, L.A. (2008) 'Cheap' c'est quoi? Immigrant teenagers in quest of multilingual competence and identity. *International Journal of Multilingualism* 5 (4), 333–356.

Keenan, E.O., Schieffelin, B.B. and Platt, M.L. (1976) Propositions across utterances and speakers. *Papers and Reports on Child Language Development* 12 (December), 127–143.

Kendall, S. (2007) Introduction: Family talk. In D. Tannen, S. Kendall and C. Gordon (eds) *Family Talk: Discourse and Identity In Four American Families* (pp. 3–23). Oxford: Oxford University Press.

King, K.A. (2000) Language ideologies and heritage language education. *International Journal of Bilingual Education and Bilingualism* 3 (3), 167–184.

King, K.A. (2001) *Language Revitalization Processes and Prospects: Quichua in the Ecuadorian Andes*. Clevedon: Multilingual Matters.

King, K.A. and Fogle, L. (2006) Bilingual parenting as good parenting: Parents' perspectives on family language policy for additive bilingualism. *International Journal of Bilingual Education and Bilingualism* 9 (6), 695–712.

King, K.A. and Gallagher, C. (2008) Love, diminutives and gender socialization in Andean motherchild narrative conversations. In A. McCabe, A. Bailey and G. Melzi (eds) *Research on the Development of Spanish Language Narratives*. New York: Cambridge University Press.

King, K.A. and Ganuza, N. (2005) Language, identity, education, and transmigration: Chilean adolescents in Sweden. *Journal of Language, Identity, and Education* 4 (3), 179–199.

King, K.A. and Logan-Terry, A. (2008) Additive bilingualism through family language policy: Ideologies, strategies and interactional outcomes. *Calidoscópio* 6 (1), 5–19.

King, K.A., Fogle, L. and Logan-Terry, A. (2008) Family language policy. *Language and Linguistics Compass* 2 (5), 907–922.

Kotler, A., Wegerif, R. and LeVoi, M. (2001) Oracy and the educational achievement of pupils with English as an additional language: The impact of bringing 'talking partners' into Bradford schools. *International Journal of Bilingual Education and Bilingualism* 4 (6), 403–419.

Kowal, M. and Swain, M. (1994) Using collaborative language production tasks to promote students' language awareness. *Language Awareness* 3 (2), 73–93.

Kramsch, C. (2010) *The Multilingual Subject*. New York: Oxford University Press.

Kritikos, E.P. (2003) Speech-language pathologists' beliefs about language assessment of bilingual/bicultural individuals. *American Journal of Speech-Language Pathology* 12 (1), 73–91.

Kulick, D. (1993) Growing up monolingual in a multilingual community: How language socialization patterns are leading to language shift in Gapun (Papua New Guinea). In K. Hyltenstam and A. Viberg (eds) *Progression and Regression in Language* (pp. 94–121). Cambridge: Cambridge University Press.

Kulick, D. (1997) *Language Shift and Cultural Reproduction: Socialization, Self and Syncretism in a Papua New Guinean Village*. Cambridge: Cambridge University Press.

Kulick, D. and Schieffelin, B. (2004) Language socialization. In A. Duranti (ed.) *A Companion to Linguistic Anthropology* (pp. 349–368). Malden, MA: Blackwell.

Labov, W. and Waletzky, J. (1967) Narrative analysis. In J. Helm (ed.) *Essays on the Verbal and Visual Arts* (pp. 12–44). Seattle: University of Washington Press.

Lantolf, J.P. (2000) *Sociocultural Theory and Second Language Learning*. Oxford: Oxford University Press.

Lantolf, J.P. and Thorne, S.L. (2006) *Sociocultural Theory and the Genesis of Second Language Development*. New York: Oxford University Press.

Lanza, E. (1992) Can bilingual two-year-olds code-switch? *Journal of Child Language* 19 (3), 633–658.

Lanza, E. (1997/2004) *Language Mixing in Infant Bilingualism*. Oxford: Oxford University Press.

Lapkin, S., Swain, M. and Psyllakis, P. (2010) The role of languaging in creating zones of proximal development (ZPDs): A long-term care resident interacts with a researcher. *Canadian Journal on Aging = La Revue Canadienne Du Vieillissement* 29 (4), 477–490.

Larsen-Freeman, D. and Cameron, L. (2008) *Complex Systems and Applied Linguistics*. Oxford: Oxford University Press.

Larson, R.W., Wiley, A.R. and Branscomb, K.R. (2006) *Family Mealtime as a Context of Development and Socialization*. San Francisco: Jossey-Bass.

Lave, J. and Wenger, E. (1991) *Situated Learning: Legitimate Peripheral Participation*. Cambridge: Cambridge University Press.

Leather, J. and van Dam, J. (2003) *Ecology of Language Acquisition*. Dordrecht: Kluwer Academic Publishers.

Lemke, J. (2000) Across the scales of time: Artifacts, activities, and meanings in ecosocial systems. *Mind, Culture, and Activity* 7 (4), 273–290.

Lemke, J. (2010) Identity, development, and desire: Critical questions. In C. Caldas-Coulthard and R. Iedema (eds) *Identity Trouble: Critical Discourse and Contestations of Identification*. London: Macmillan Palgrave.

Levine, E. (1995) *I Hate English!* New York: Scholastic Paperbacks.

Levy, C. (2010) Russia calls for halt on U.S. adoptions. *The New York Times* – Online document: http://www.nytimes.com/2010/04/10/world/europe/10russia.html?_r=1&

Lin, A.M.Y. (2007) *Problematizing Identity: Everyday Struggles in Language, Culture, and Education.* London: Routledge.

Lo, A. and Kim, J. (2011) Manufacturing citizenship: Metapragmatic framings of language competencies in media images of mixed race men in South Korea. *Discourse & Society* 22 (4), 440–457.

Luykx, A. (2003) Weaving languages together: Family language policy and gender socialization in bilingual Aymara households. In R. Bayley and S. Schecter (eds) *Language Socialization in Bilingual and Multilingual Societies* (pp. 25–43). Clevedon: Multilingual Matters.

Luykx, A. (2005) Children as socializing agents: Family language policy in situations of language shift. In J. Cohen, K.T. McAlister, K. Rolstad and J. MacSwan (eds) *ISB4: Proceedings of the 4th International Symposium on Bilingualism* (pp. 1407–1414). Somerville, MA: Cascadilla Press.

MacSwan, J. (2000) The threshold hypothesis, semilingualism, and other contributions to a deficit view of linguistic minorities. *Hispanic Journal of Behavioral Sciences* 22 (1), 3–45.

MacWhinney, B. (2000) *The CHILDES Project: Tools for Analyzing Talk* (3rd edn). Mahwah, NJ: Lawrence Erlbaum.

Magady, N. (2004) International adoptees: Are they ESOL? *MIDTESOL Matters.* Online document: http://www.midtesol.org/Newsletter/2004spr-International_Adoptions.htm

Martin-Jones, M. and Romaine, S. (1986) Semilingualism: A half-baked theory of communicative competence. *Applied Linguistics* 7 (1), 26–38.

McCarty, T. (2009) The youngest policymakers: An ethnographic look at language practices and ideologies among American Indian youth. Paper presented at AAAL 2009, Denver, CO.

McDermott, R.P. and Tylbor, H. (1995) On the necessity of collusion in conversation. In D. Tedlock and B. Mannheim (eds) *The Dialogic Emergence of Culture* (pp. 218–236). Urbana, IL: University of Illinois Press.

McKay, S.L. and Wong, S.C. (1996) Multiple discourses, multiple identities: Investment and agency in second-language learning among Chinese adolescent immigrant students. *Harvard Educational Review* 66 (3), 577–608.

Mehan, H. (1979) *Learning Lessons.* Cambridge, MA: Harvard University Press.

Melosh, B. (2002) *Strangers and Kin: The American Way of Adoption.* Cambridge, MA: Harvard University Press.

Mennen, I. and Stansfield, J. (2006) Speech and language therapy service delivery for bilingual children: A survey of three cities in Great Britain. *International Journal of Language & Communication Disorders* 41 (6), 635–652.

Michaels, S. (1981) Sharing time: Children's narrative styles and differential access to literacy. *Language in Society* 10, 423–42.

Miller, B.C., Xitao, F., Grotevant, H.D., Christensen, M., Coyl, D. and van Dulmen, M. (2000) Adopted adolescents' overrepresentation in mental health counseling: Adoptees' problems or parents' lower threshold for referral? *Journal of the American Academy of Child and Adolescent Psychiatry* 39 (12), 1504–1510.

Morita, N. (2004) Negotiating participation and identity in second language academic communities. *TESOL Quarterly* 38 (4), 573–603.

Myers-Scotton, C. (1993) Common and uncommon ground: Social and structural factors in codeswitching. *Language in Society* 22 (4), 475–503.

Nelson, K. (1990) The psychological and social origins of autobiographical memory. *Psychological Sciences* 4 (1), 7–14.

Nicoladis, E. and Grabois, H. (2002) Learning English and losing Chinese: A case study of a child adopted from China. *International Journal of Bilingualism* 6 (4), 441–454.

Ninio, A. and Bruner, J. (1976) The achievement and antecedents of labeling. *Journal of Child Language* 5, 1–15.

Ninio, A. and Snow, C. (1996) *Pragmatic Development*. Boulder, CO: Westview Press.

Norris, S. (2005) Habitus, social identity, the perception of male domination – and agency? In S. Norris and R. Jones (eds) *Discourse in Action: Introducing Mediated Discourse Analysis* (pp. 183–198). London: Routledge.

Norris, S. and Jones, R. (eds) (2005) *Discourse in Action: Introducing Mediated Discourse Analysis*. London: Routledge.

Norton Pierce, B. (1995) Social identity, investment, and language learning. *TESOL Quarterly* 29 (1), 9–32.

Norton, B. and Toohey, K. (2001) Changing perspectives on good language learners. *TESOL Quarterly* 35 (2), 307–22.

Nystrand, M., Wu, L.L., Gamoran, A., Zeiser, S. and Long, D.A. (2003) Questions in time: Investigating the structure and dynamics of unfolding classroom discourse. *Discourse Processes* 35 (2), 135–198.

Ochs, E. (1988) *Culture and Language Development: Language Acquisition and Language Socialization in a Samoan Village*. New York: Cambridge University Press.

Ochs, E. and Capps, L. (2001) *Living Narrative: Creating Lives in Everyday Storytelling*. Cambridge, MA: Harvard University Press.

Ochs, E. and Schieffelin, B. (1984) Language acquisition and socialization: Three developmental stories and their implications. In R. Shweder and R. LeVine (eds) *Culture Theory: Essays on Mind, Self, and Emotion* (pp. 276–320). Cambridge: Cambridge University Press.

Ochs, E. and Schieffelin, B. (2008) Language socialization: An historical overview. In P.A. Duff and N.H. Hornberger (eds) *Encyclopedia of Language and Education* (2nd edn), *Volume 8: Language Socialization* (pp. 3–15). Norwell, MA: Springer.

Ochs, E. and Taylor, C. (1992) Family narrative as political activity. *Discourse & Society* 3 (3), 301–340.

Ochs, E. and Taylor, C. (1995) The 'father knows best' dynamic in family dinnertime narratives. In K. Hall and M. Bucholtz (eds) *Gender Articulated: Language and the Socially Constructed Self*. London: Routledge.

Ochs, E., Taylor, C., Rudolph, D. and Smith, R. (1992) Story-telling as a theory-building activity. *Discourse Processes* 15 (1), 671–681.

Office of Immigration Statistics. (2004) *2003 Yearbook Of Immigration Statistics* – Online document: http://uscis.gov/graphics/shared/aboutus/statistics/2003Yearbook.pdf.

Ohara, Y. (2001) Finding one's voice in Japanese: A study of the pitch levels of L2 users. In A. Pavlenko (ed.) *Multilingualism, Second Language Learning, and Gender* (pp. 231–256). Berlin: Mouton De Gruyter.

Pasquandrea, S. (2008) *Più lingue, più identità.Code-switching e costruzione identitaria in famiglie di emigrati italiani*. Guerra Edizioni: Perugia.

Pavlenko, A. and Lantolf, J.P. (2000) Second language learning as participation and the (re) construction of selves. In J.P. Lantolf (ed.) *Sociocultural Theory and Second Language Learning* (pp. 155–178). Oxford: Oxford University Press.

Peal, E. and Lambert, W.E. (1962) The relation of bilingualism to intelligence. *Psychological Monographs* 76, 1–23.

Peräkylä, A. (1997/2003) Validity and reliability in research based on tapes and transcripts. In D. Silverman (ed.) *Qualitative Analysis: Issues of Theory and Method* (pp. 201–220). London: Sage.

Pertman, A. (2001) *Adoption Nation: How the Adoption Revolution Is Transforming America.* New York: Basic Books.

Peters, A.M. and Boggs, S.T. (1986) Interactional routines as cultural influences upon language. In B. Schieffelin and E. Ochs (eds) *Language Socialization Across Cultures* (pp. 80–97). New York: Cambridge University Press.

Philips, S. (2001) Participant structures and communicative competence: Warm Springs children in community and classroom. In A. Duranti (ed.) *Linguistic Anthropology: A Reader* (pp. 302–317). Malden, MA: Wiley-Blackwell.

Philips, S.U. (1992) *The Invisible Culture: Communication in Classroom and Community on the Warm Springs Indian Reservation.* Prospect Heights: Waveland Press.

Pizer, G., Walters, K. and Meier, R.P. (2007) Bringing up baby with baby signs: Language ideologies and socialization in hearing families. *Sign Language Studies* 7 (4), 387–430.

Polich, L. (2005) *The Emergence of Deaf Community in Nicaragua: "With Sign Language You Can Learn So Much."* Washington, DC: Gallaudet University Press.

Pollock, K. and Price, J. (2005) Phonological skills of children adopted from China: Implications for assessment. *Seminars in Speech and Language* 26 (1), 54–63.

Poole, D. (1992) Language socialization in the second language classroom. *Language Learning* 42 (4), 593–616.

Princiotta, D. and Bielick, S. (2006) *Homeschooling in the United States: 2003,* (NCES 2006-042) U.S. Department of Education. National Center for Education Statistics, Washington, DC.

Rampton, B. (1996) Dichotomies, difference, and ritual in second language learning and teaching. *Applied Linguistics* 20 (3), 316–340.

Rogoff, B. (1990) *Apprenticeship in Thinking: Cognitive Development in Social Context.* New York: Oxford University Press.

Russell, B. (2009) Madonna, Malawi and adoption madness. *Los Angeles Times* – Online document: http://articles.latimes.com/2009/apr/06/opinion/oe-russell6

Rymes, B. (1997) Second language socialization: A new approach to second language acquisition research. *Journal of Intensive English Studies* 11 (spring–fall), 143–155.

Rymes, B. and Pash, D. (2001) Questioning identity: The case of one second-language learner. *Anthropology & Education Quarterly* 32 (3), 276–300.

Sato, C. (1990) *The Syntax of Conversation in Interlanguage Development.* Tübingen: Gunter Narr Verlag Tübingen.

Schieffelin, B. (1990) *The Give and Take of Everyday Life: Language Socialization of Kaluli Children.* Cambridge: Cambridge University Press.

Schieffelin, B. and Ochs, E. (eds) (1986) *Language Socialization Across Cultures.* New York: Cambridge University Press.

Schiffrin, D. (2002) Mother and friends in a Holocaust life story. *Language in Society* 31 (3), 309–353.

Scollon, S. (2005) Agency distributed through time, space and tools: Bentham, Babbage and the census. In S. Norris and R. Jones (eds) *Discourse in Action: Introducing Mediated Discourse Analysis* (pp. 172–182). London: Routledge.

Scollon, R. and Scollon, S.W. (1981) *Narrative, Literacy and Face in Interethnic Communication.* Norwood, NJ: Ablex Publishing.

Shin, S. (2011) Transnational adoptees, community heritage language schools, and identity. Paper presentation at the International Symposium on Bilingualism 8, Oslo, Norway.

Shin, S.J. and Milroy, L. (2000) Conversational codeswitching among Korean-English bilingual children. *International Journal of Bilingualism* 4 (3), 351–383.

Shohamy, E. (2006) *Language Policy: Hidden Agendas and New Approaches* (illustrated edition). London: Routledge.

Simpson, R. (2009) United Nations of Brangelina: Pitt and Jolie's rainbow family arrives in Japan. *Mail Online* – Online document: http://www.dailymail.co.uk/tvshowbiz/article-1129321/United-Nations-Brangelina-Pitt-Jolies-rainbow-family-arrives-Japan.html

Snedeker, J., Geren, J. and Shafto, C.L. (2007) Starting over: International adoption as a natural experiment in language development. *Psychological Science* 18 (1), 79–87.

Snow et al. (1987) *Second Language Learners' Formal Definitions : An Oral Language Correlate of School Literacy*. Los Angeles, CA: Center for Language Education and Research, UCLA.

Spolsky, B. (2004) *Language Policy*. Cambridge: Cambridge University Press.

Stake, R.E. (2000) Case studies. In N.K. Denzin and Y.S. Lincoln (eds) *Handbook Of Qualitative Research* (pp. 134–164). Thousand Oaks, CA: Sage.

Strauss, A. and Corbin, J. (1990) *Basics of Qualitative Research: Grounded Theory Procedures and Techniques*. Newbury Park, CA: Sage.

Stryker, R. (2000) Ethnographic solutions to the problems of Russian adoptees. *Anthropology of East Europe Review* 18 (2), 79–84.

Stryker, R. (2004) Forging family, fixing family: Adoption and the cultural politics of reactive attachment disorder. Unpublished PhD dissertation: University of California, Berkeley.

Stryker, R. (2010) *The Road to Evergreen: Adoption, Attachment Therapy, and the Promise of Family*. Ithaca, NY: Cornell University Press.

Stryker, R. (2011) The war at home: Affective economics and transnationally adoptive families in the United States. *International Migration* 49 (6), 25–49.

Swain, M. (2000) The output hypothesis and beyond: Mediating acquisition through collaborative dialogue. In J.P. Lantolf (ed.) *Sociocultural Theory and Second Language Learning* (pp. 97–114). Oxford: Oxford University Press.

Swain, M. (2006) Languaging, agency and collaboration in advanced second language proficiency. In H. Byrnes (ed.) *Advanced Language Learning: The Contribution of Halliday and Vygotsky* (pp. 95–108). London: Continuum.

Swain, M. and Lapkin, S. (1998) Interaction and second language learning: Two adolescent French immersion students working together. *Modern Language Journal* 82, 320–337.

Tannen, D. (2007) Power maneuvers and connection maneuvers in family interaction. In D. Tannen, S. Kendall and C. Gordon (eds) *Family Talk: Discourse and Identity in Four American Families* (pp. 27–48). Oxford: Oxford University Press.

Tannen, D. and Goodwin, M.H. (2006) Introduction [Special issue entitled Family discourse, framing family]. *Text and Talk* 26 (4/5), 407–409.

Tannen, D., Kendall, S. and Gordon, C. (eds) (2007) *Family Talk: Discourse and Identity in Four American Families*. Oxford: Oxford University Press.

Tarone, E. and Liu, G-Q. (1996) Situational context, variation, and second language acquisition theory. In G. Cook and B. Seidlhoffer (eds) *Principle and Practice in Applied Linguistics* (pp. 107–124). Oxford: Oxford University Press.

Thorne, S.L. (2000) Second language acquisition theory and the truth(s) about relativity. In J.P. Lantolf (ed.) *Sociocultural Theory and Second Language Learning* (pp. 219–243). Oxford: Oxford University Press.

Tomasello, M. and Stahl, D. (2004) Sampling children's spontaneous speech: How much is enough? *Journal of Child Language* 31, 101–121.

Toohey, K. (2000) *Learning English at School: Identity, Social Relations, and Classroom Practice.* Clevedon: Multilingual Matters.

Torras, M. and Gafaranga, J. (2002) Social identities and language alternation in non-formal institutional bilingual talk: Trilingual service encounters in Barcelona. *Language in Society* 31 (4), 527–48.

Tuominen, A. (1999) Who decides the home language? A look at multilingual families. *International Journal of the Sociology of Language* 140, 59–76.

U.S. Census Bureau News. (2007) Single-parent households showed little variation since 1994, Census Bureau reports. Online document: http://www.census.gov/Press-release/www/releases/archives/families_households/009842.html

U.S. Department of Immigration Statistics. (2009) Yearbook of Immigration Statistics. Online document: http://www.dhs.gov/files/statistics/publications/yearbook.shtm

Vaidyanathan, R. (1988) Development of forms and functions of interrogatives in children: A longitudinal study in Tamil. *Journal of Child Language* 15, 533–549.

Valadez, C.M., MacSwan, J. and Martínez, C. (2000) Toward a new view of low-achieving bilinguals: A study of linguistic competence in designated 'semilinguals'. *The Bilingual Review/ La Revista Bilingüe* 25 (3), 238–248.

van Ijzendoorn, M. and Juffer, F. (2005) Adoption is a successful natural intervention enhancing adopted children's IQ and school performance. *Current Directions in Psychological Science* 14 (6), 326–330.

van Lier, L. (2004) *The Ecology and Semiotics of Language Learning: A Sociocultural Perspective.* Boston: Kluwer Academic.

van Lier, L. (2007) Action-based teaching, autonomy and identity. *Innovation in Language Learning and Teaching* 1 (1), 46–65.

Vandivere, S., Malm, K. and Radel, L. (2009) Adoption USA: A chartbook based on the 2007 national survey of adoptive parents (Washington, DC: The U.S. department of health and human services, office of the assistant secretary for planning and evaluation, 2009). Online document: http://aspe.hhs.gov/hsp/09/NSAP/chartbook/chartbook.cfm?id=2

Volkman, T.A. (2005) Introduction: New geographies of kinship. In T.A. Volkman, K. Johnson, B. Yngvesson, L. Kendall and L. Cartwright (eds) *Cultures of Transnational Adoption* (pp. 1–22). Durham, NC: Duke University Press.

Volkman, T.A., Johnson, K., Yngvesson, B., Kendall, L. and Cartwright, L. (eds) (2005) *Cultures of Transnational Adoption.* Durham, NC: Duke University Press.

Vygotsky, L.S. (1986) *Thought and Language – Revised Edition* (A. Kozulin, ed.). Cambridge, MA: MIT Press.

Warren, S.B. (1992) Lower threshold for referral for psychiatric treatment for adopted adolescents. *Journal of the American Academy for Child and Adolescent Psychiatry* 31, 512–527.

Watson-Gegeo, K.A. (2004) Mind, language, and epistemology: Toward a language socialization paradigm for SLA. *The Modern Language Journal* 88 (3), 331–350.

Watson-Gegeo, K.A. and Gegeo, D.W. (1986) Calling-out and repeating routines in Kwara'ae chidren's language socialization. In B. Schieffelin and E. Ochs (eds) *Language Socialization Across Cultures* (pp. 17–50). New York: Cambridge University Press.

Watson, N. (2006) Negotiating social and academic identities: Russian immigrant adolescents in the United States. Unpublished PhD thesis: University of Colorado at Denver.

Willett, J. (1995) Becoming first graders in an L2: An ethnographic study of L2 socialization. *TESOL Quarterly* 29 (3), 473–503.

Wilson, B. (2007) Homeschooling – older child adoption. Online document: http://www. parentingtheadopted.com/homeschooling-older-child-adoption/

Wong Fillmore, L. (2000) Loss of family languages: Should educators be concerned? *Theory into Practice* 39 (4), 203–210.

Woolard, K.A. (1998) Introduction: Language ideology as a field of inquiry. In B. Schieffelin, K. Woolard and P. Kroskrity (eds) *Language Ideologies: Practice and Theory* (pp. 3–48). Oxford: Oxford University Press.

Yngvesson, B. (2010) *Belonging in an Adopted World: Race, Identity, and Transnational Adoption*. Chicago, IL: University Of Chicago Press.

Zentella, A.C. (1997) *Growing Up Bilingual: Puerto Rican Children in New York*. Malden, MA: Blackwell.

Zentella, A.C. (2005) *Building on Strength: Language and Literacy in Latino Families and Communities*. New York: Teachers College Press.

Zilles, A.M.S. and King, K.A. (2005) Self-presentation in sociolinguistic interviews: Identities and language variation in Panambi, Brazil. *Journal of Sociolinguistics* 9 (1), 74–94.

Index